that salty air
TIM SIEVERT

Top Shelf Productions

ISBN 978-1-60309-005-6

1. Nautical Fiction
2. Graphic Novels

That Salty Air © 2008 Timothy Siwert

Published by Top Shelf Productions,
PO Box 1282, Marietta, Georgia
30061-1282, United States of America.

Publishers: Brett Warnock and Chris Staros

Top Shelf Productions® and the Top Shelf logo are
registered trademarks of Top Shelf Productions, Inc.
Visit our online catalog at www.TopShelfComix.com

First Printing, April 2008 . Printed in Canada.

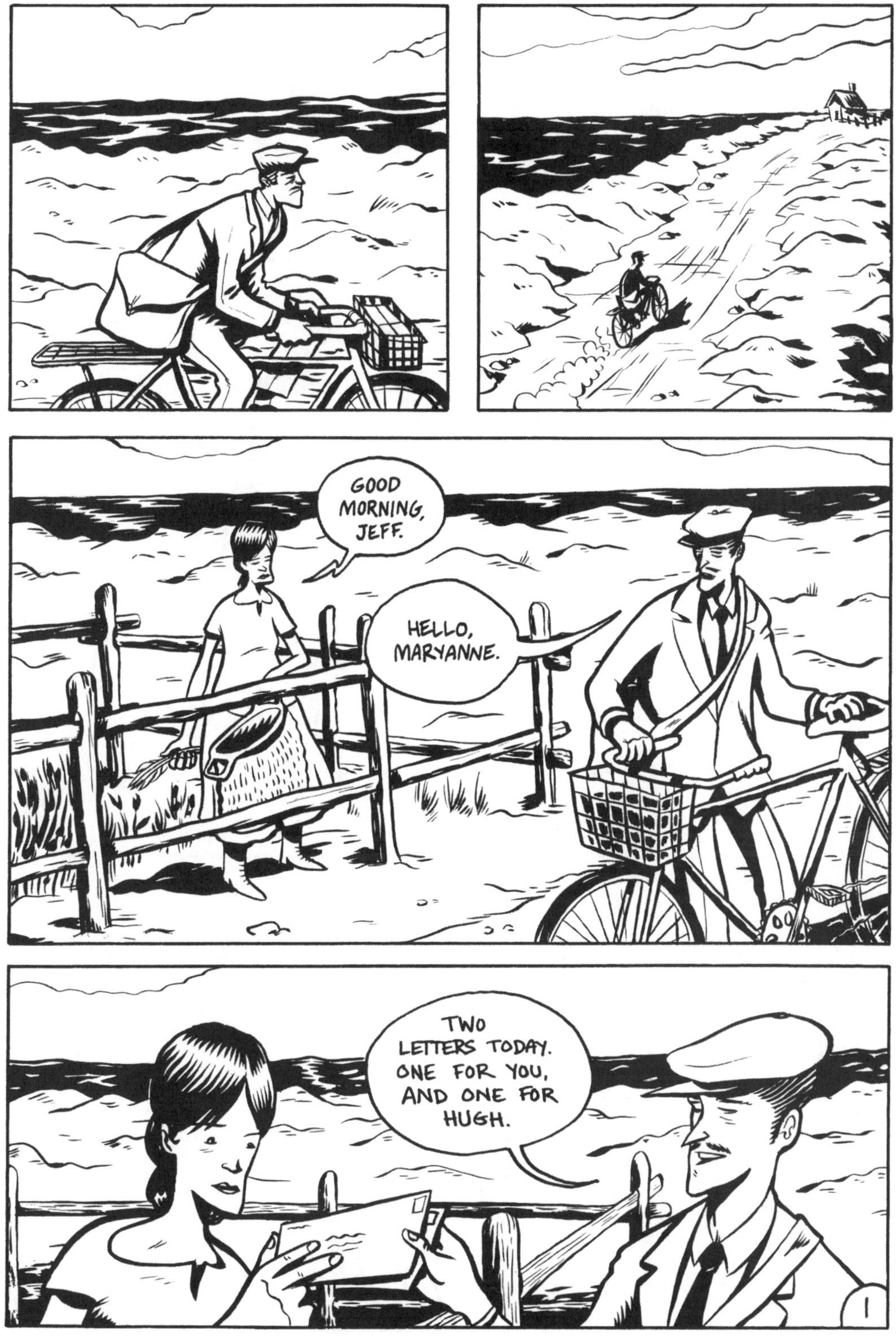
GOOD MORNING, JEFF.
HELLO, MARYANNE.
TWO LETTERS TODAY. ONE FOR YOU, AND ONE FOR HUGH.

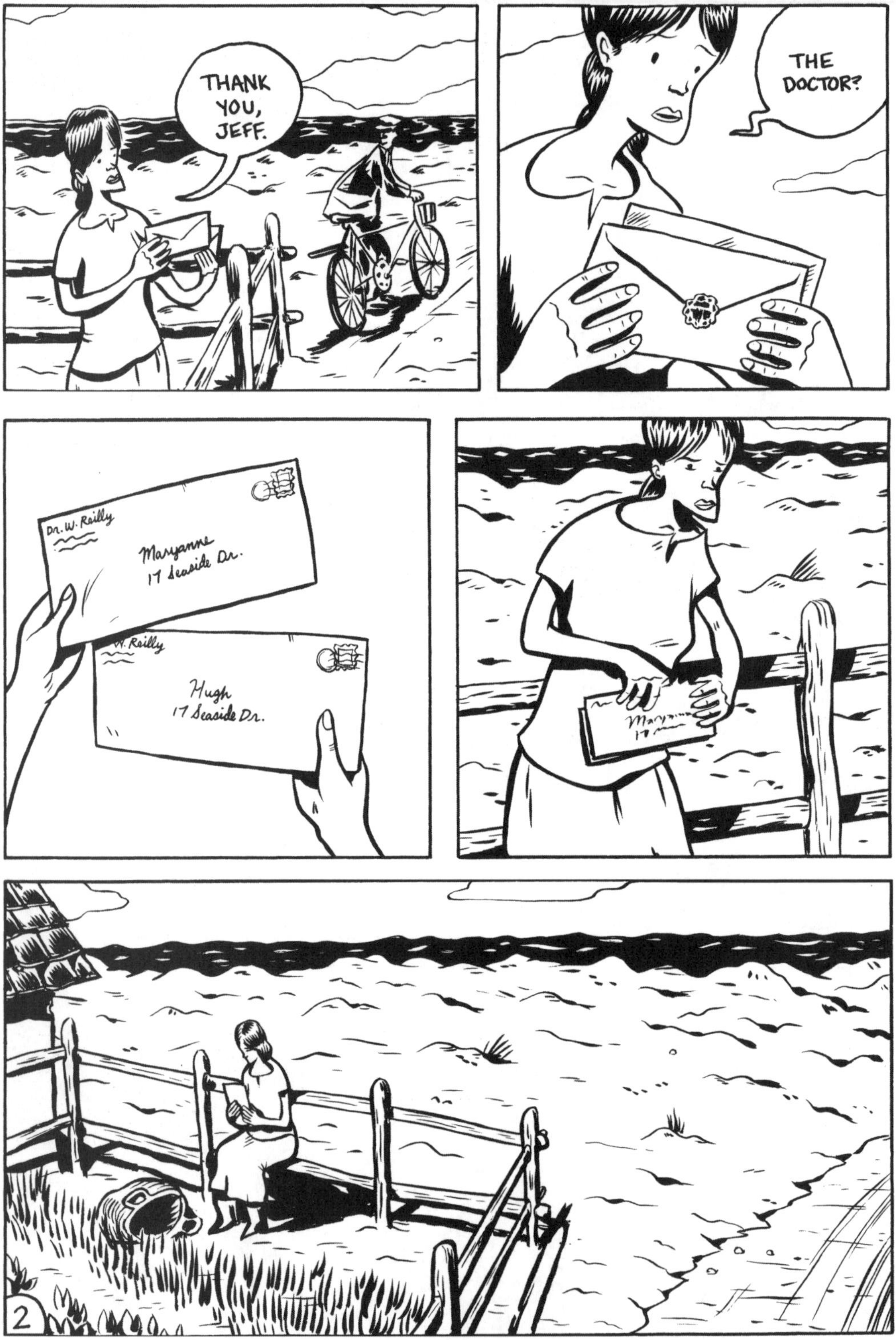
THANK YOU, JEFF.
THE DOCTOR?
Dr. W. Reilly
Maryanne
17 Seaside Dr.
W. Reilly
Hugh
17 Seaside Dr.

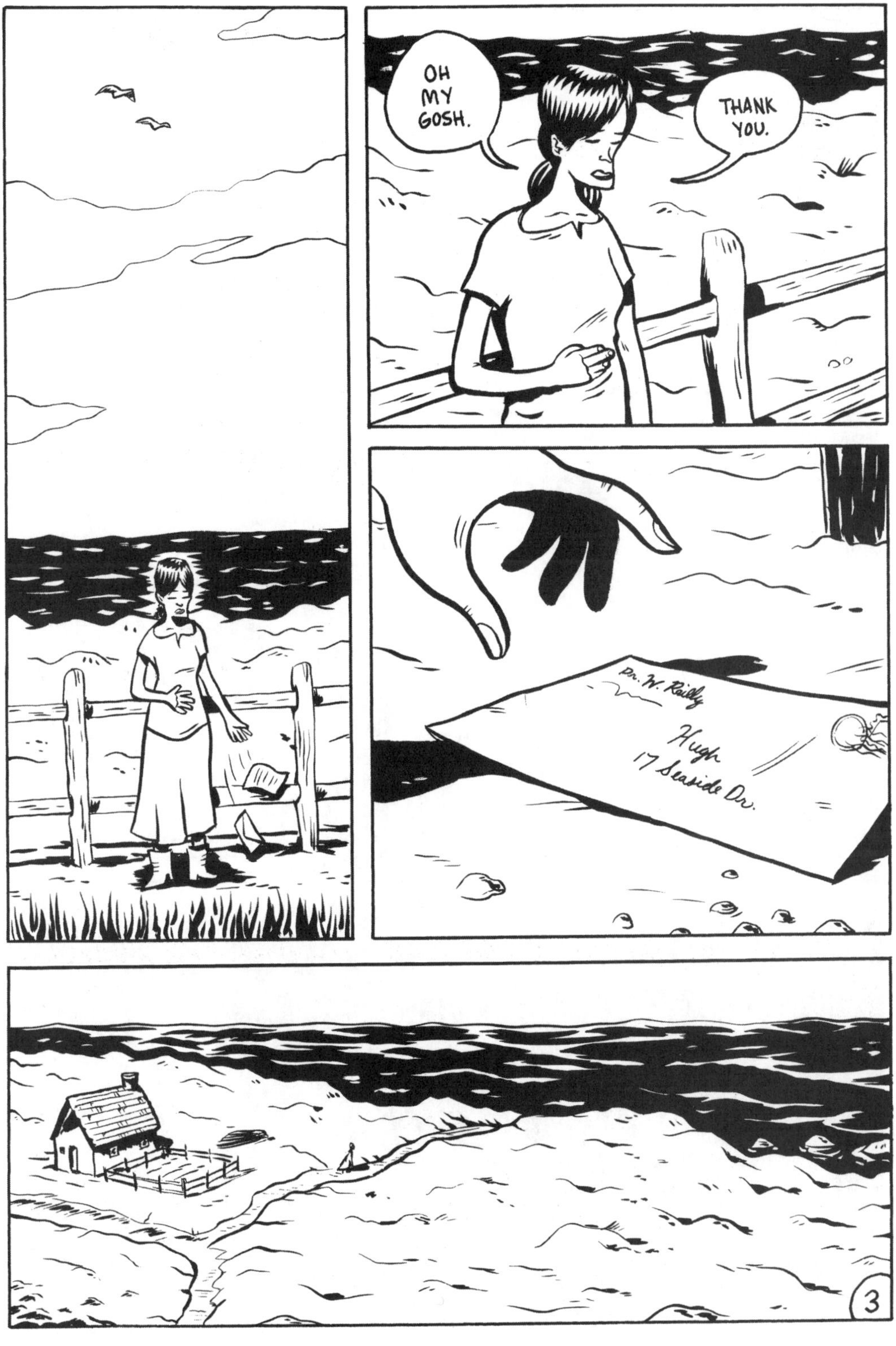
OH MY GOSH.
THANK YOU.
Dr. W. Railly
Hugh
17 Seaside Dr.
3

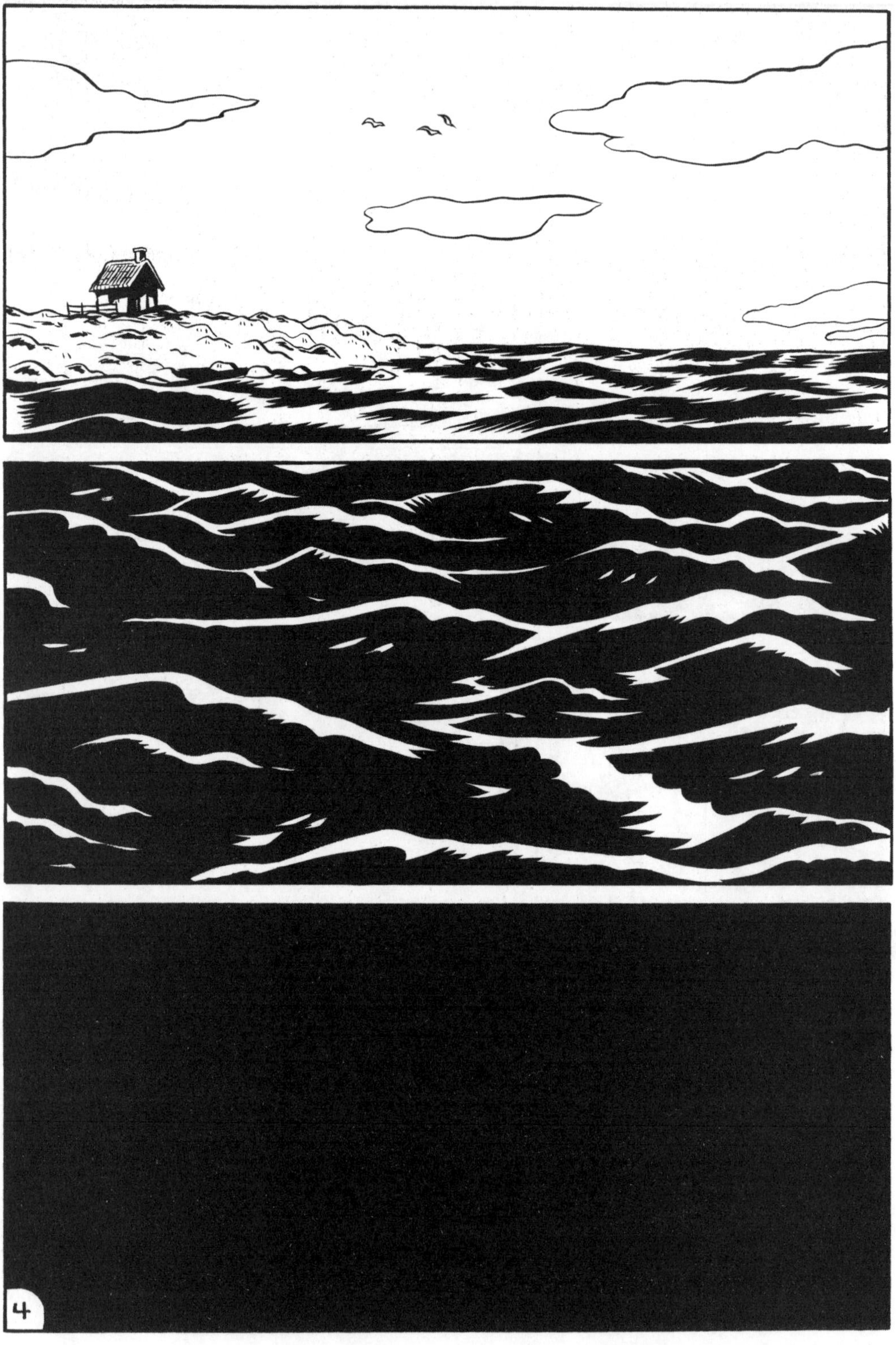

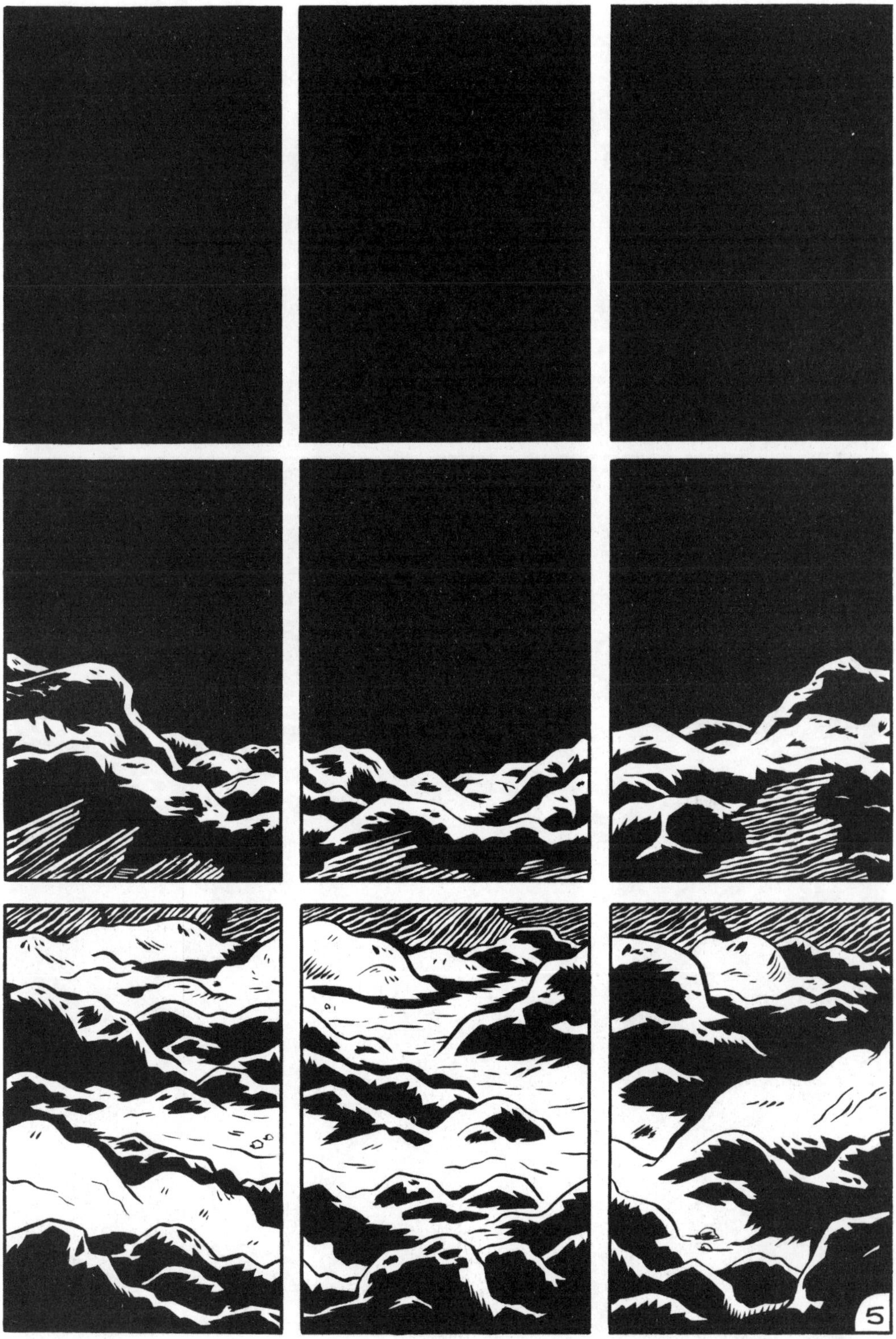
5

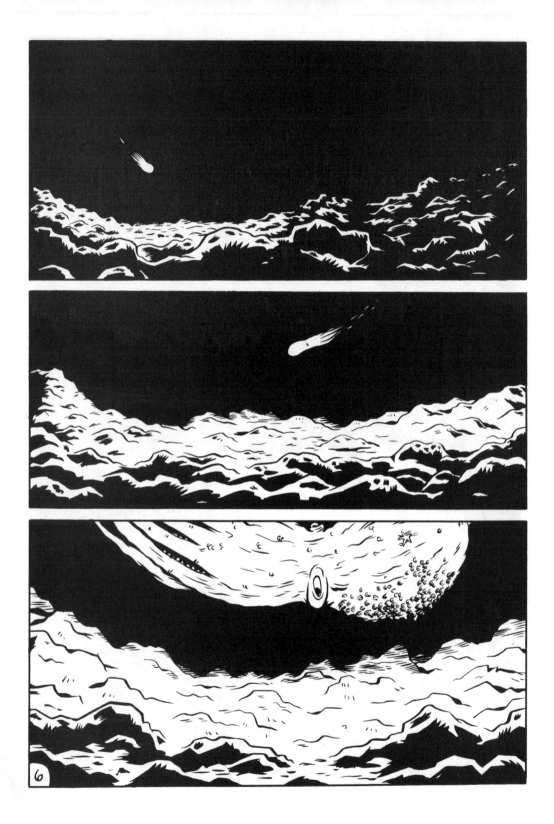

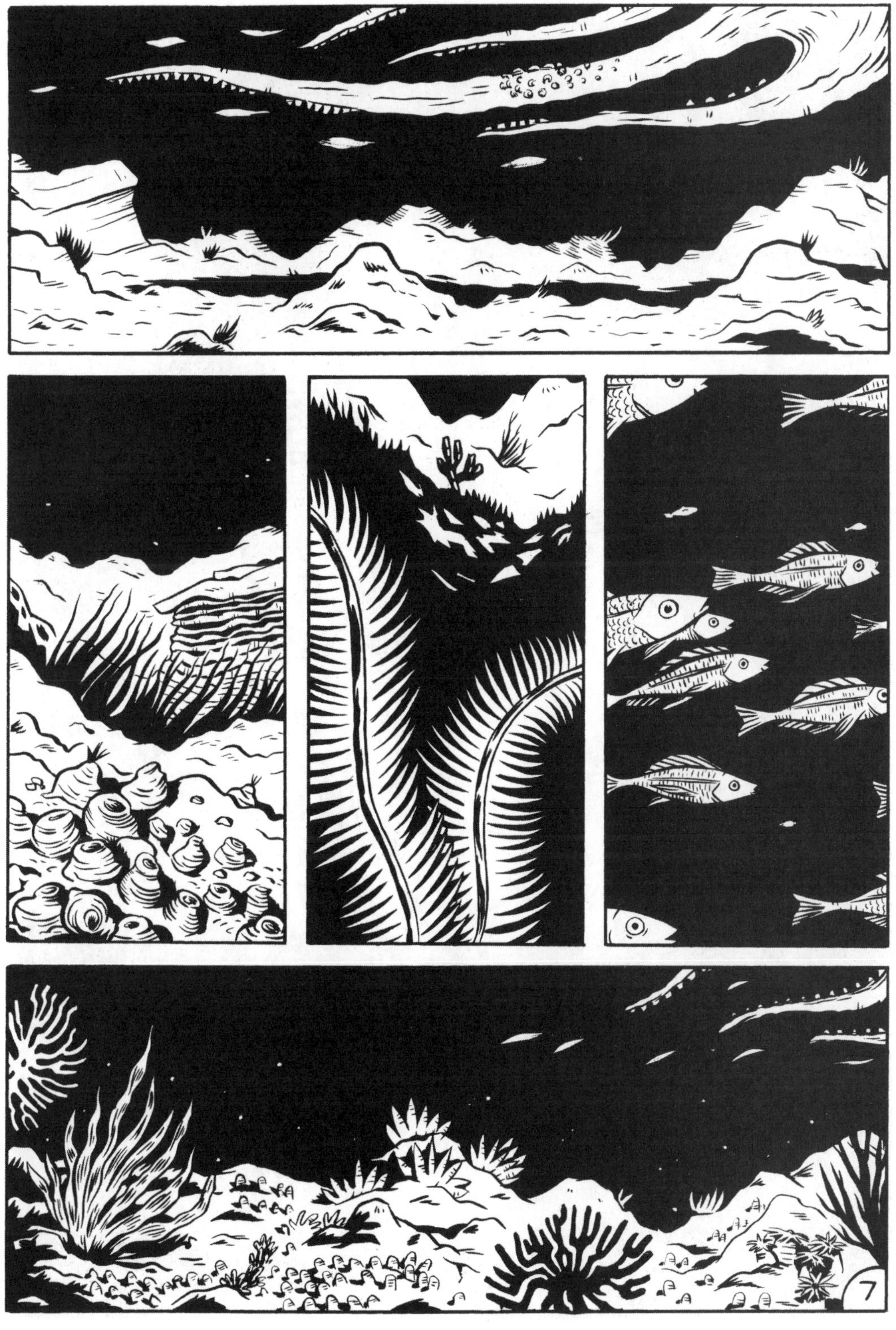

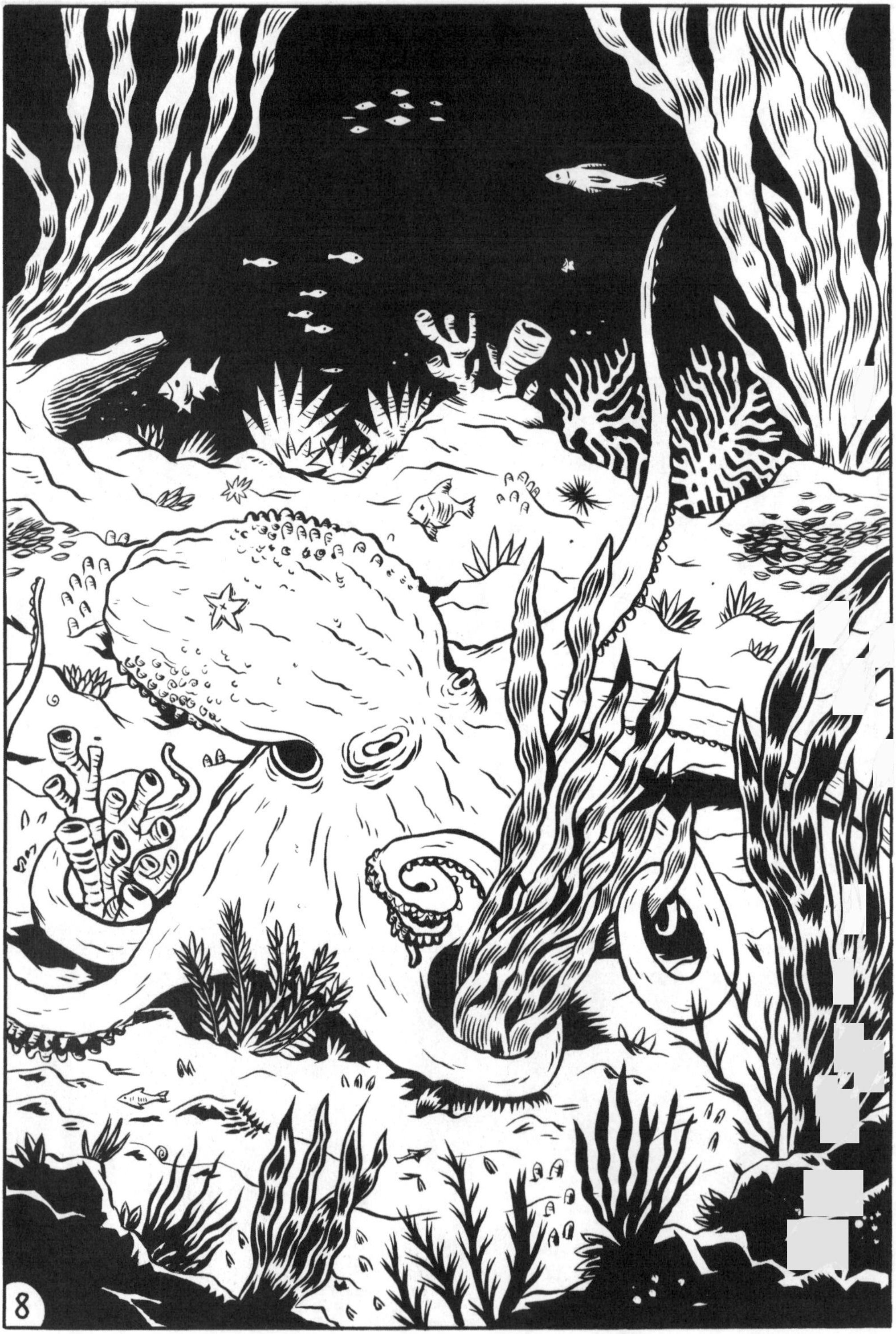

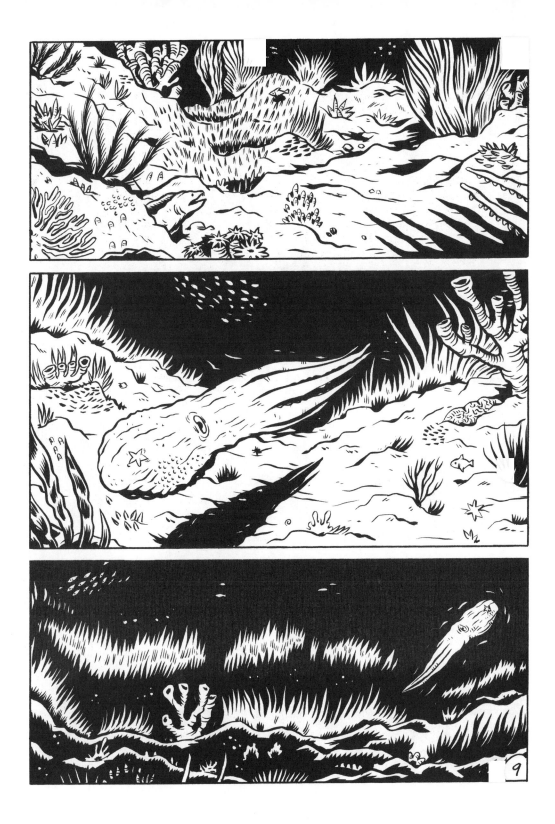

9

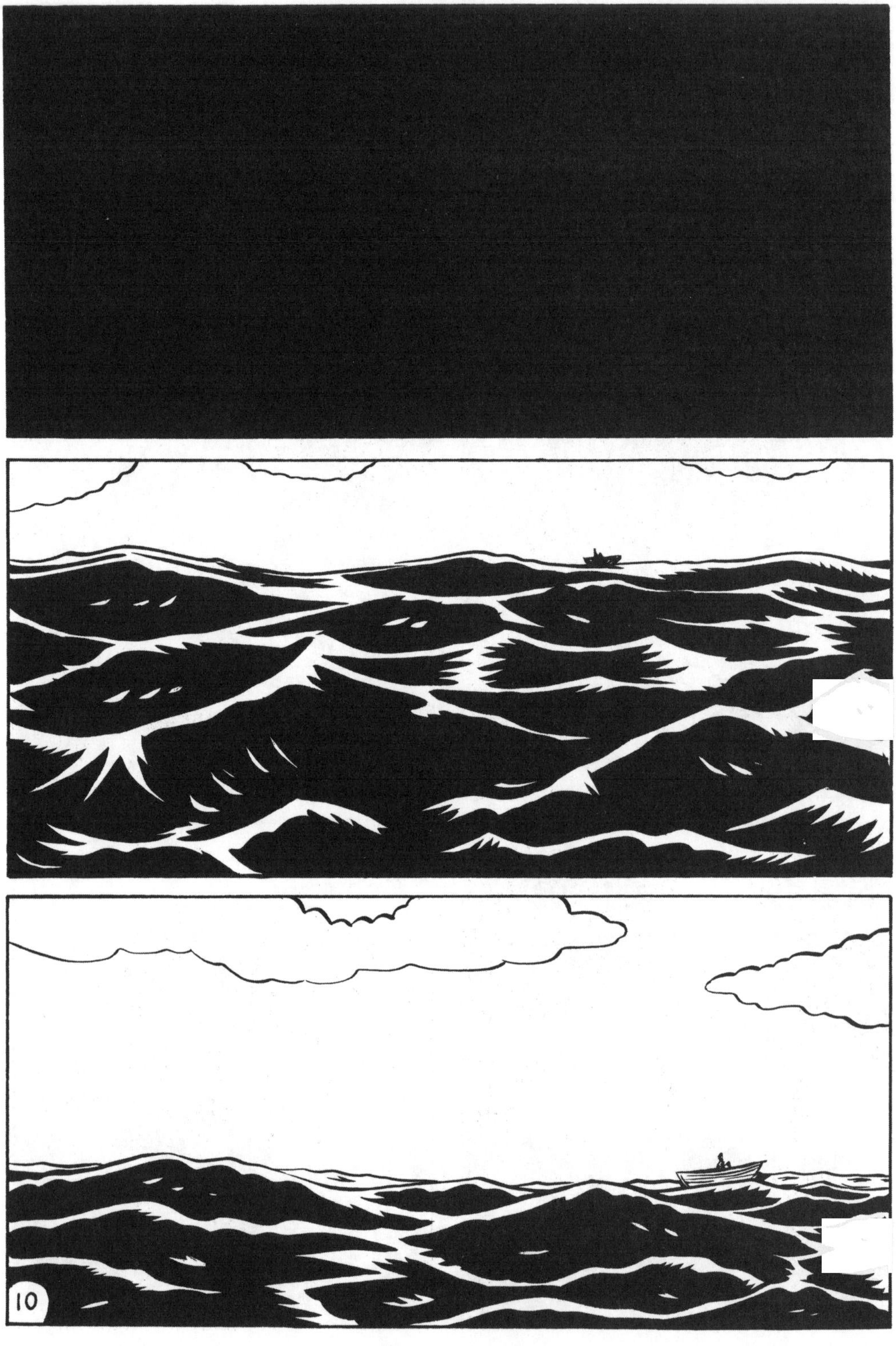

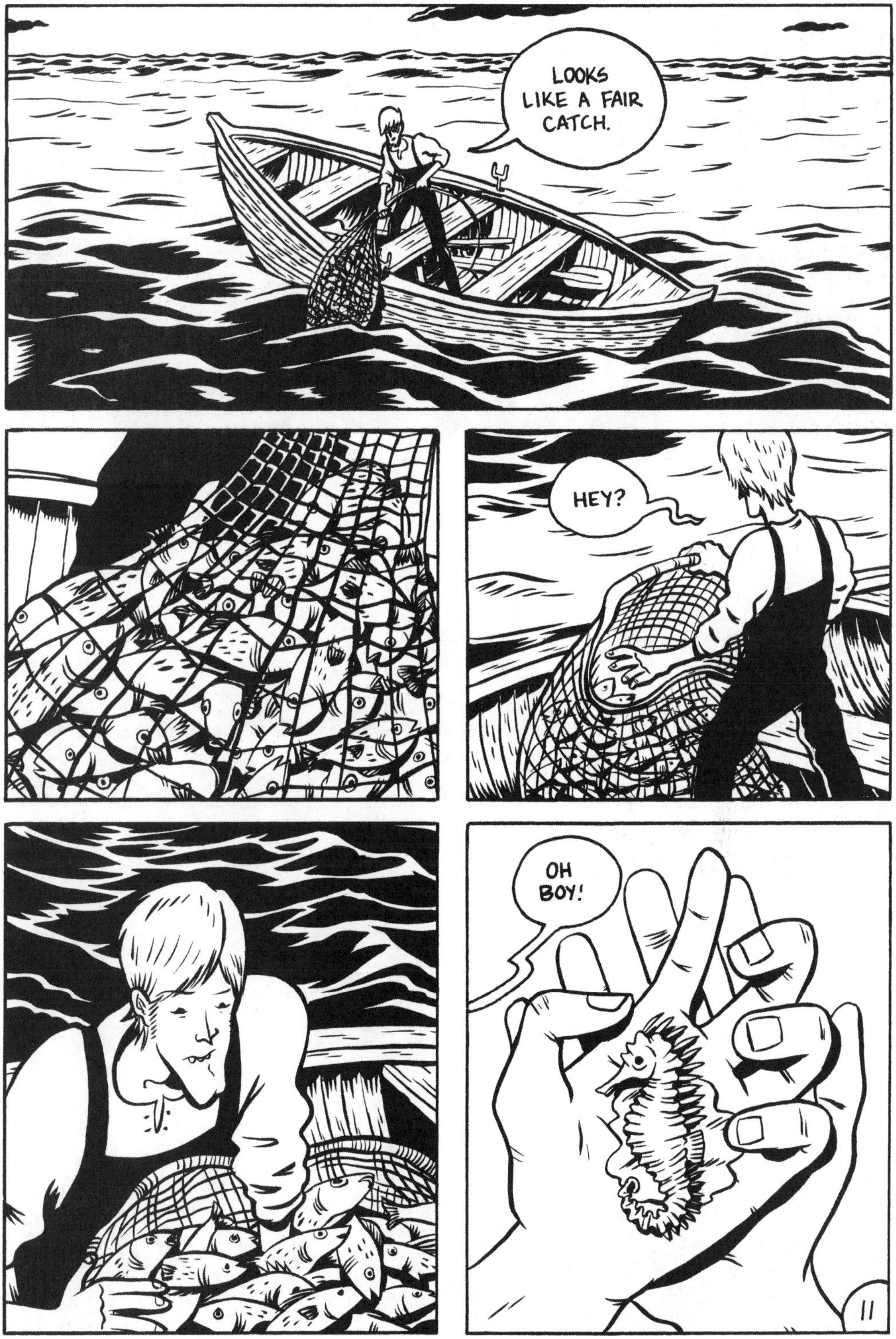
LOOKS LIKE A FAIR CATCH.
HEY?
OH BOY!

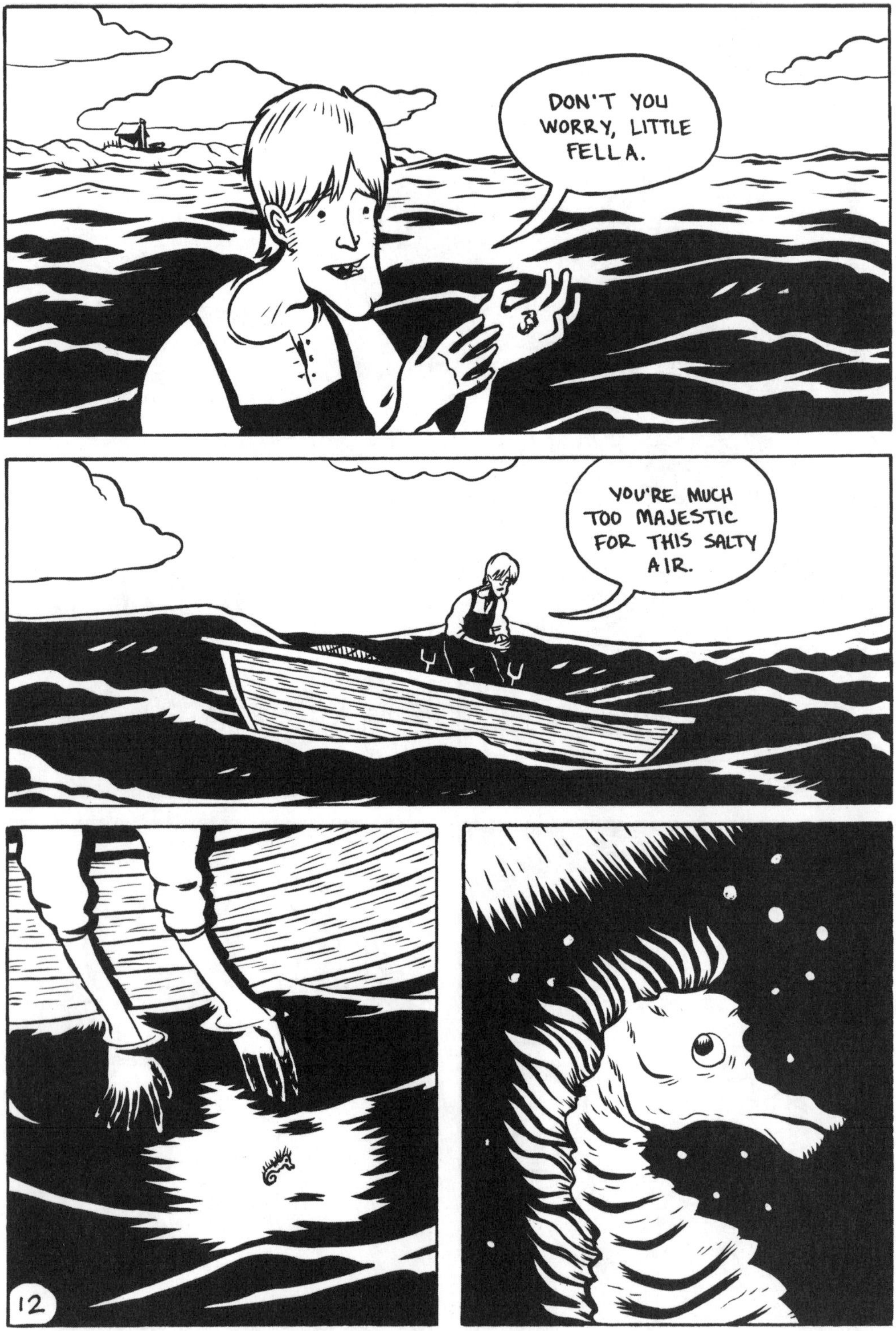
DON'T YOU WORRY, LITTLE FELLA.
YOU'RE MUCH TOO MAJESTIC FOR THIS SALTY AIR.

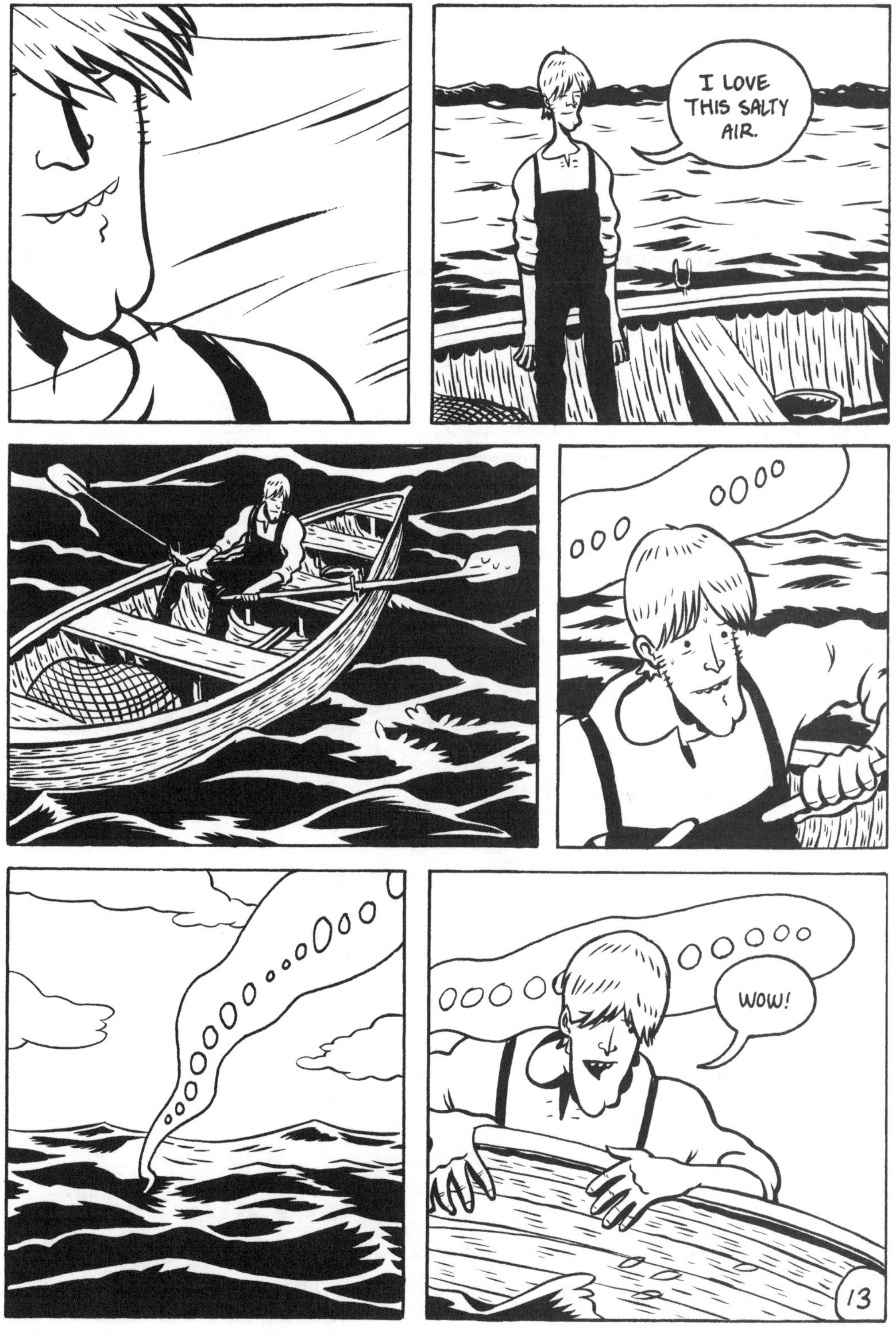
I LOVE THIS SALTY AIR.
WOW!
13

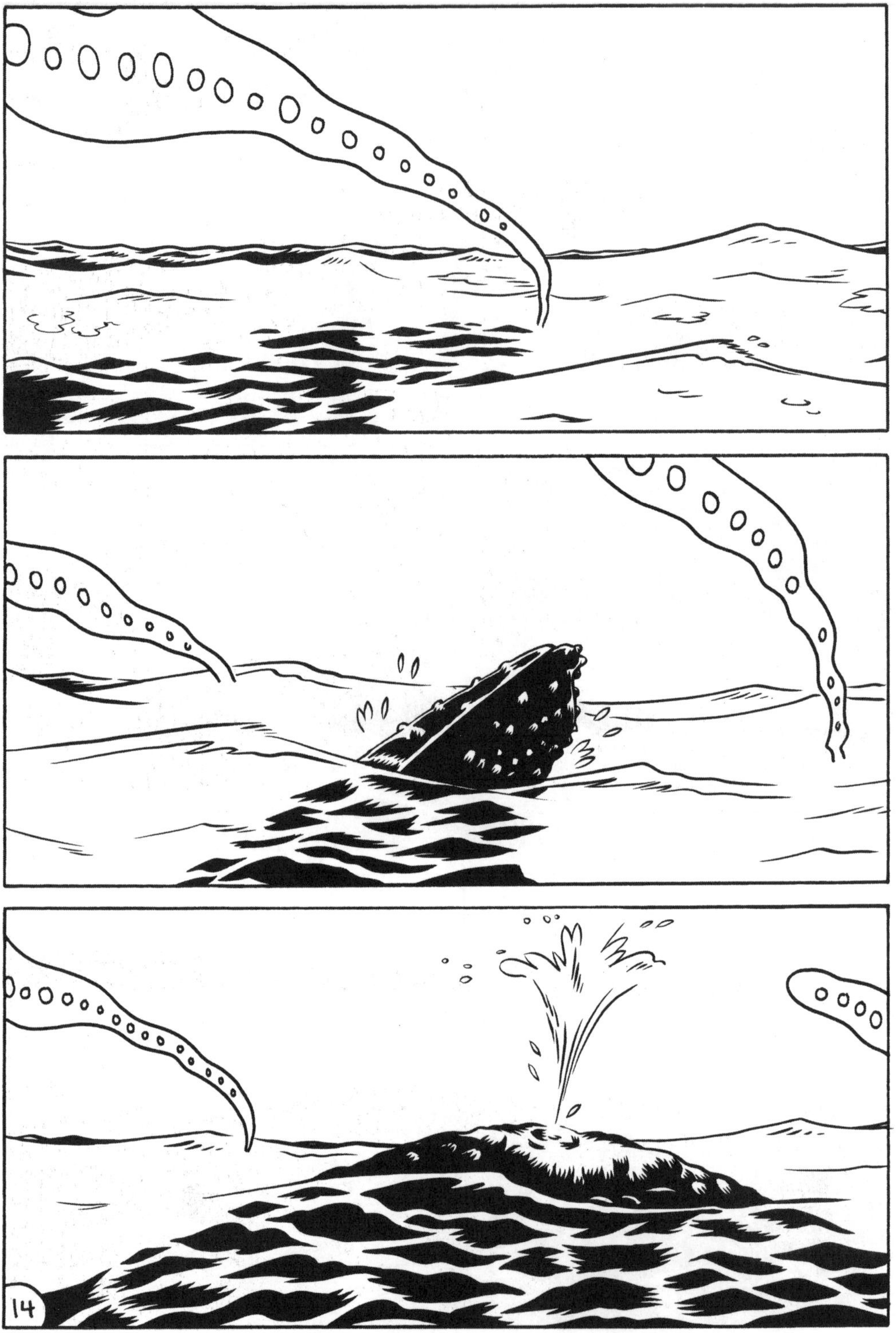

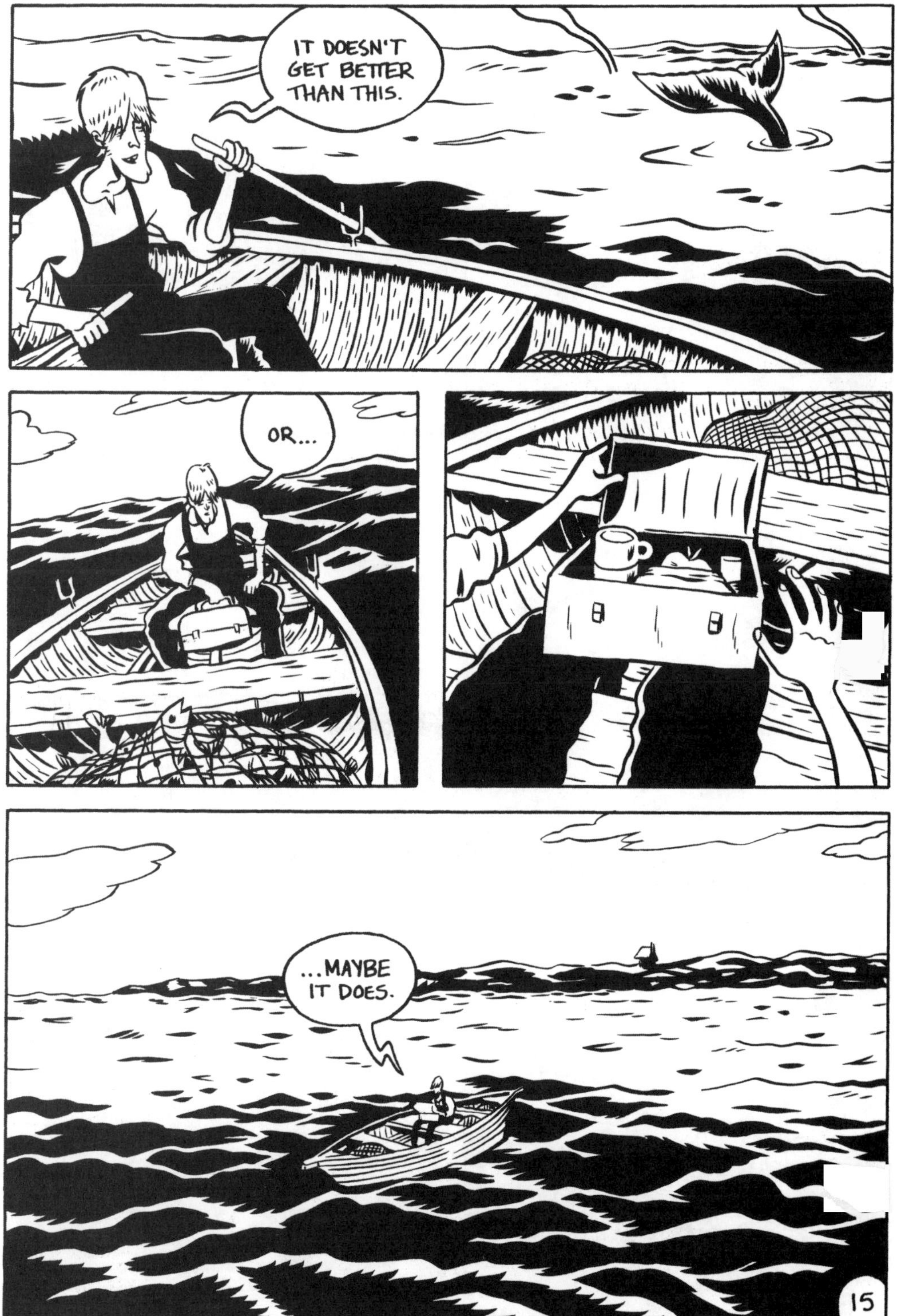
IT DOESN'T GET BETTER THAN THIS.
OR...
...MAYBE IT DOES.

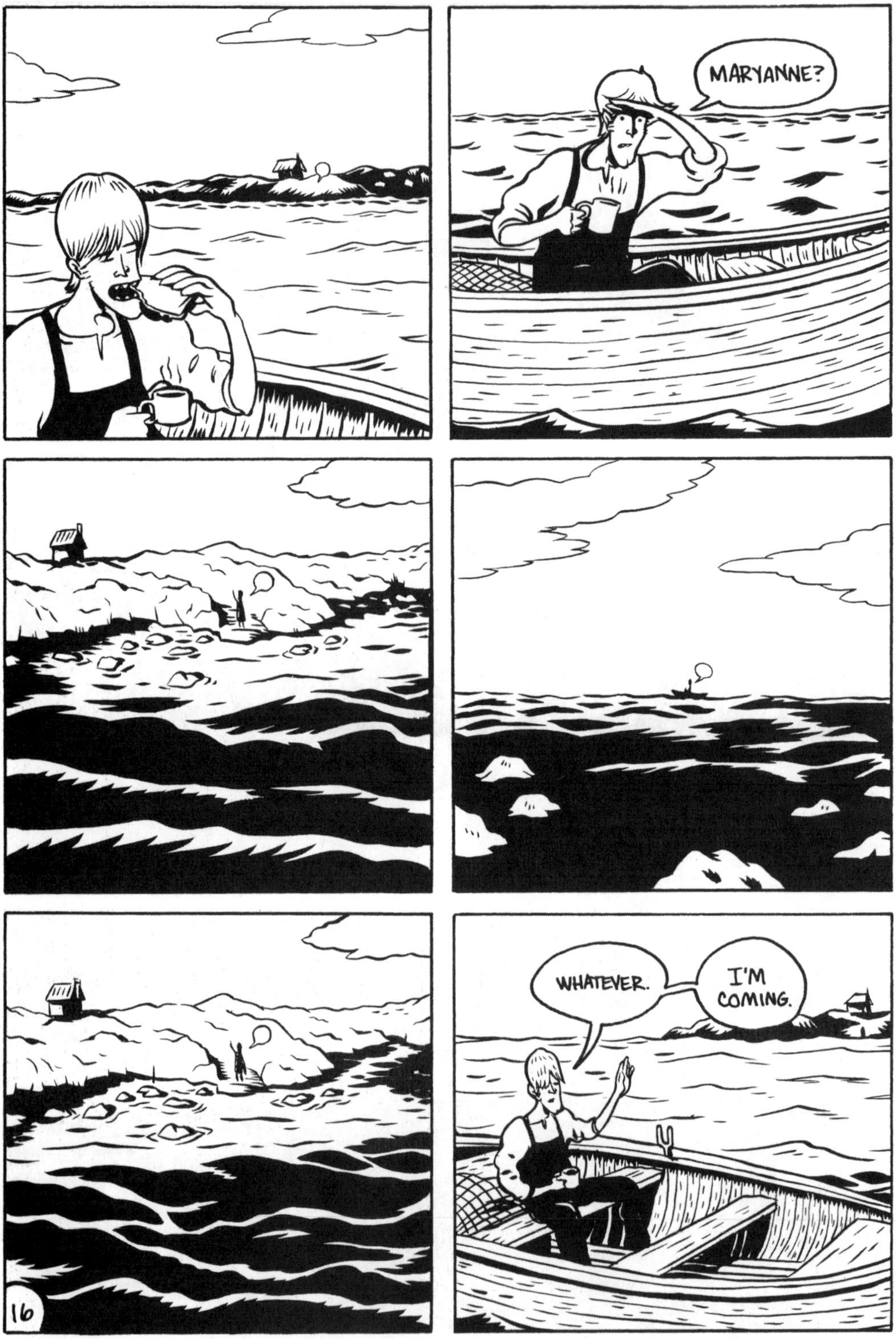
MARYANNE?
WHATEVER.
I'M COMING.

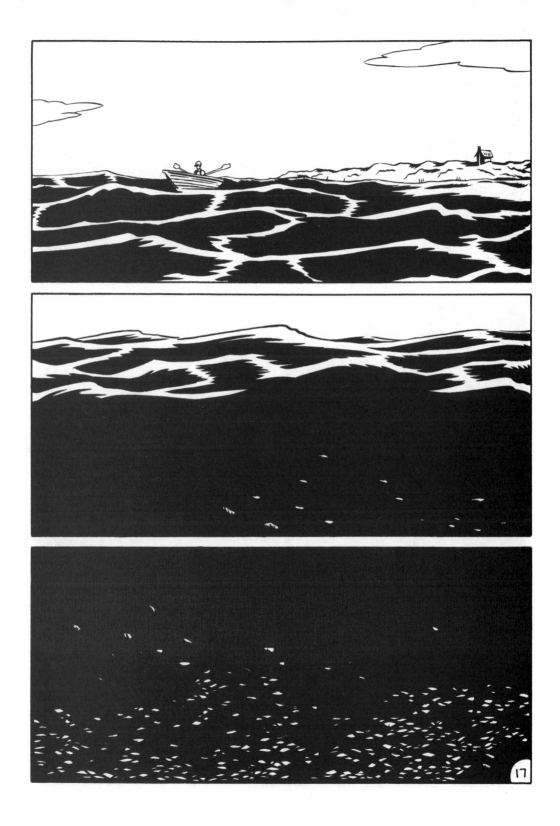

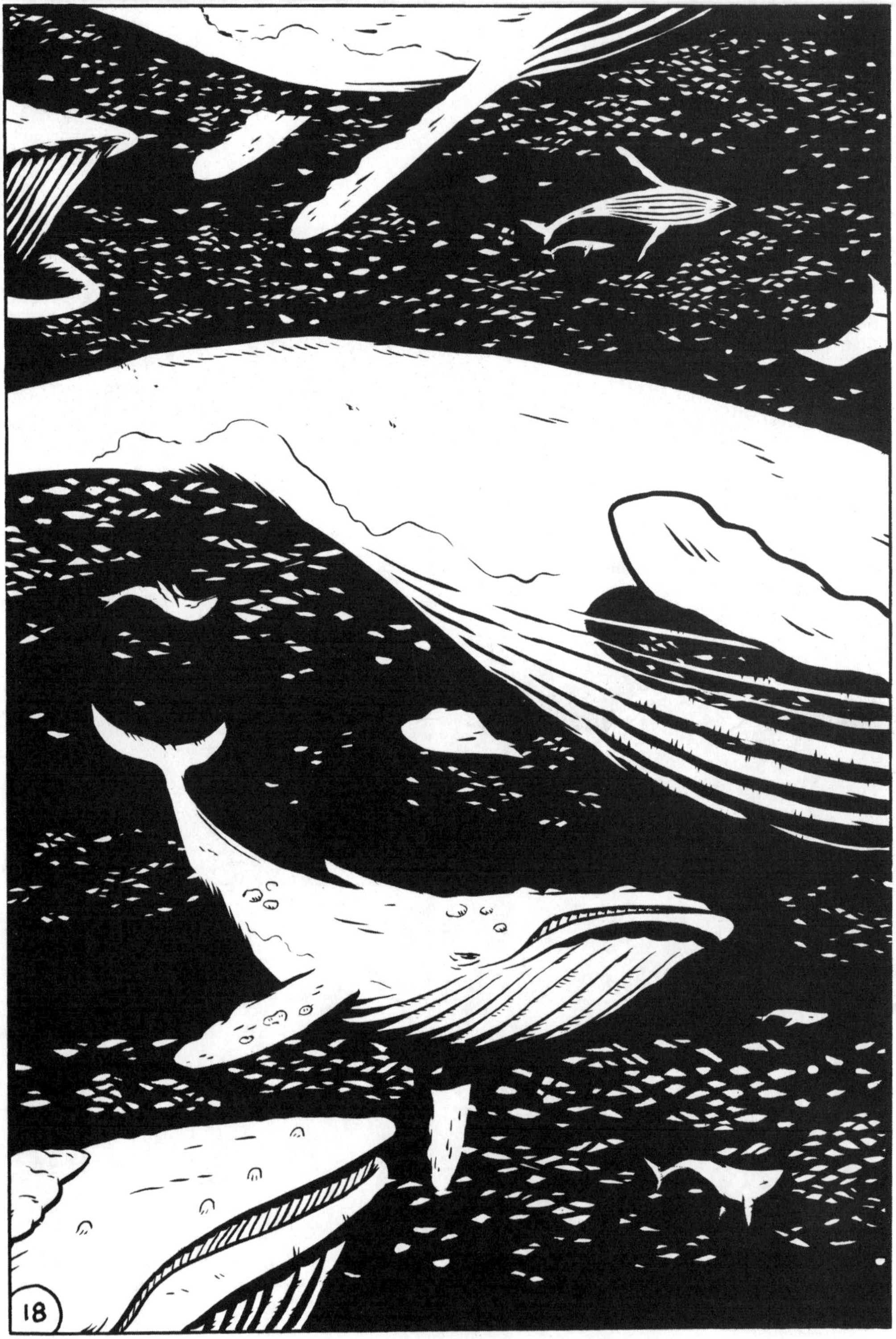

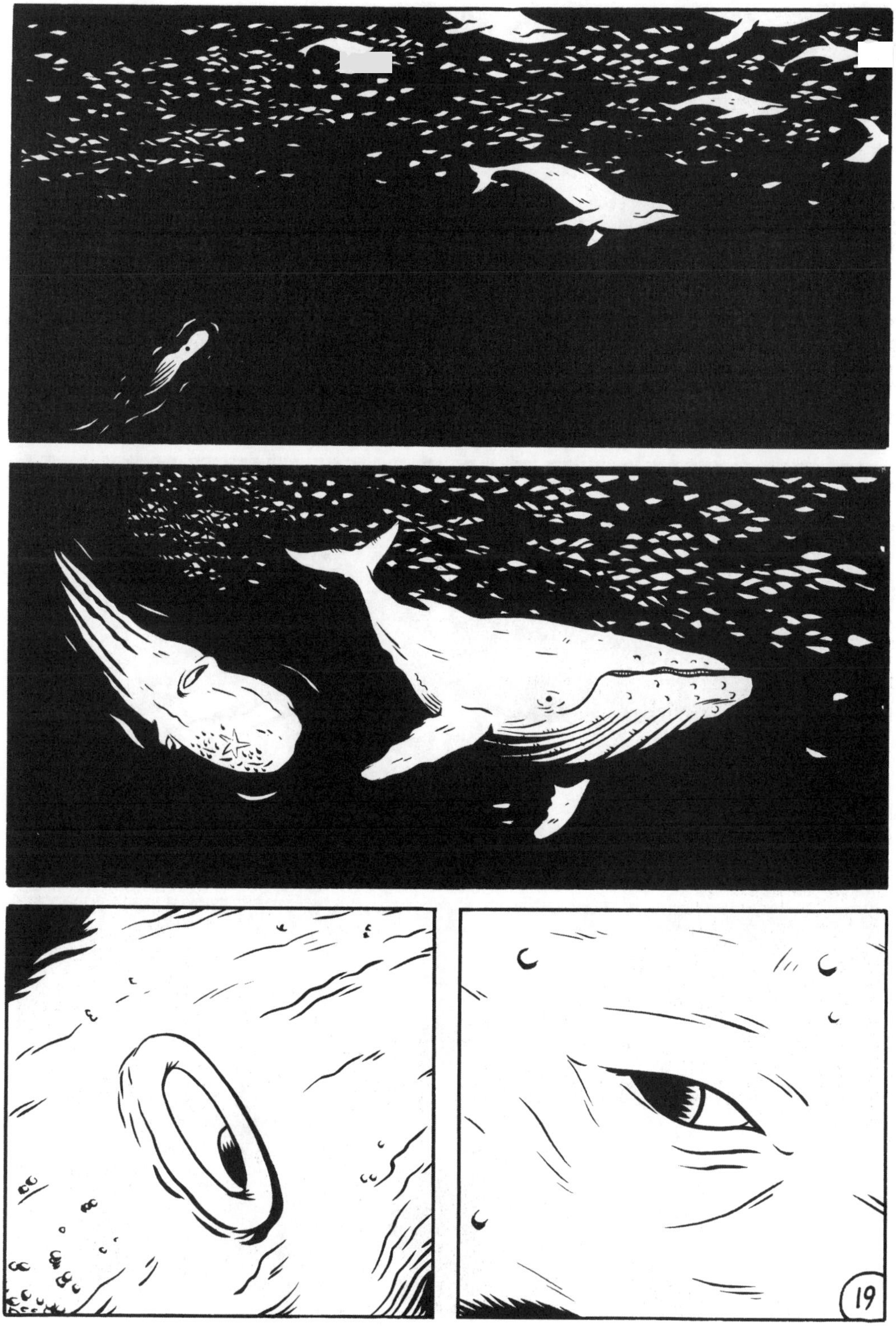

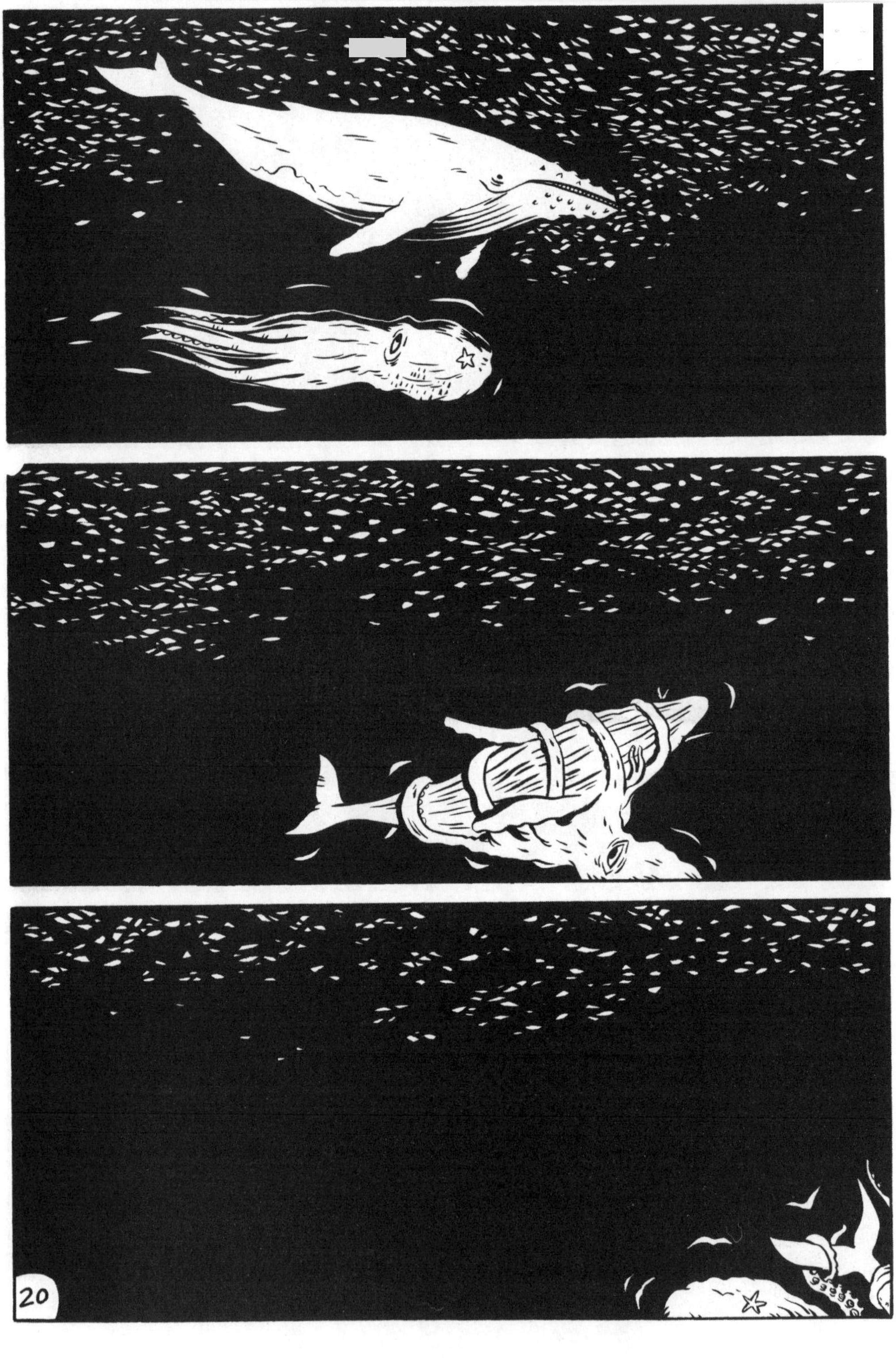

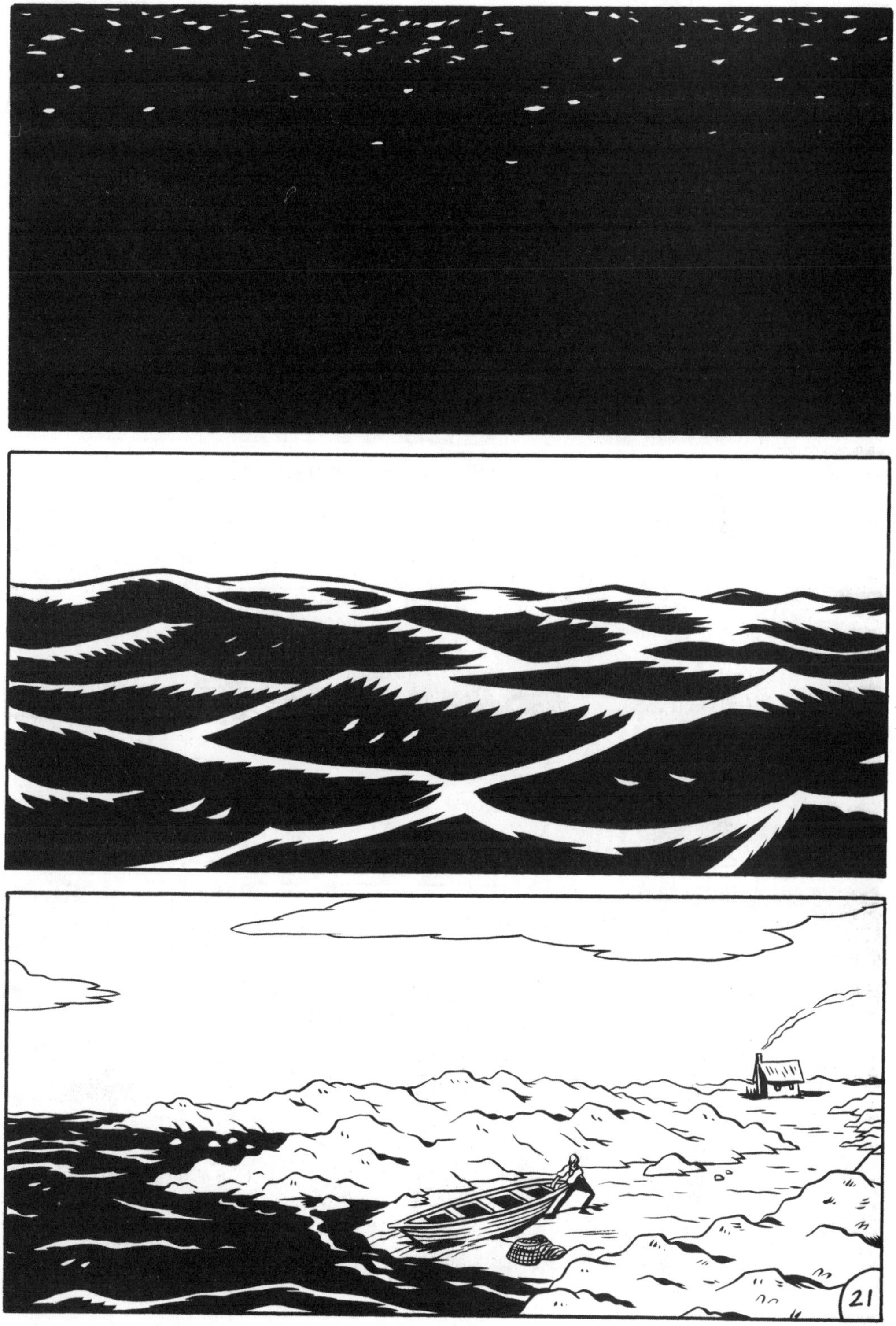

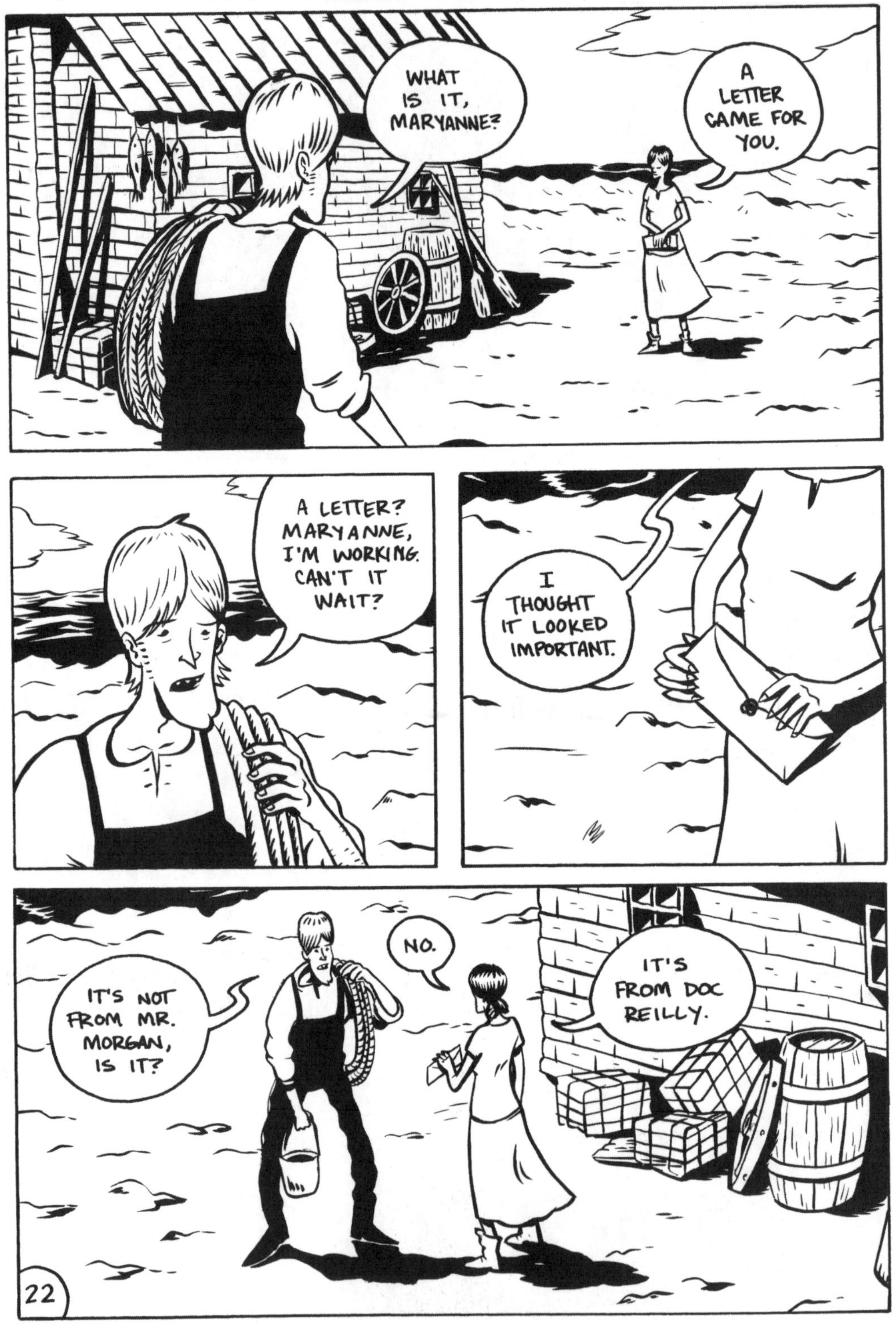

WHAT IS IT, MARYANNE?
A LETTER CAME FOR YOU.
A LETTER? MARYANNE, I'M WORKING. CAN'T IT WAIT?
I THOUGHT IT LOOKED IMPORTANT.
IT'S NOT FROM MR. MORGAN, IS IT?
NO.
IT'S FROM DOC REILLY.

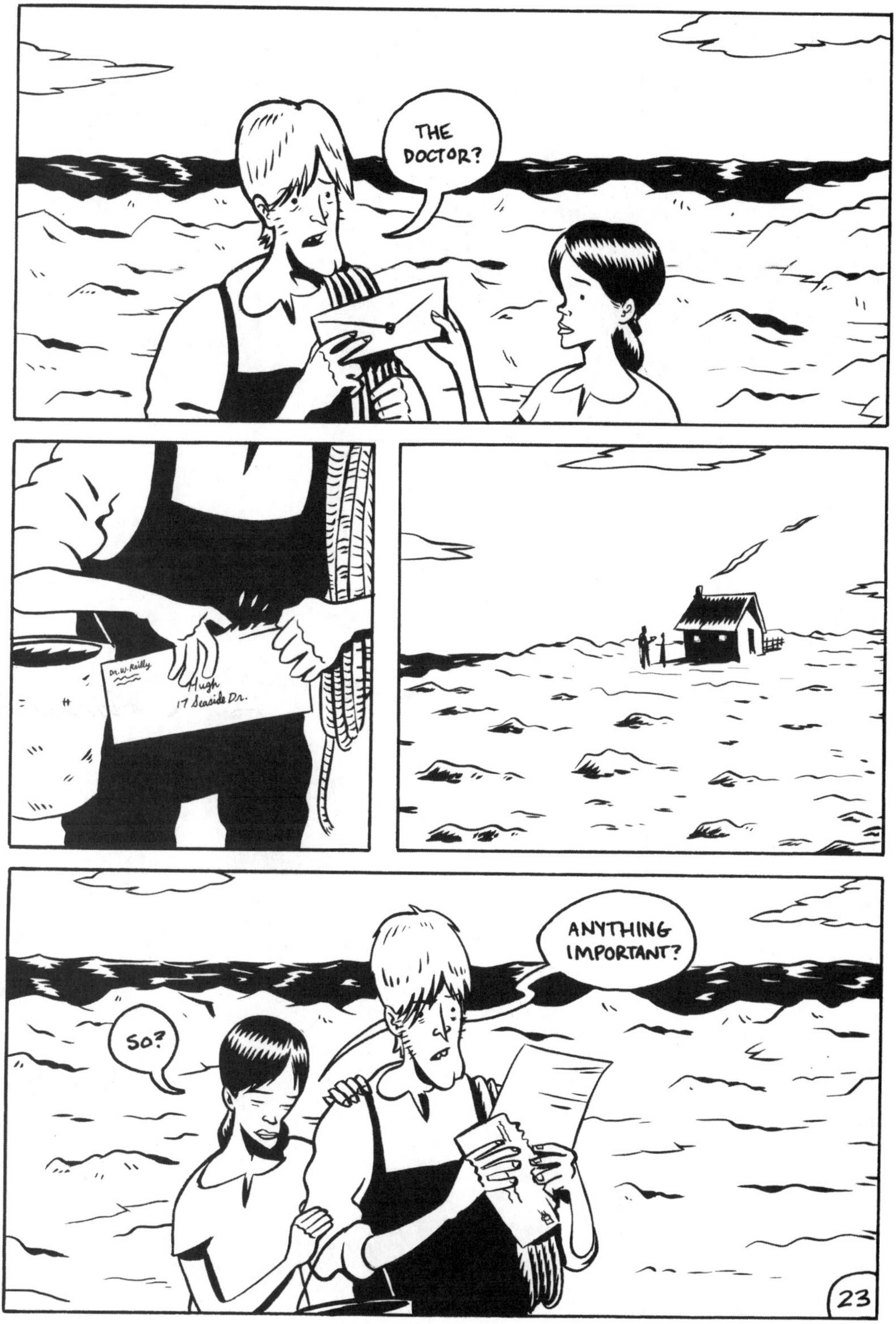
THE DOCTOR?
Dr. W. Railly
Hugh
17 Seaside Dr.
ANYTHING IMPORTANT?
SO?

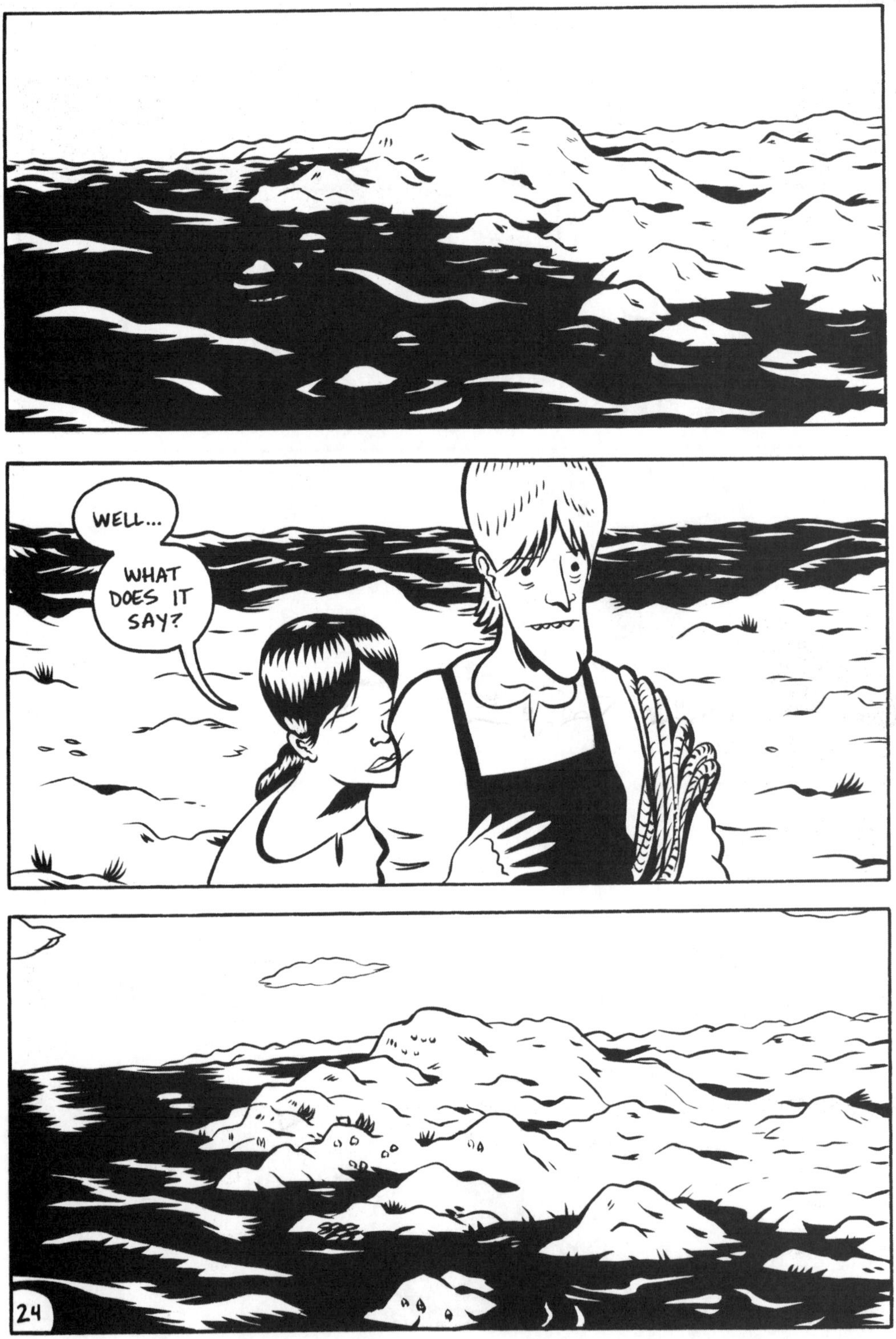
WELL...
WHAT DOES IT SAY?

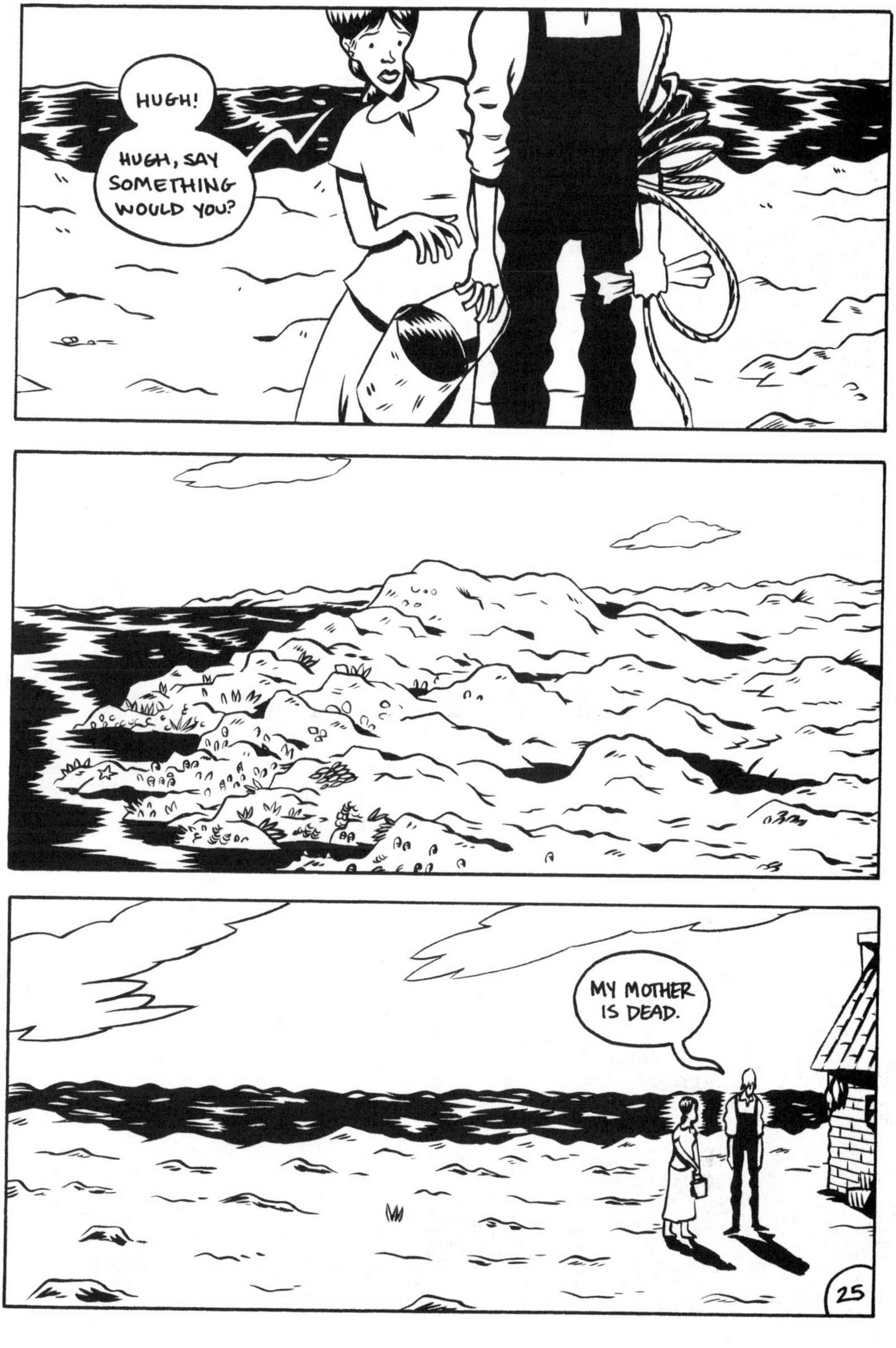
HUGH!
HUGH, SAY SOMETHING WOULD YOU?
MY MOTHER IS DEAD.

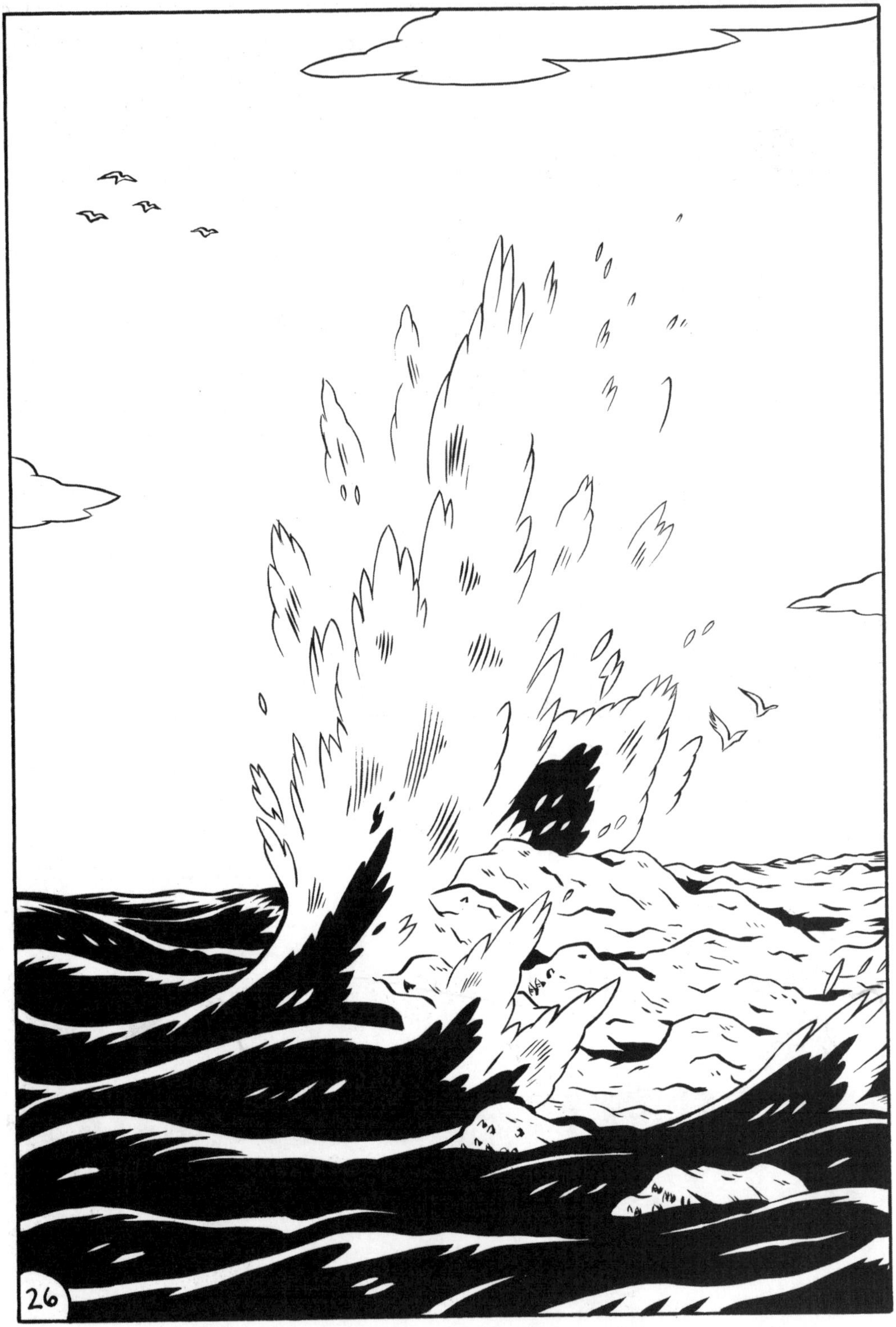

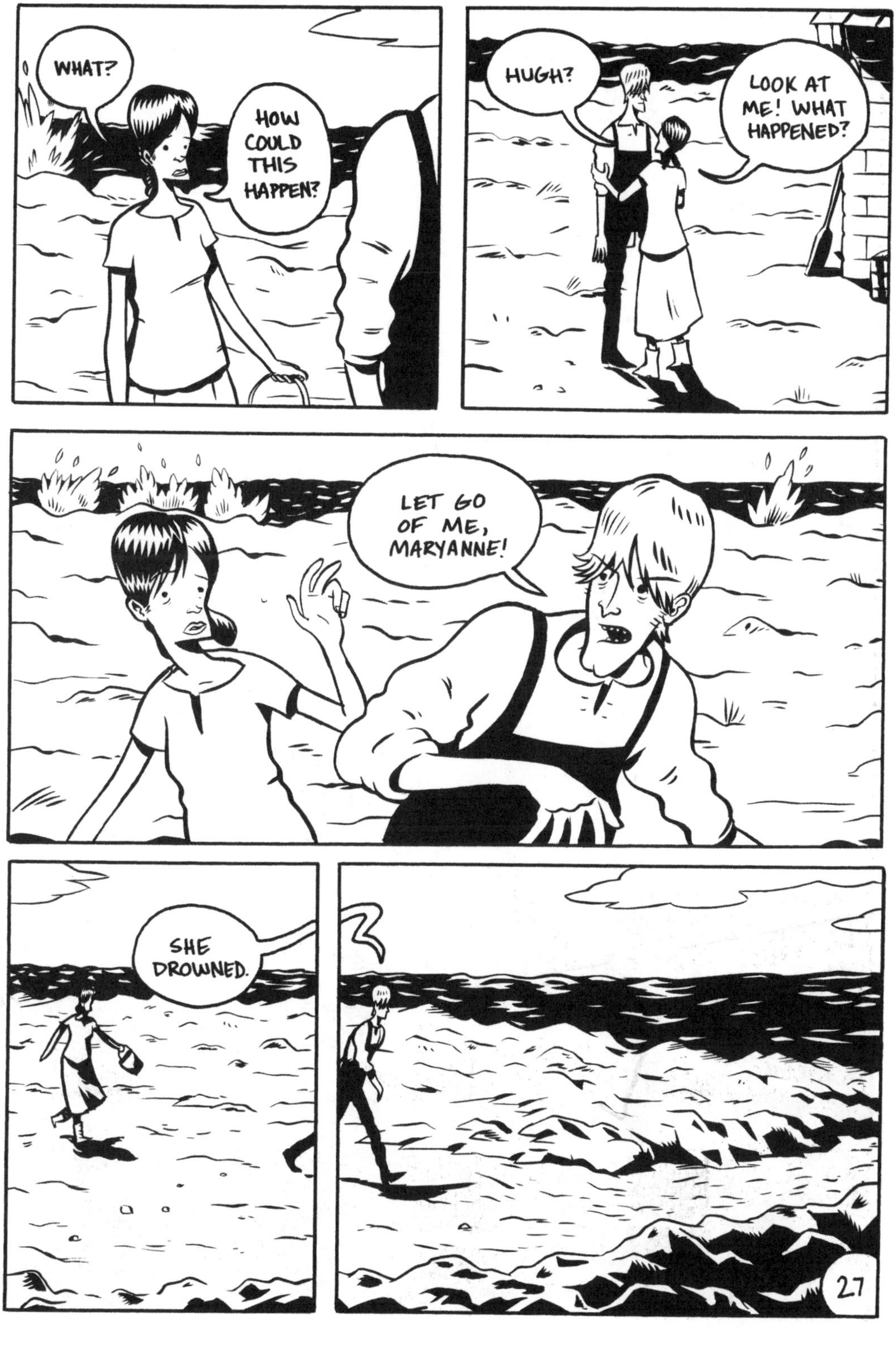
WHAT?
HOW COULD THIS HAPPEN?
HUGH?
LOOK AT ME! WHAT HAPPENED?
LET GO OF ME, MARYANNE!
SHE DROWNED.

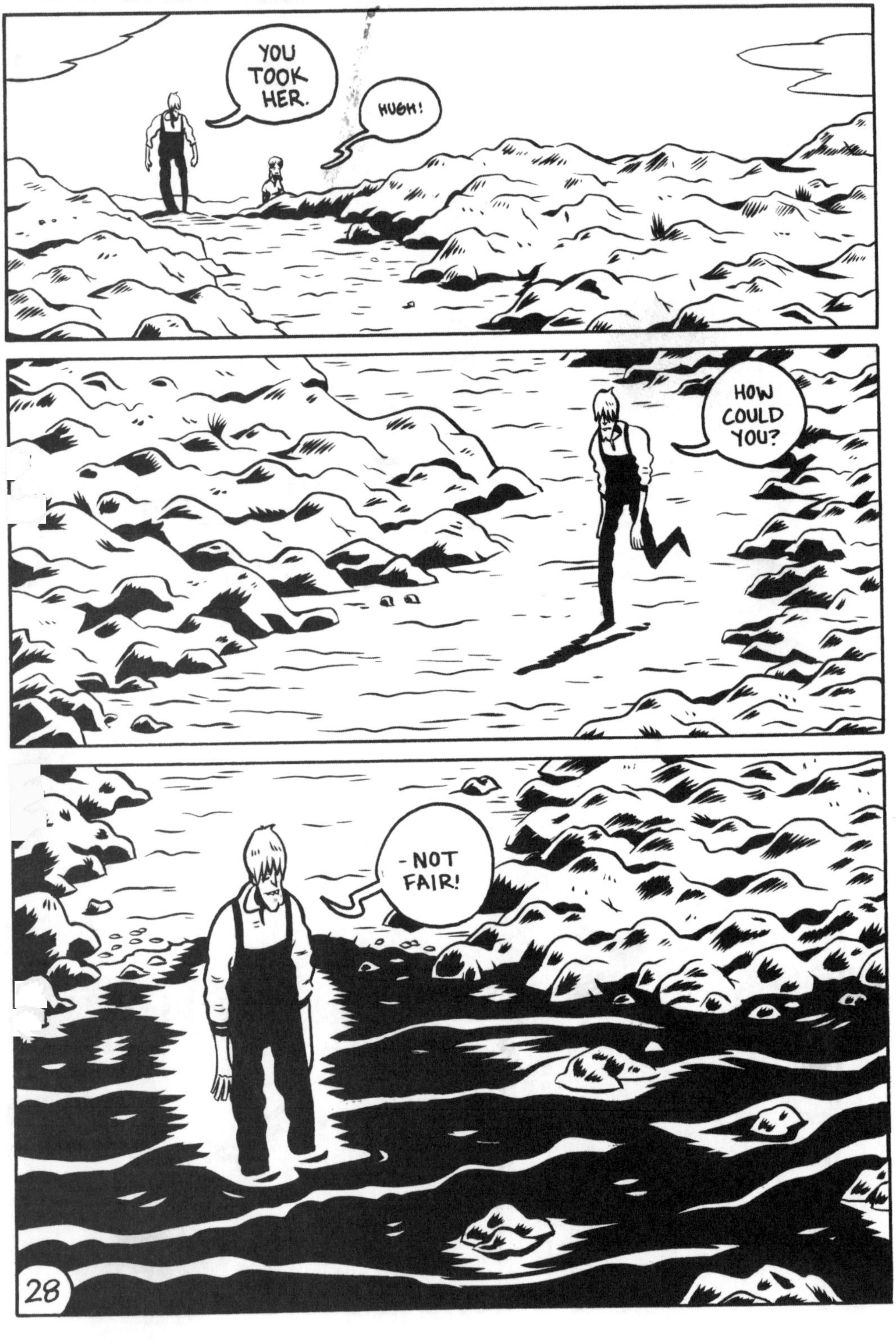
YOU TOOK HER.
HUGH!
HOW COULD YOU?
-NOT FAIR!

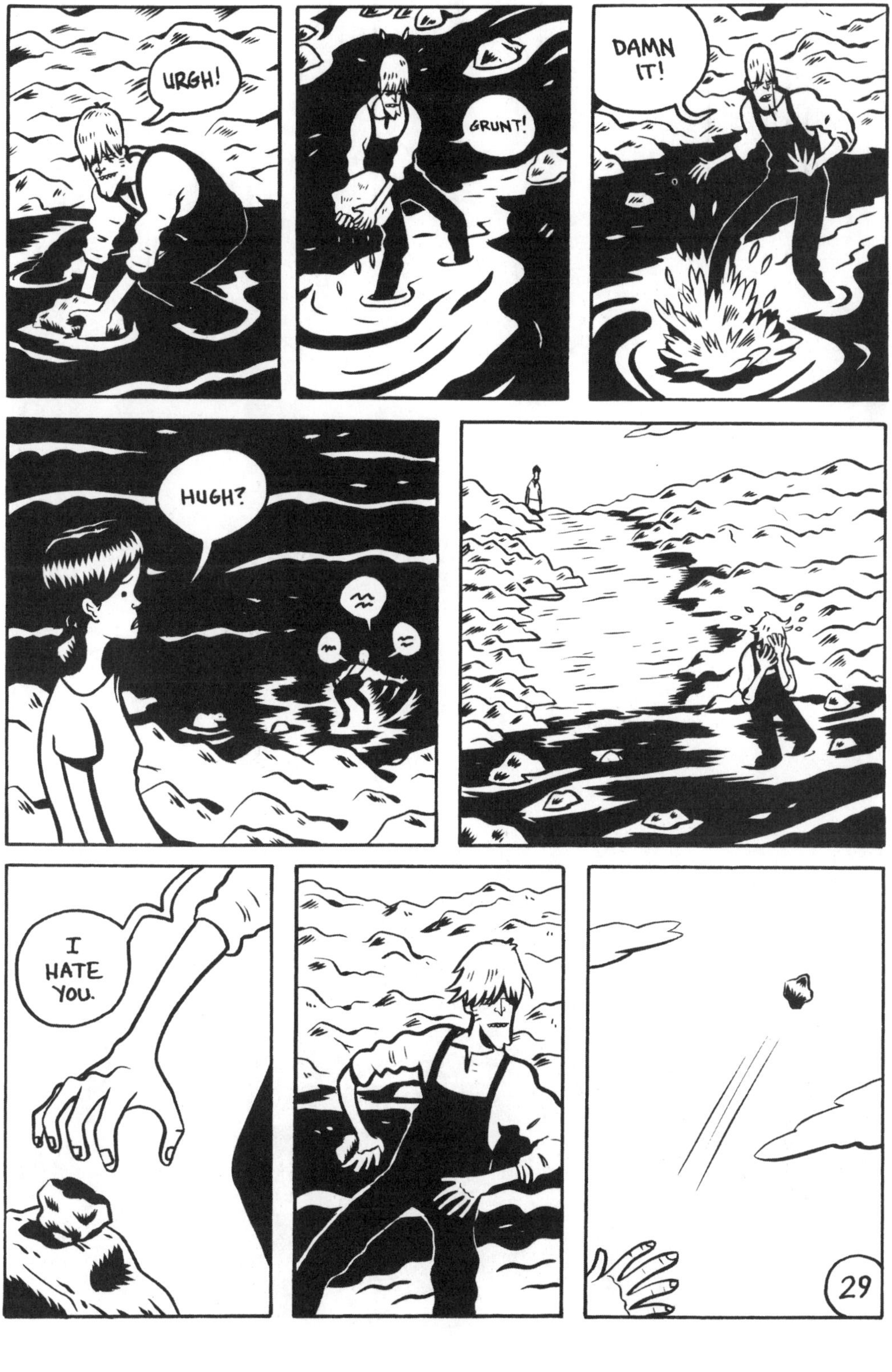
URGH!
GRUNT!
DAMN IT!
HUGH?
I HATE YOU.

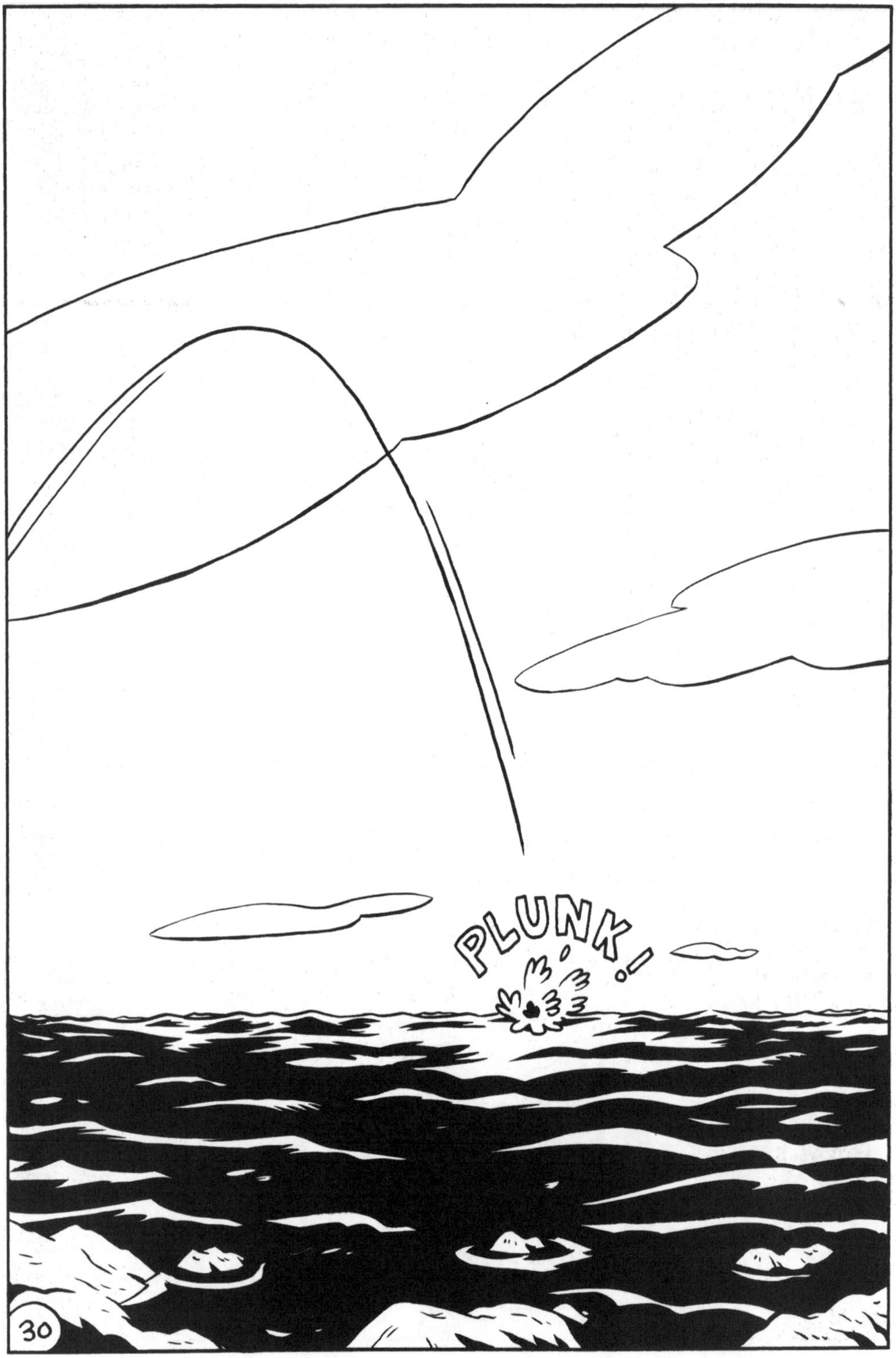
PLUNK!

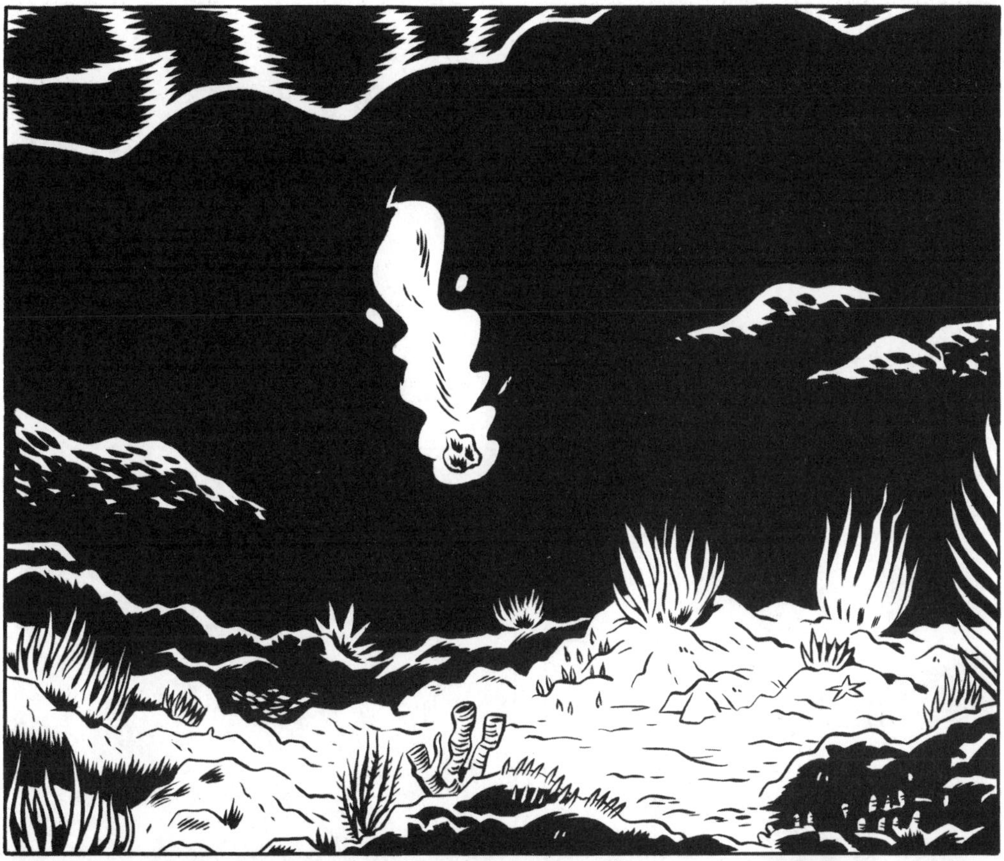

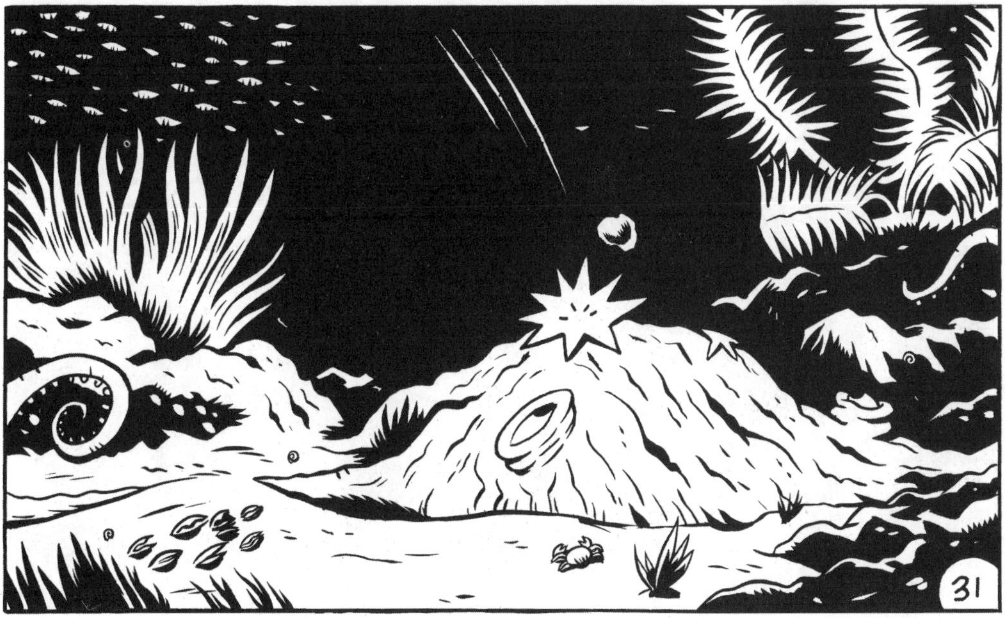

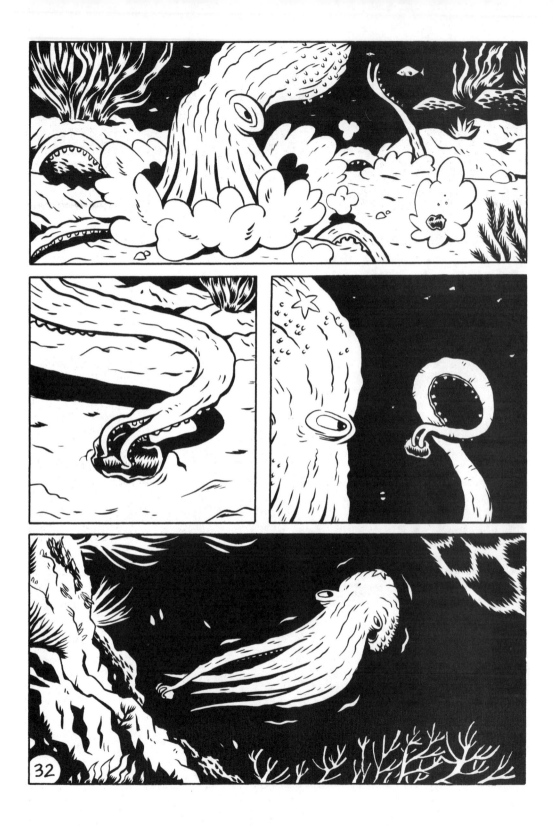

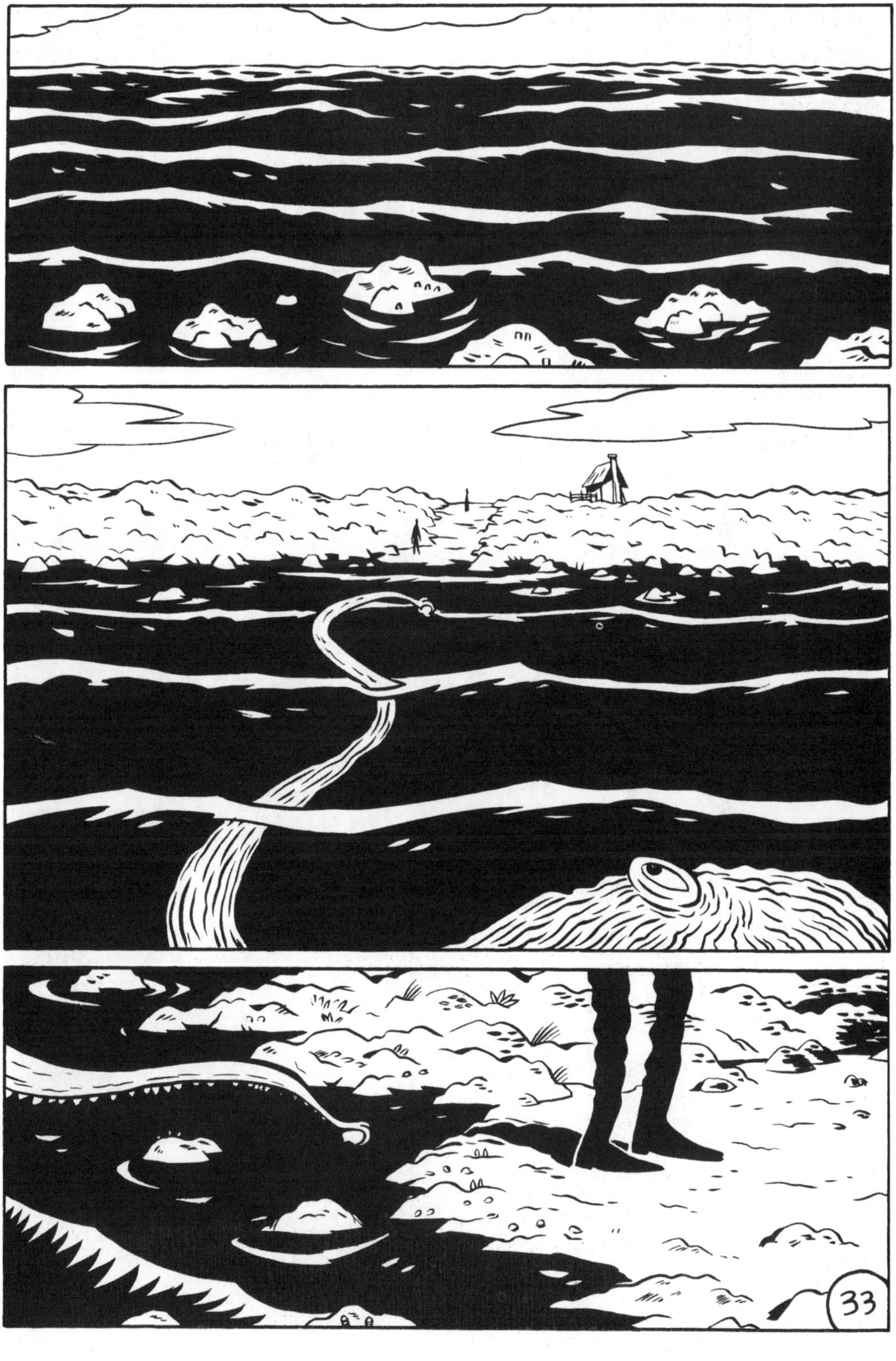

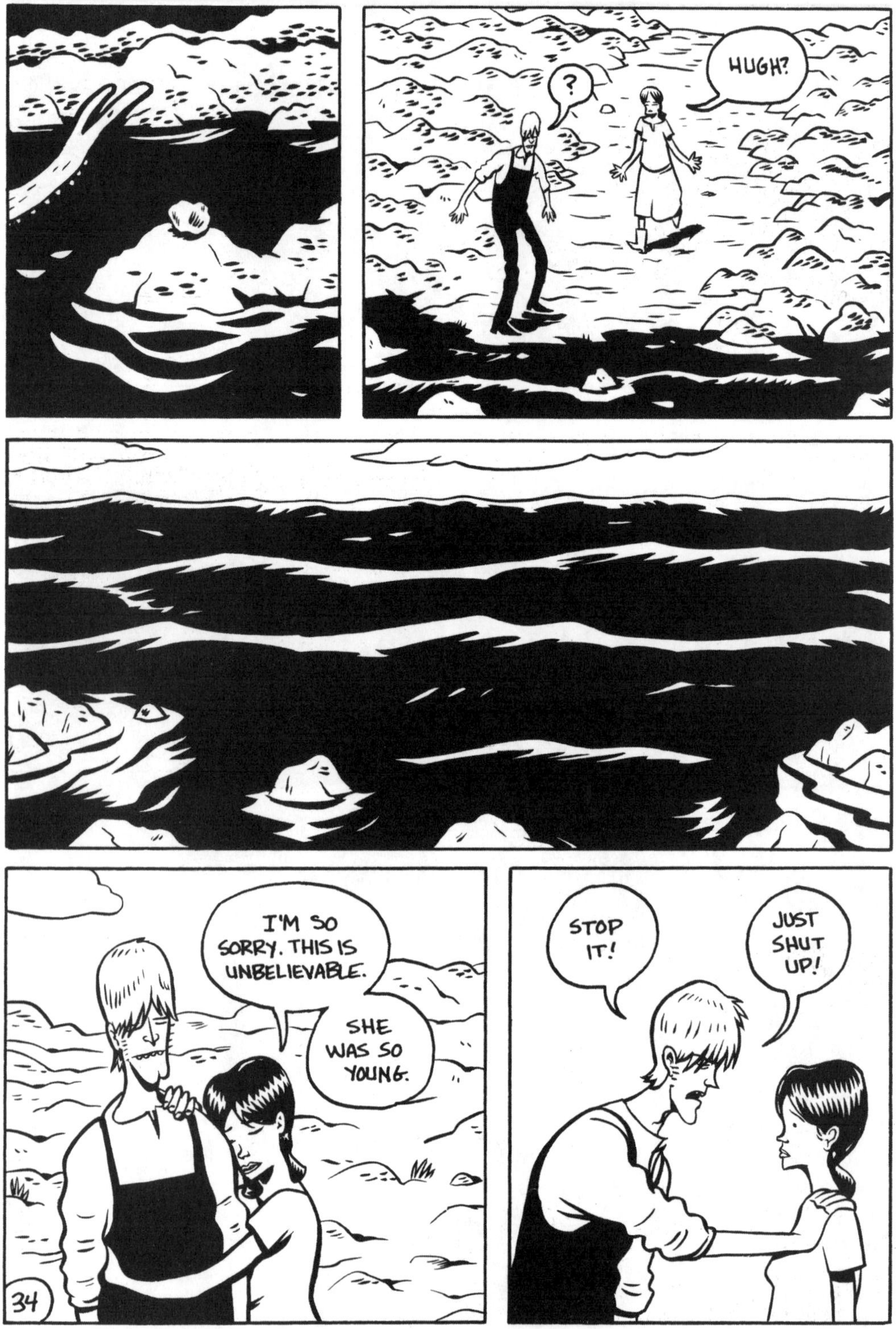
?
HUGH?
I'M SO SORRY. THIS IS UNBELIEVABLE.
SHE WAS SO YOUNG.
STOP IT!
JUST SHUT UP!

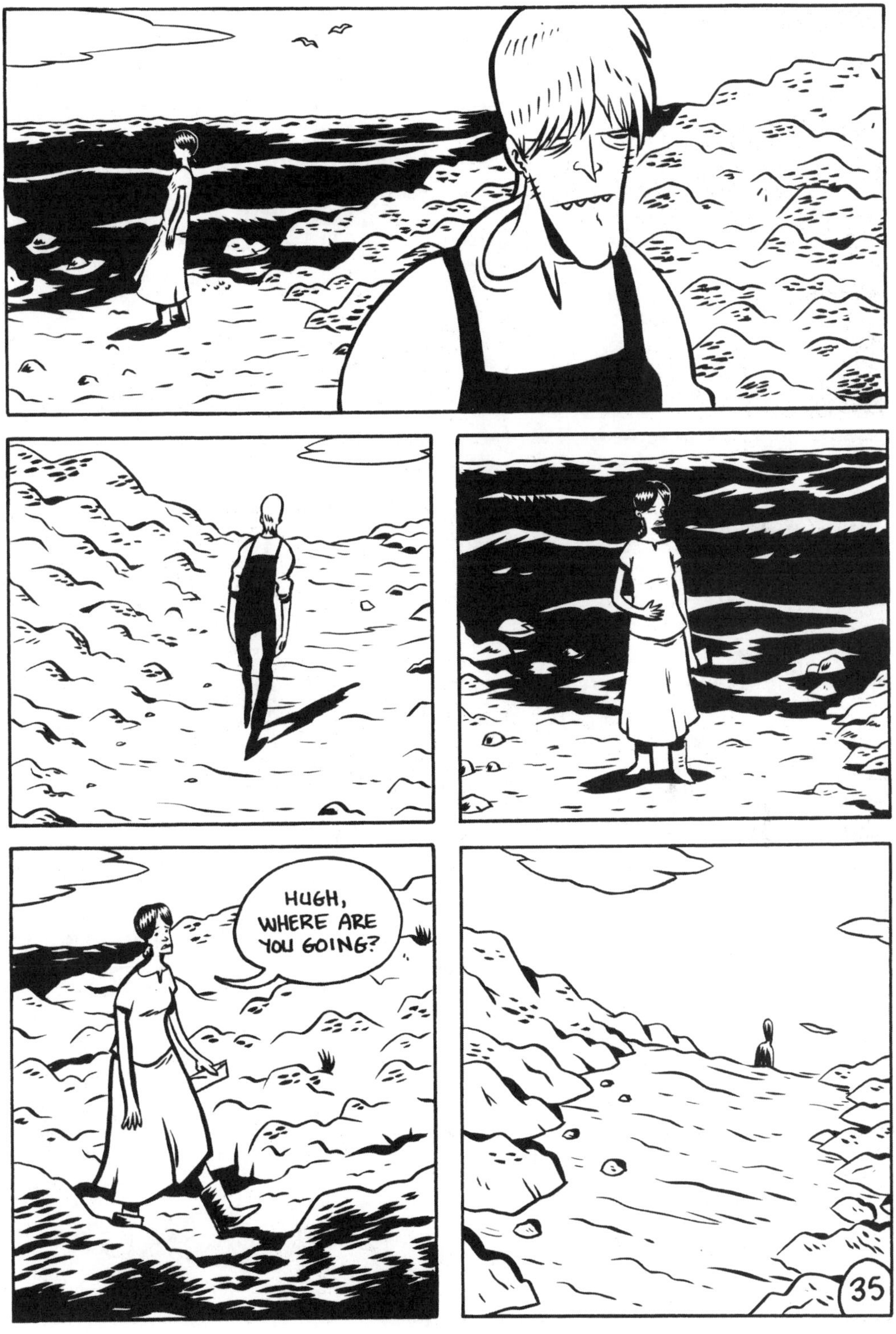
HUGH,
WHERE ARE
YOU GOING?
35

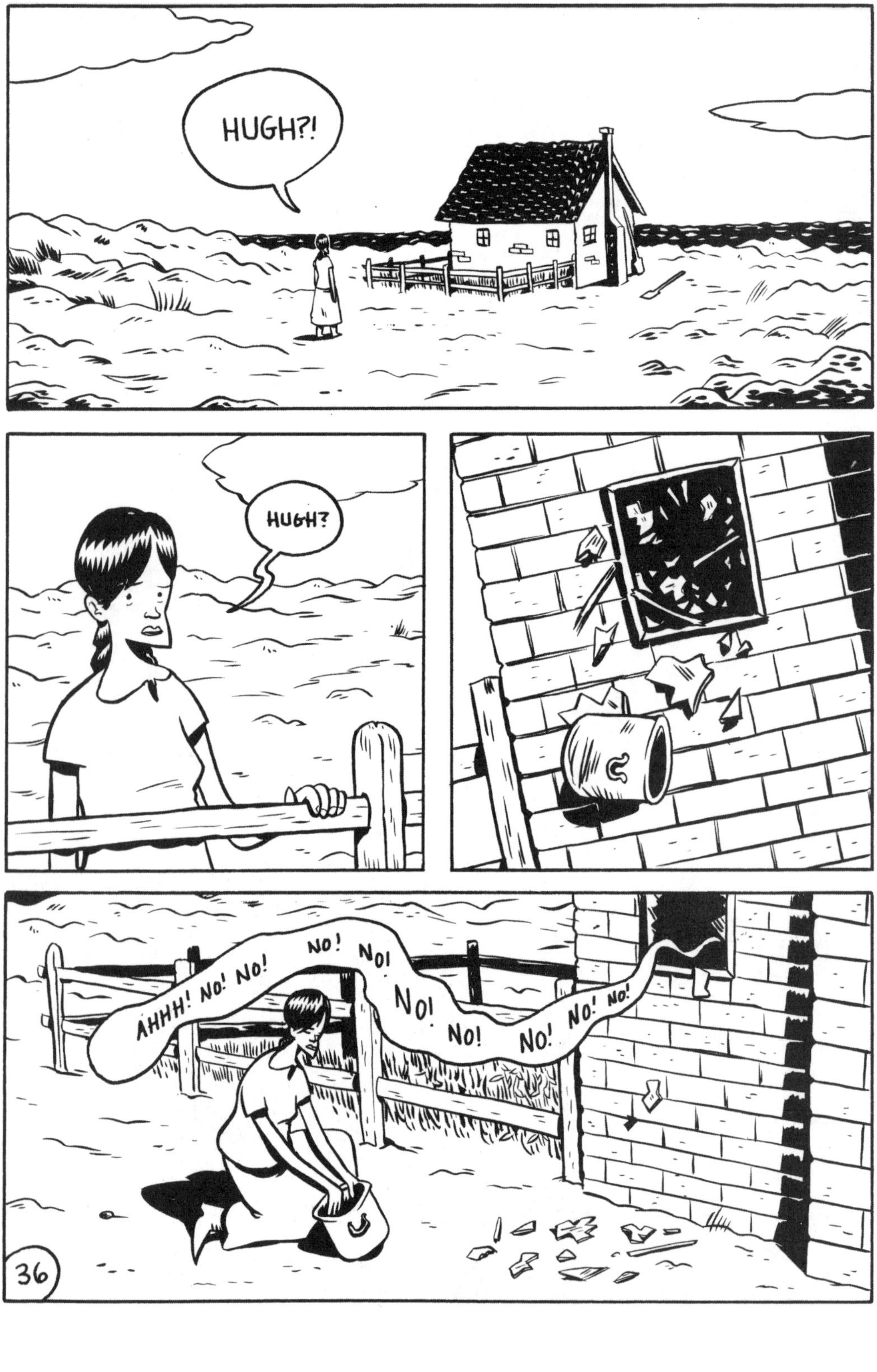
HUGH?!
HUGH?
AHHH! NO! NO! NO! NO! NO! NO! NO! NO! NO!

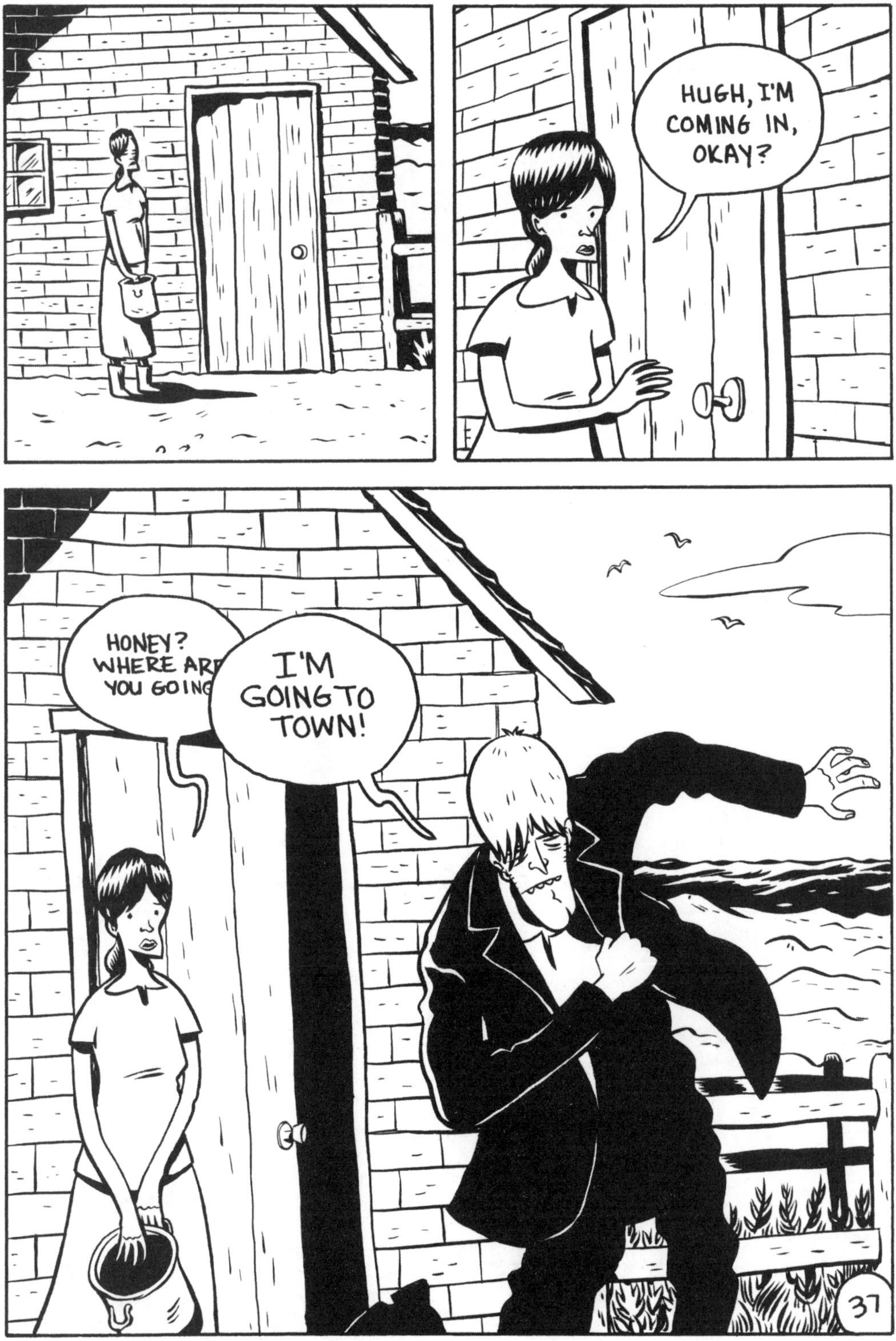
HUGH, I'M COMING IN, OKAY?
HONEY? WHERE AR YOU GOING
I'M GOING TO TOWN!

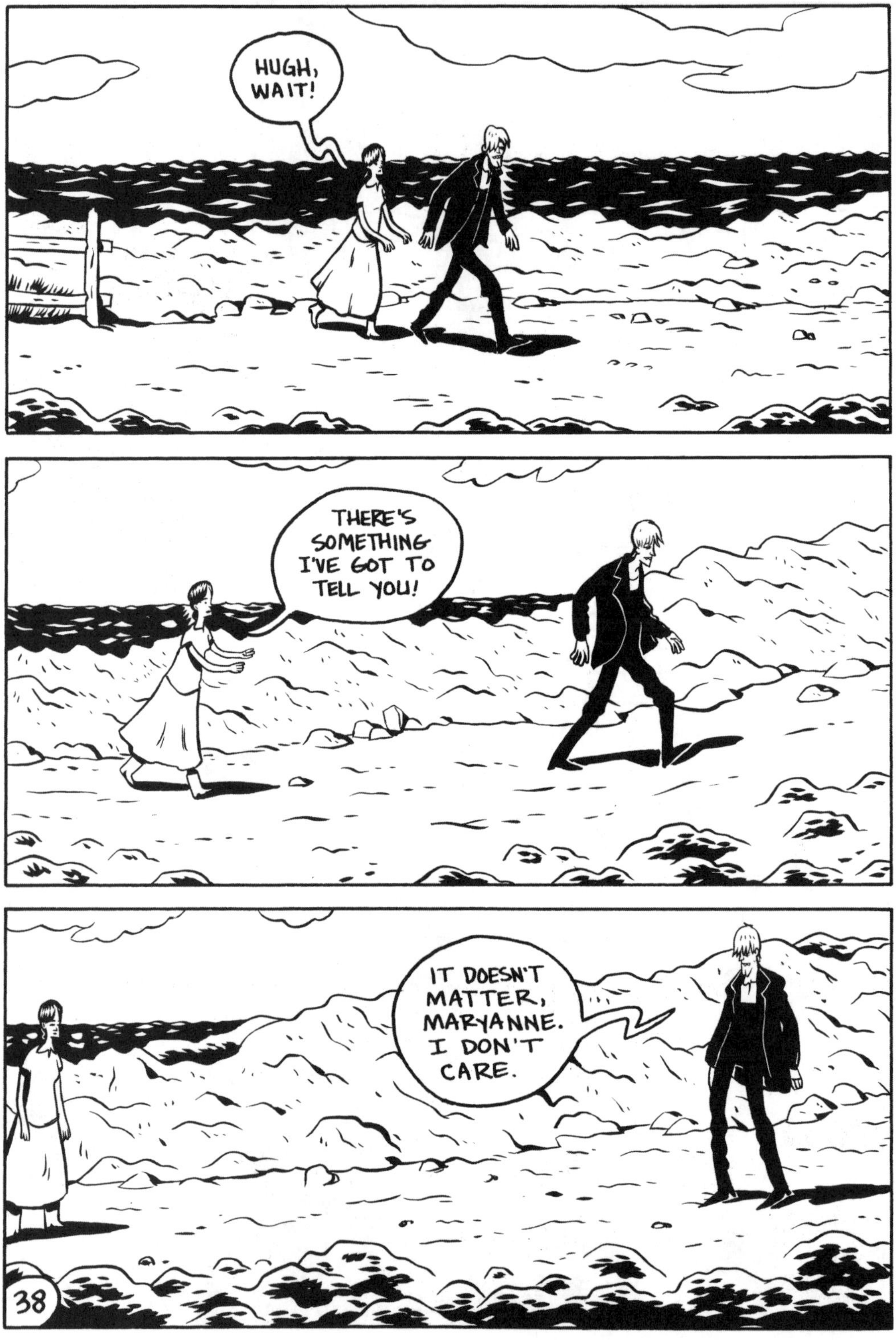
HUGH, WAIT!
THERE'S SOMETHING I'VE GOT TO TELL YOU!
IT DOESN'T MATTER, MARYANNE. I DON'T CARE.

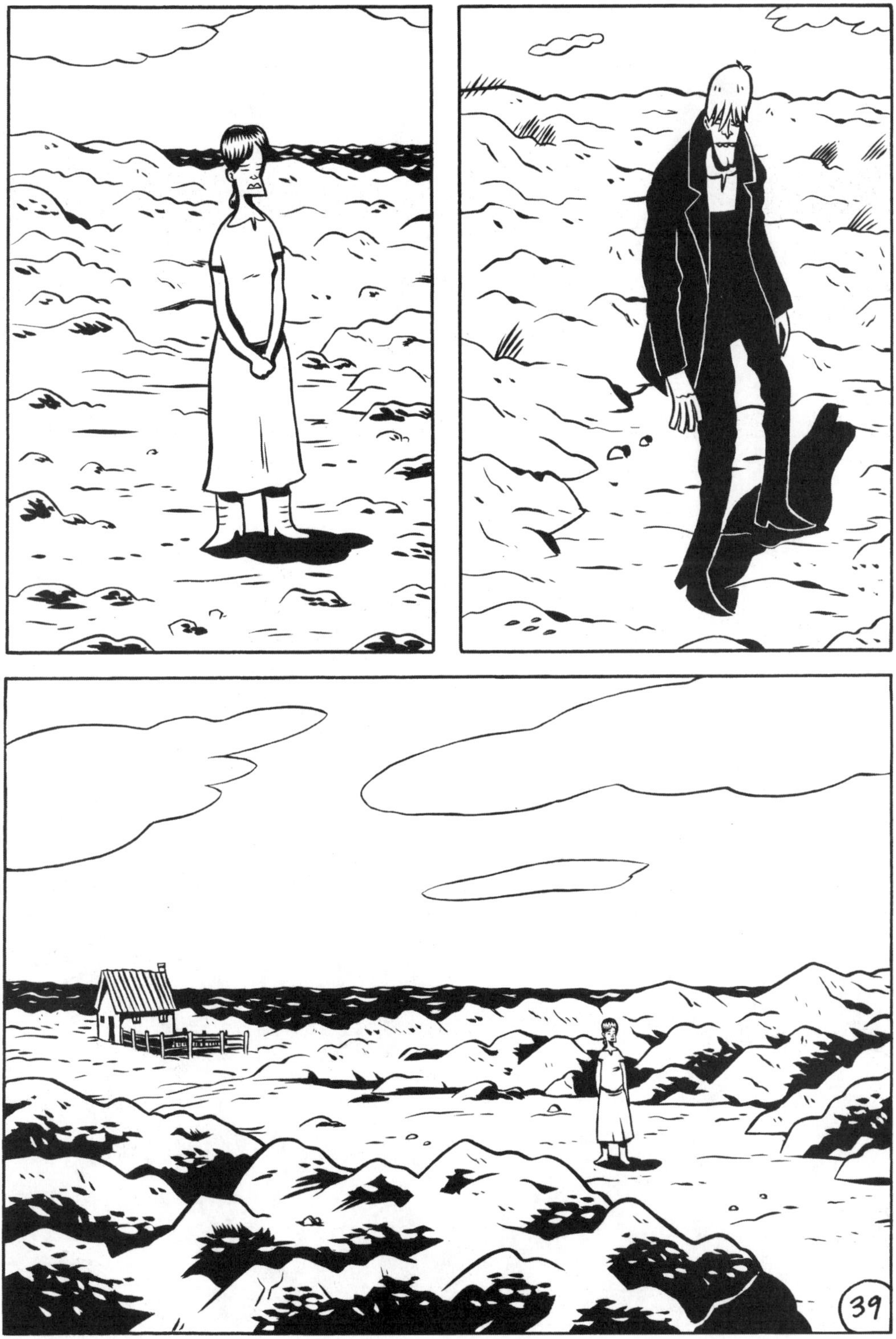

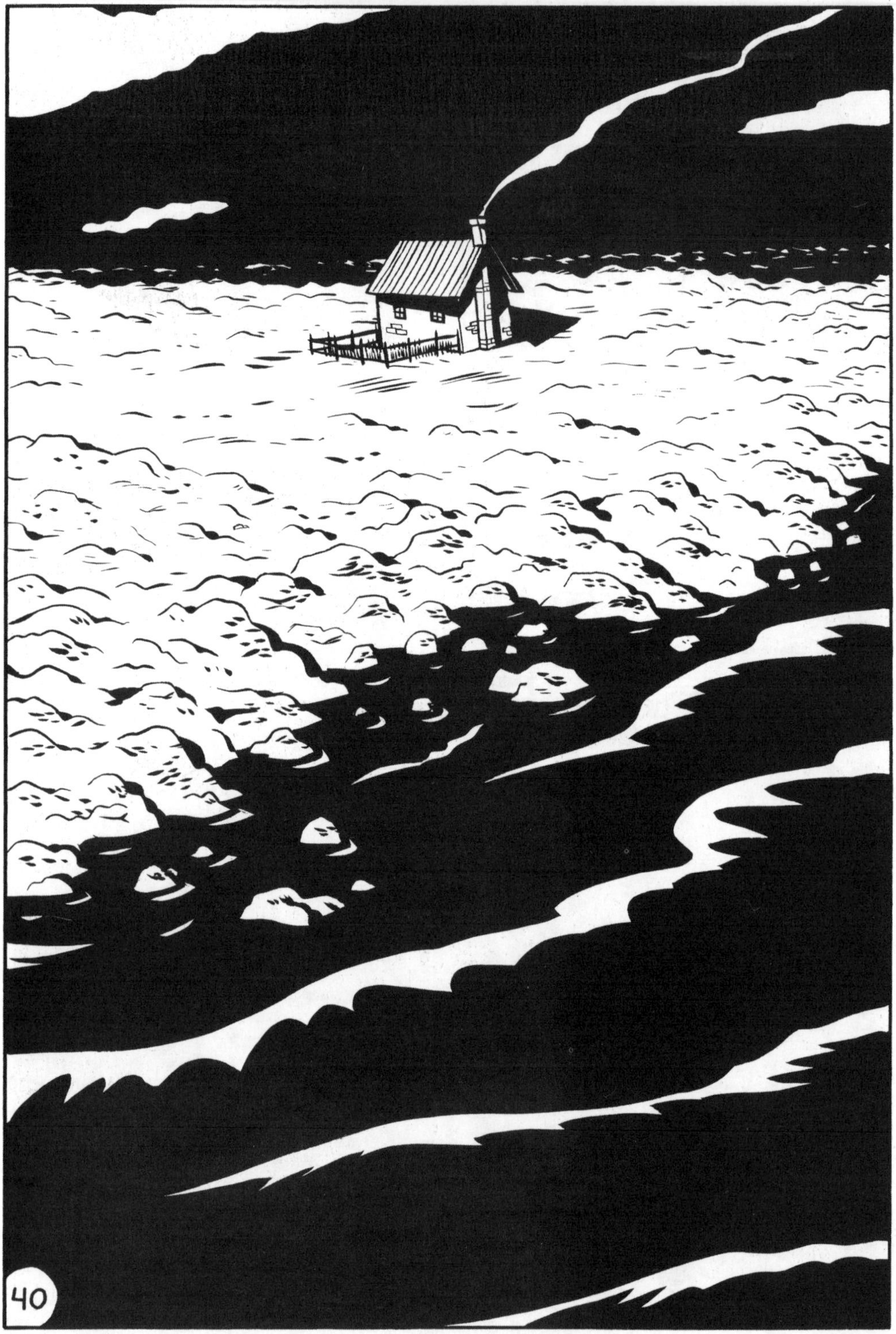

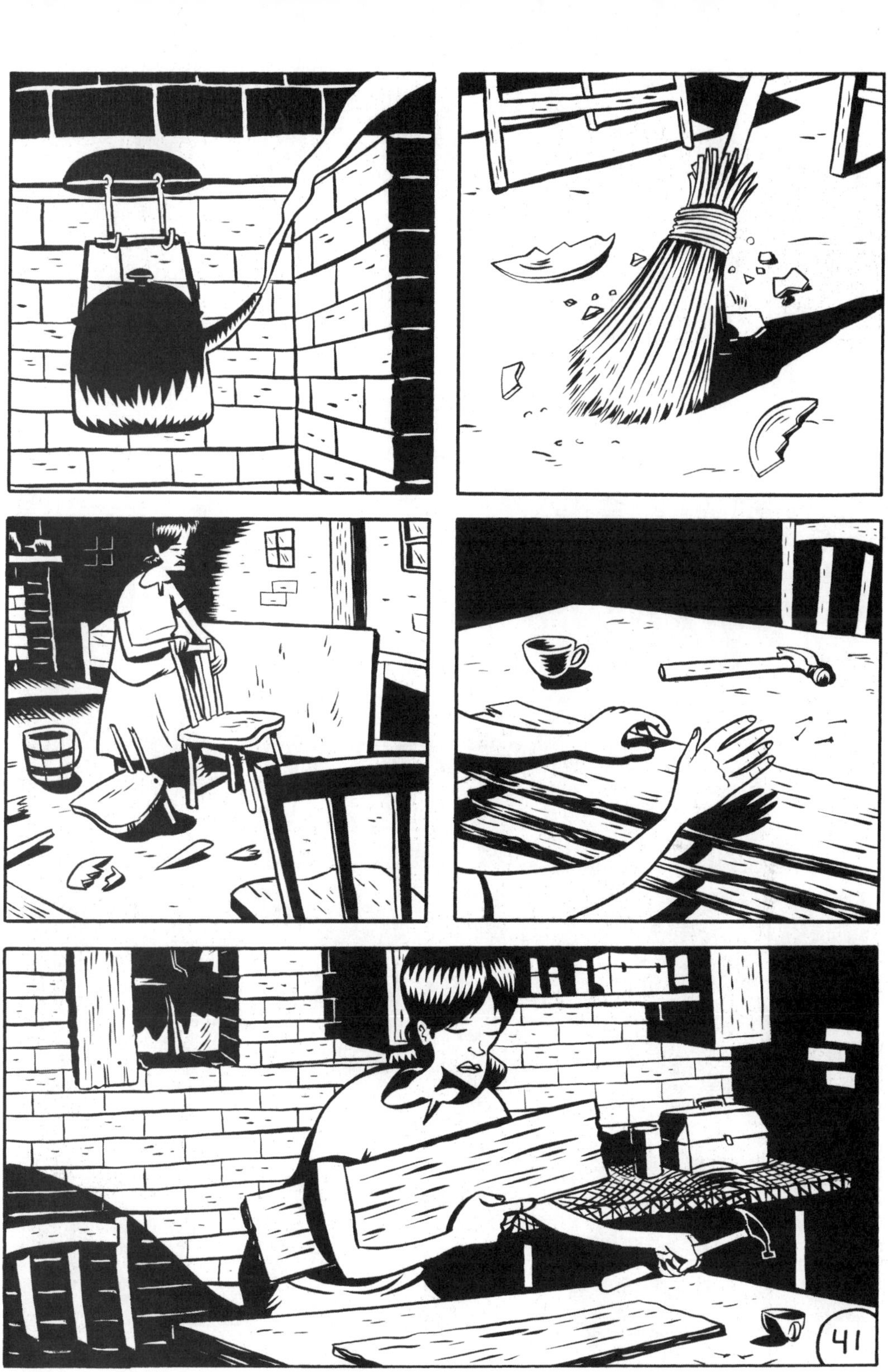

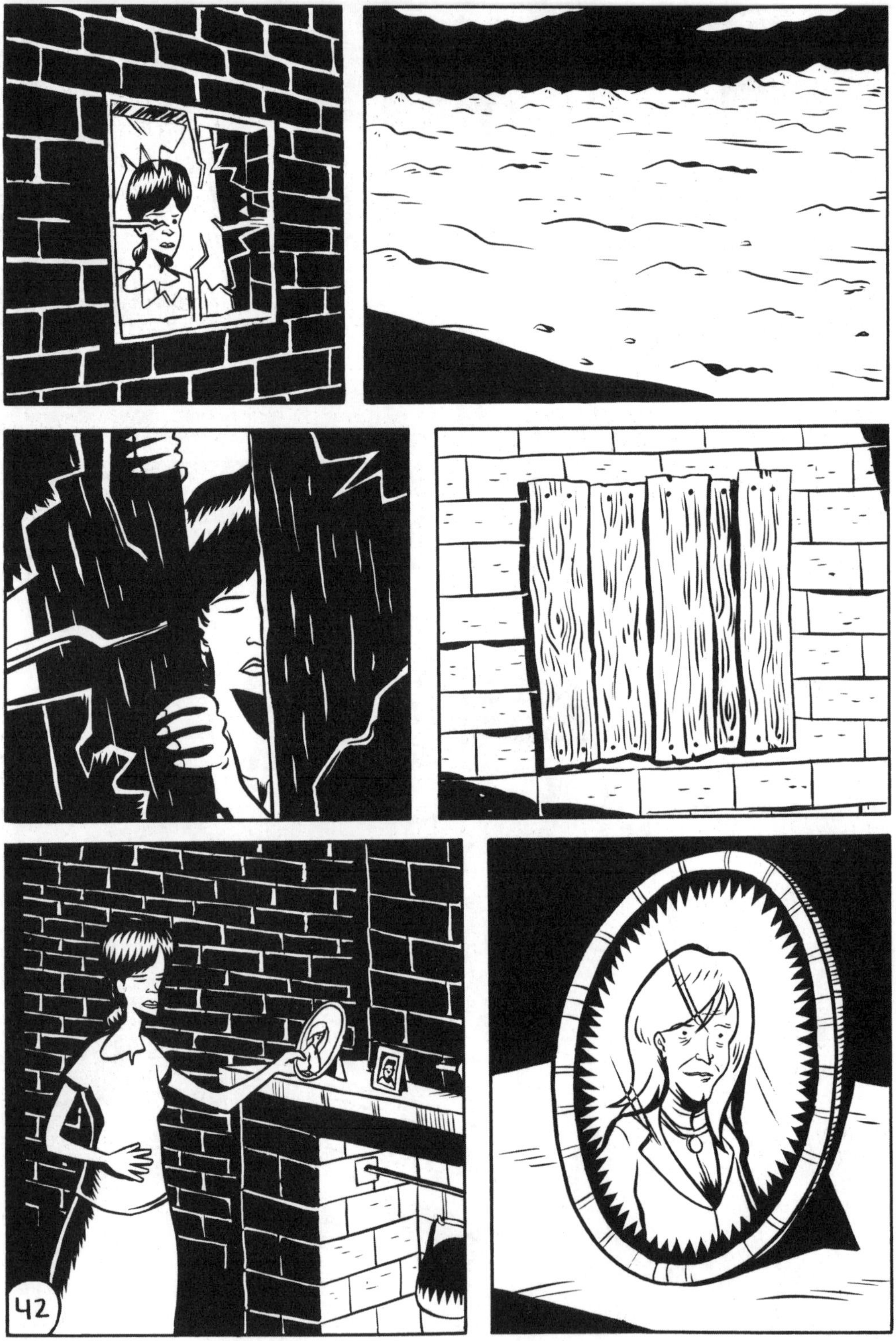

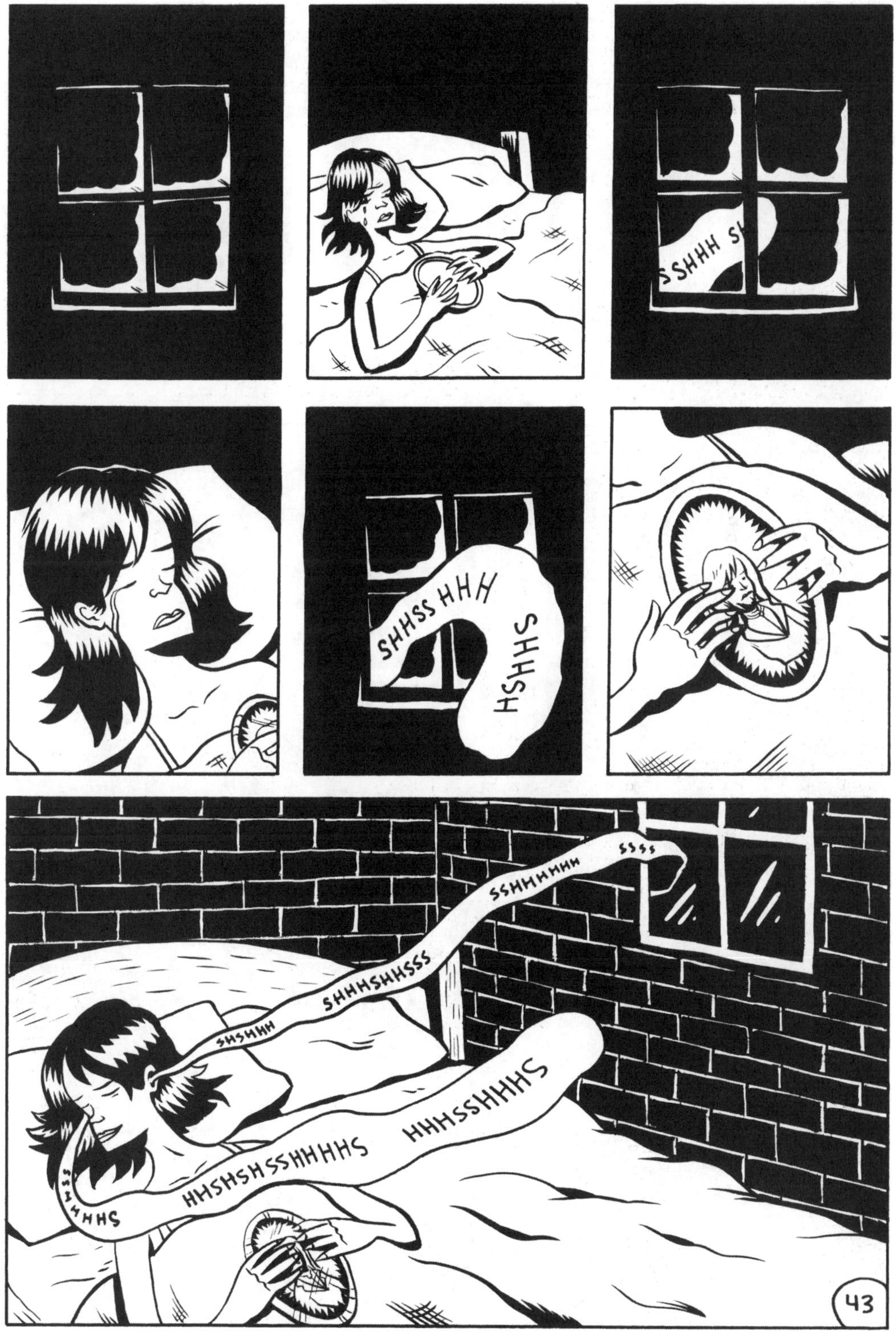
SSHHH SH
SHHSS HHH
SSSS
SSHHHHHHH
SHHHSHHSSS
SHSHHH

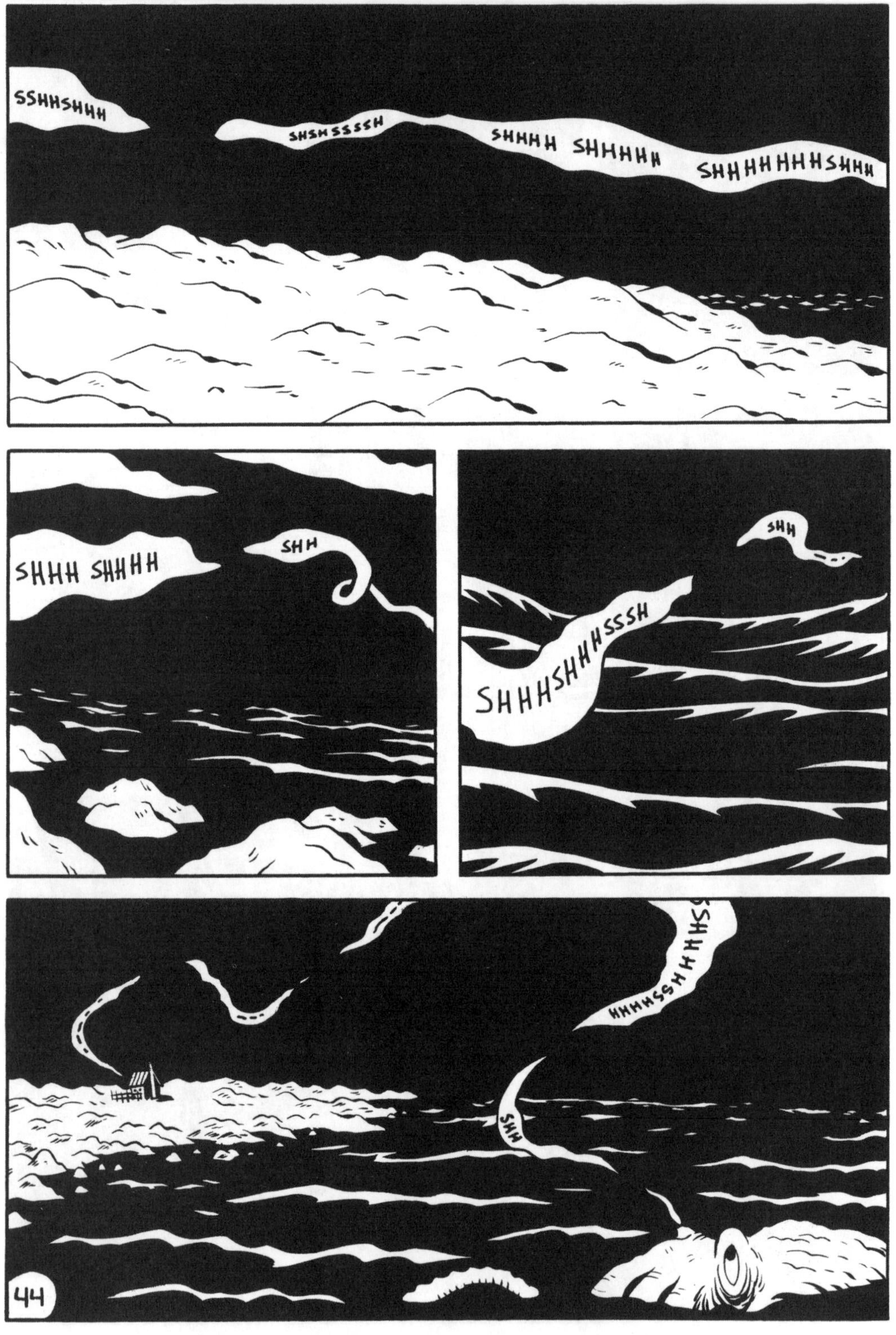
SSHHSHHH
SHSHSSSSH
SHHHH SHHHHH
SHHHHHHHSHHH
SHHH SHHHH
SHH
SHH
SHHHSHHHSSSH
SSHHHHSSHHHHH
SHH

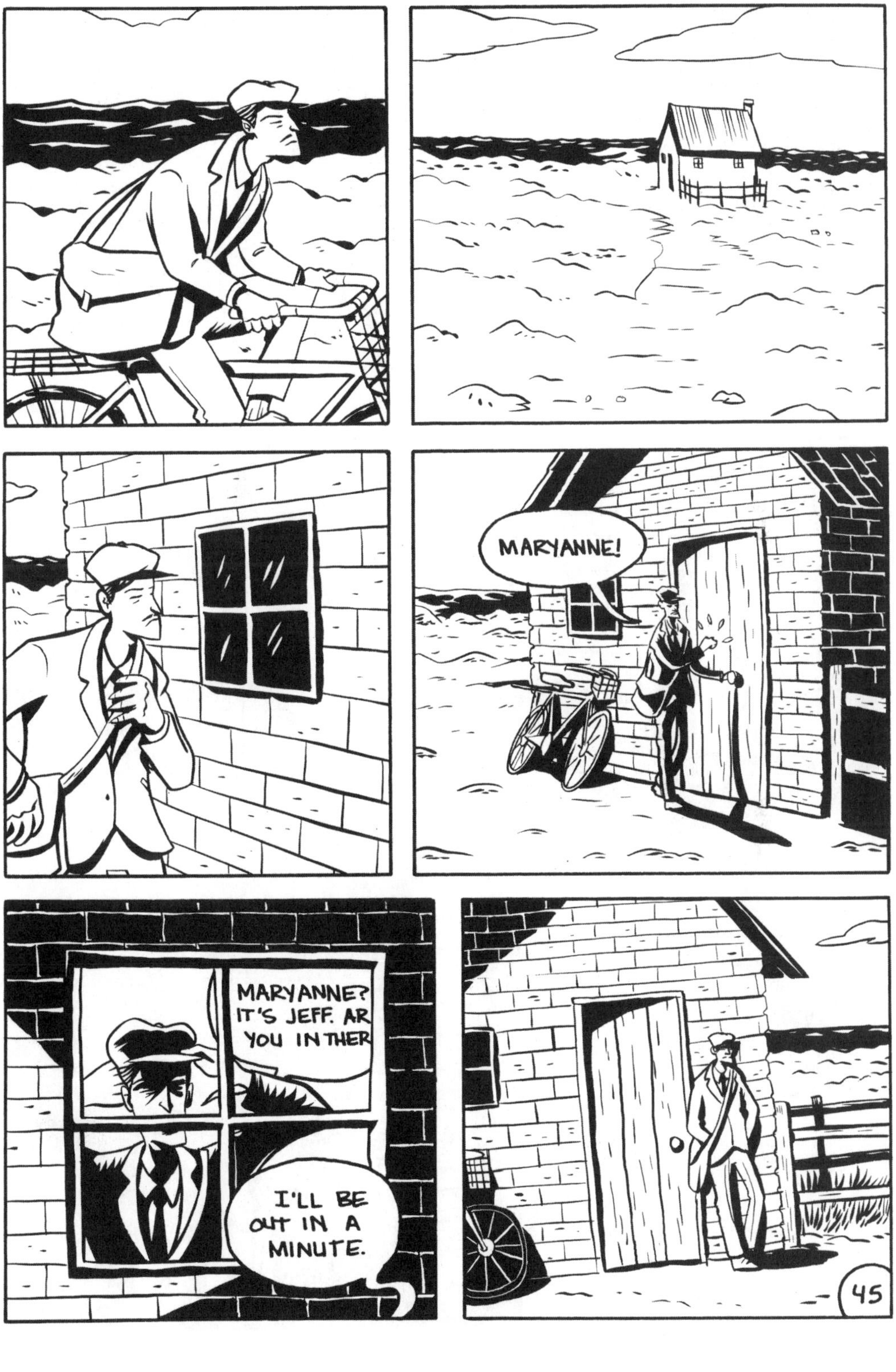
MARYANNE!
MARYANNE? IT'S JEFF. AR YOU IN THER
I'LL BE OUT IN A MINUTE.

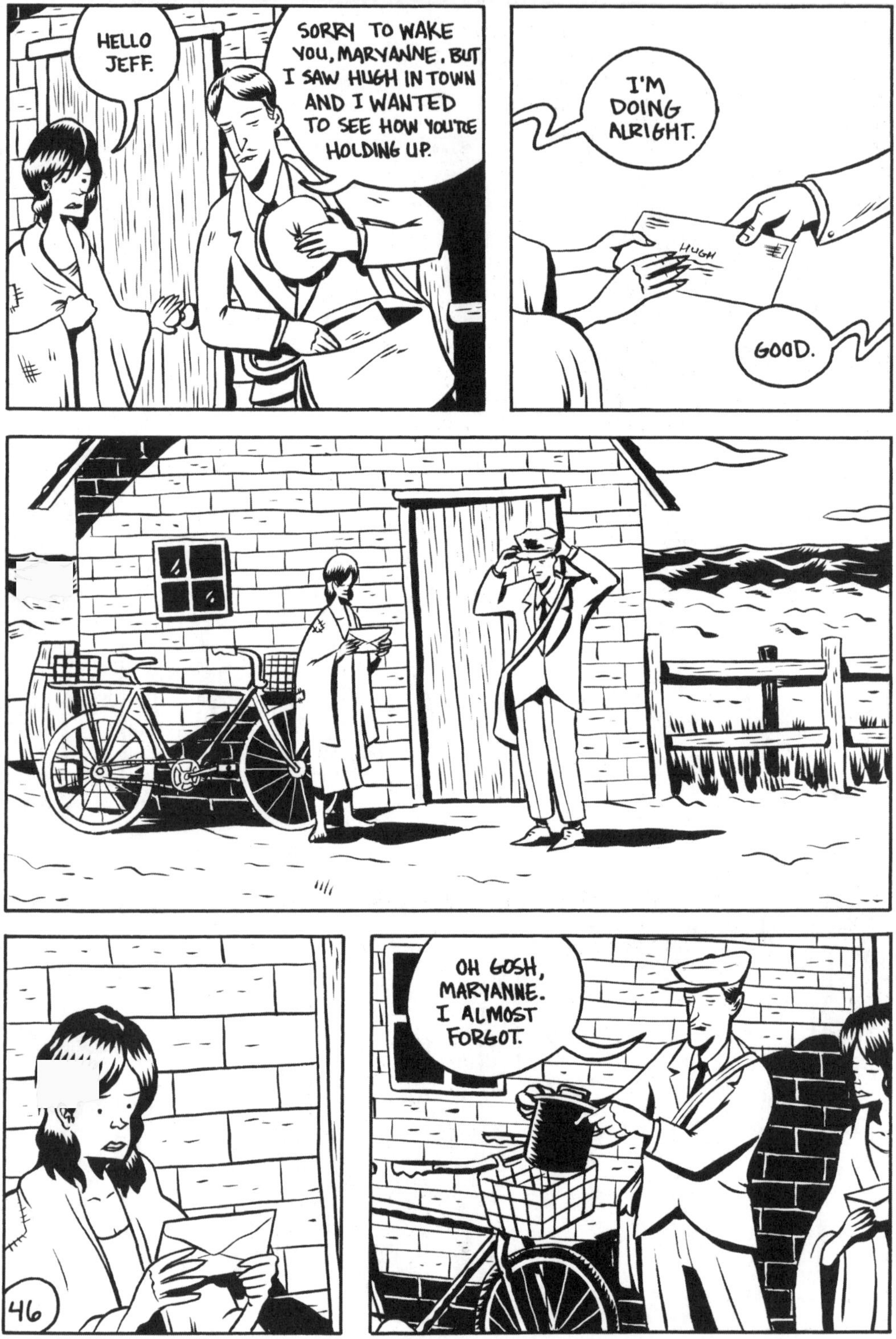
HELLO JEFF.
SORRY TO WAKE YOU, MARYANNE, BUT I SAW HUGH IN TOWN AND I WANTED TO SEE HOW YOU'RE HOLDING UP.
I'M DOING ALRIGHT.
HUGH
GOOD.
OH GOSH, MARYANNE. I ALMOST FORGOT.

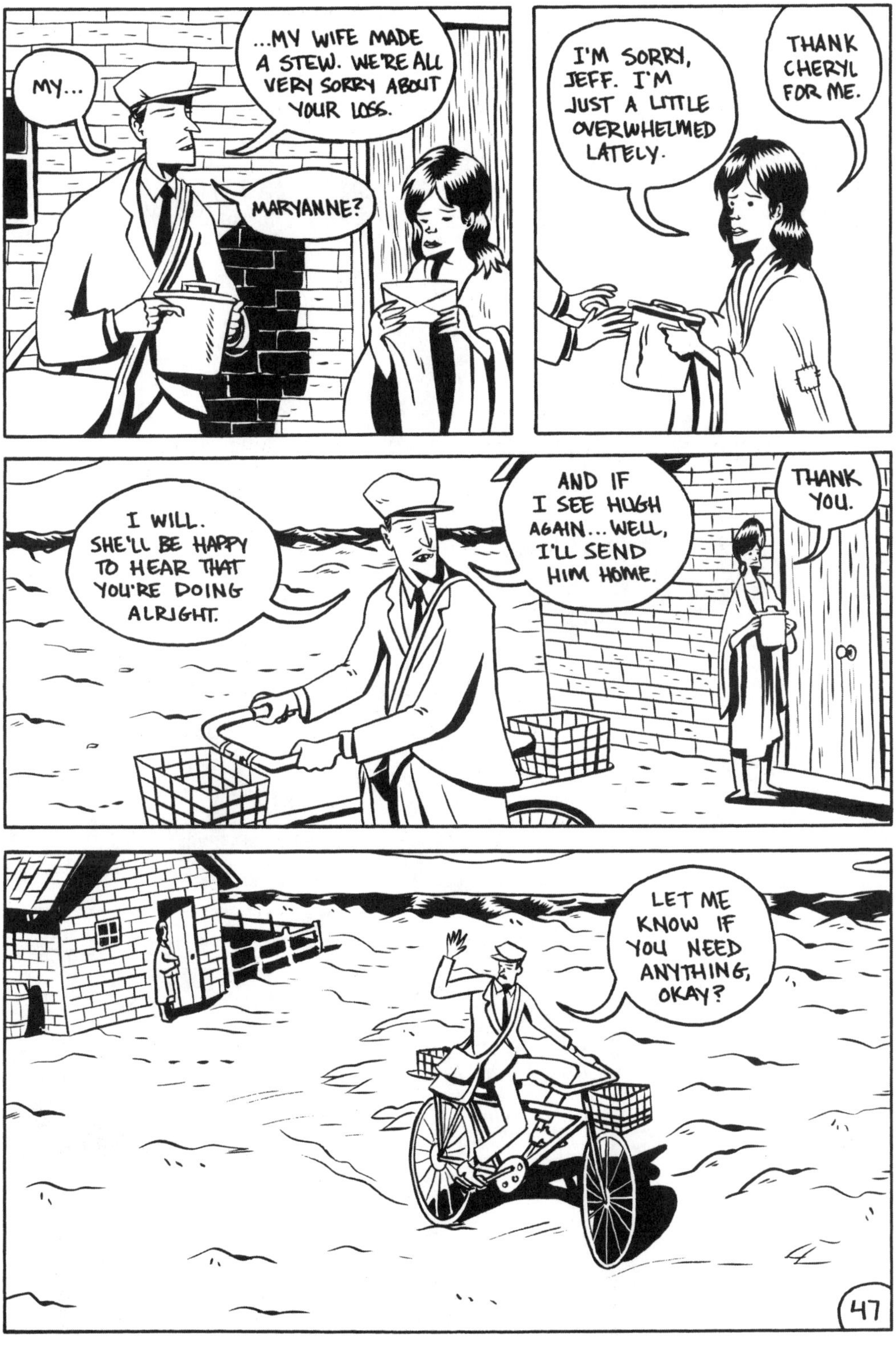
MY...
...MY WIFE MADE A STEW. WE'RE ALL VERY SORRY ABOUT YOUR LOSS.
MARYANNE?
I'M SORRY, JEFF. I'M JUST A LITTLE OVERWHELMED LATELY.
THANK CHERYL FOR ME.
I WILL. SHE'LL BE HAPPY TO HEAR THAT YOU'RE DOING ALRIGHT.
AND IF I SEE HUGH AGAIN... WELL, I'LL SEND HIM HOME.
THANK YOU.
LET ME KNOW IF YOU NEED ANYTHING, OKAY?

Hugh,
The money that you owe me is now four weeks overdue. Further delay in payment will result in your immediate eviction from my property.
I will be arriving on the sixteenth to collect my money in full.
- Nataniel Morgan
DAMN IT.

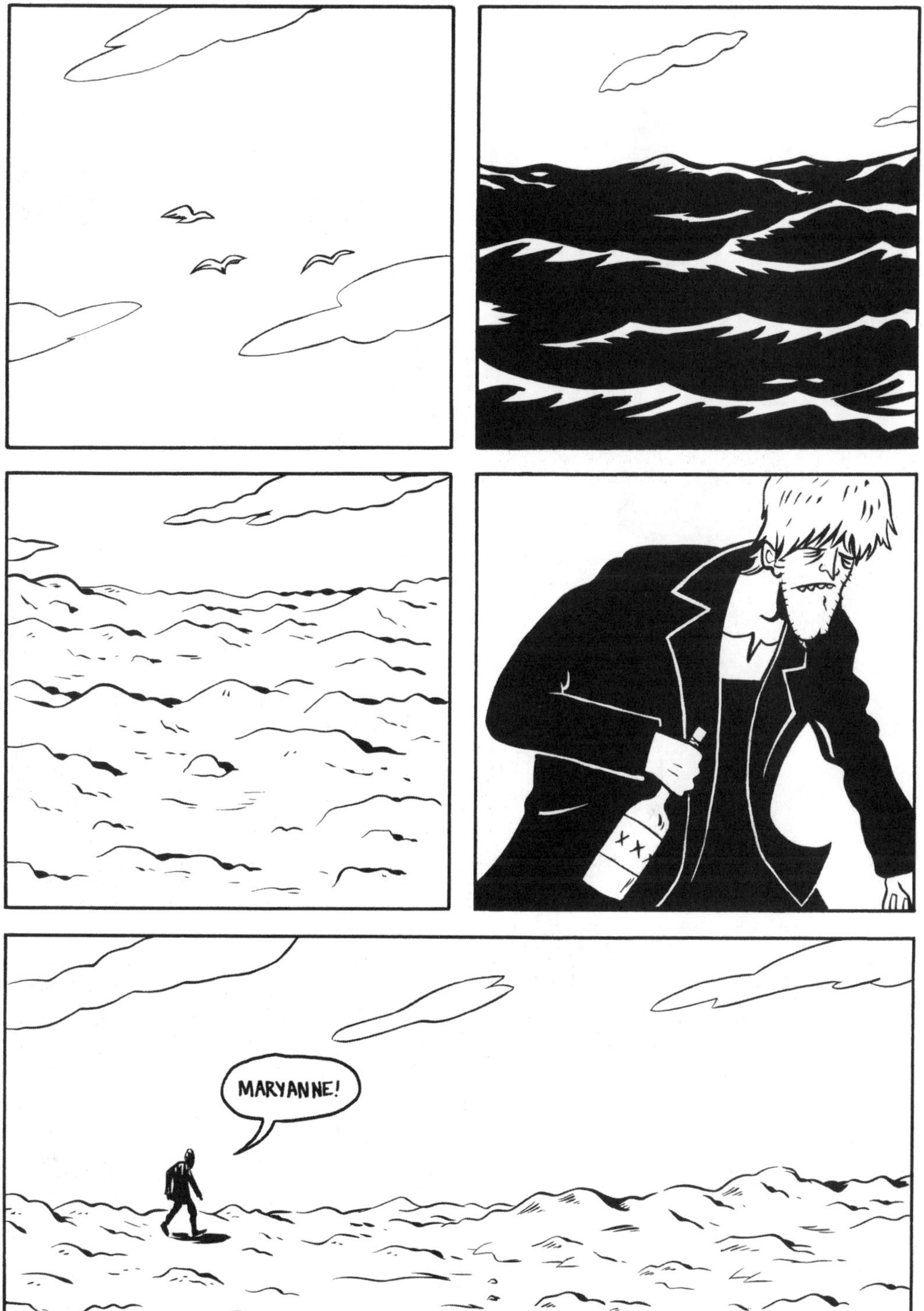
MARYANNE!

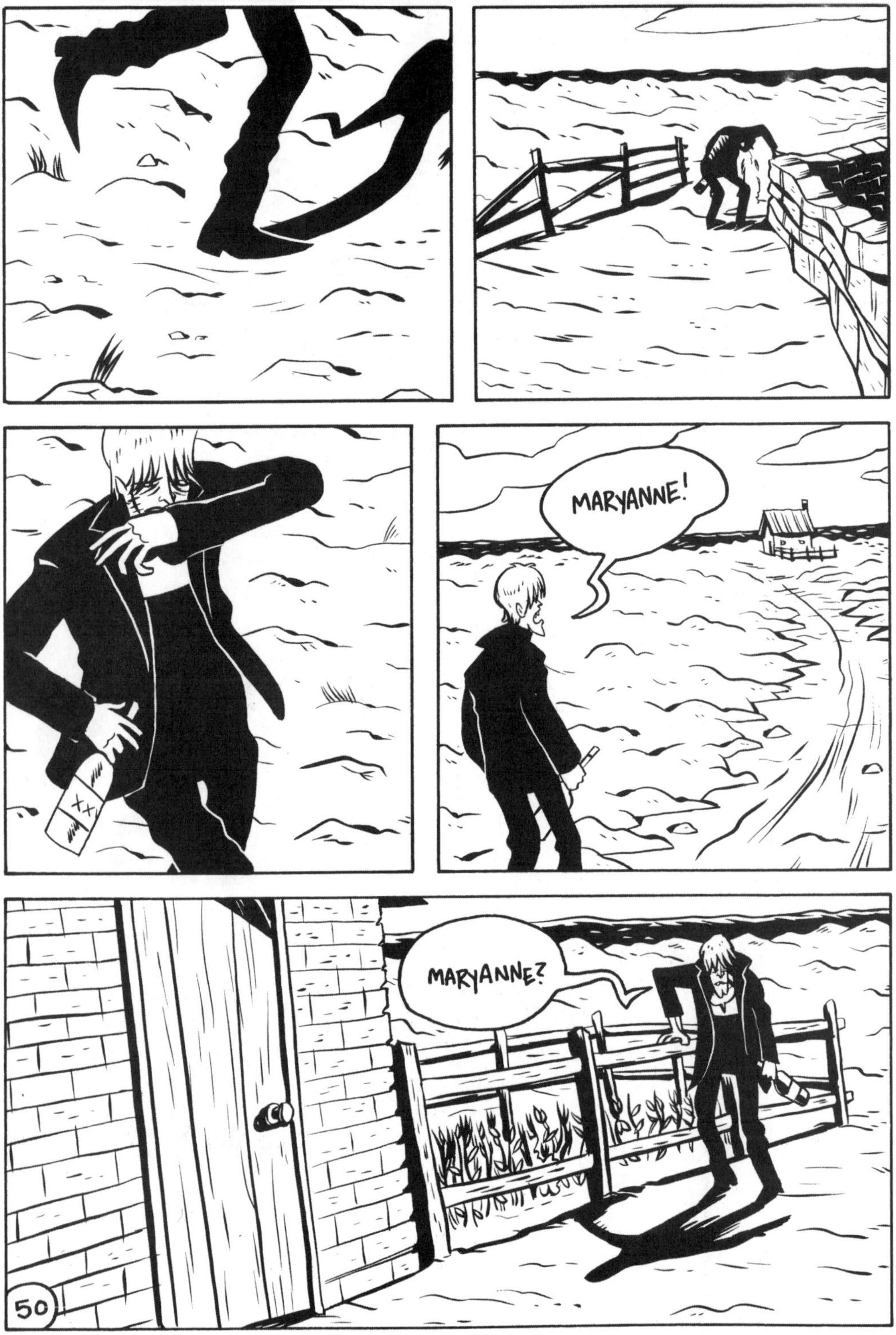
MARYANNE!
MARYANNE?

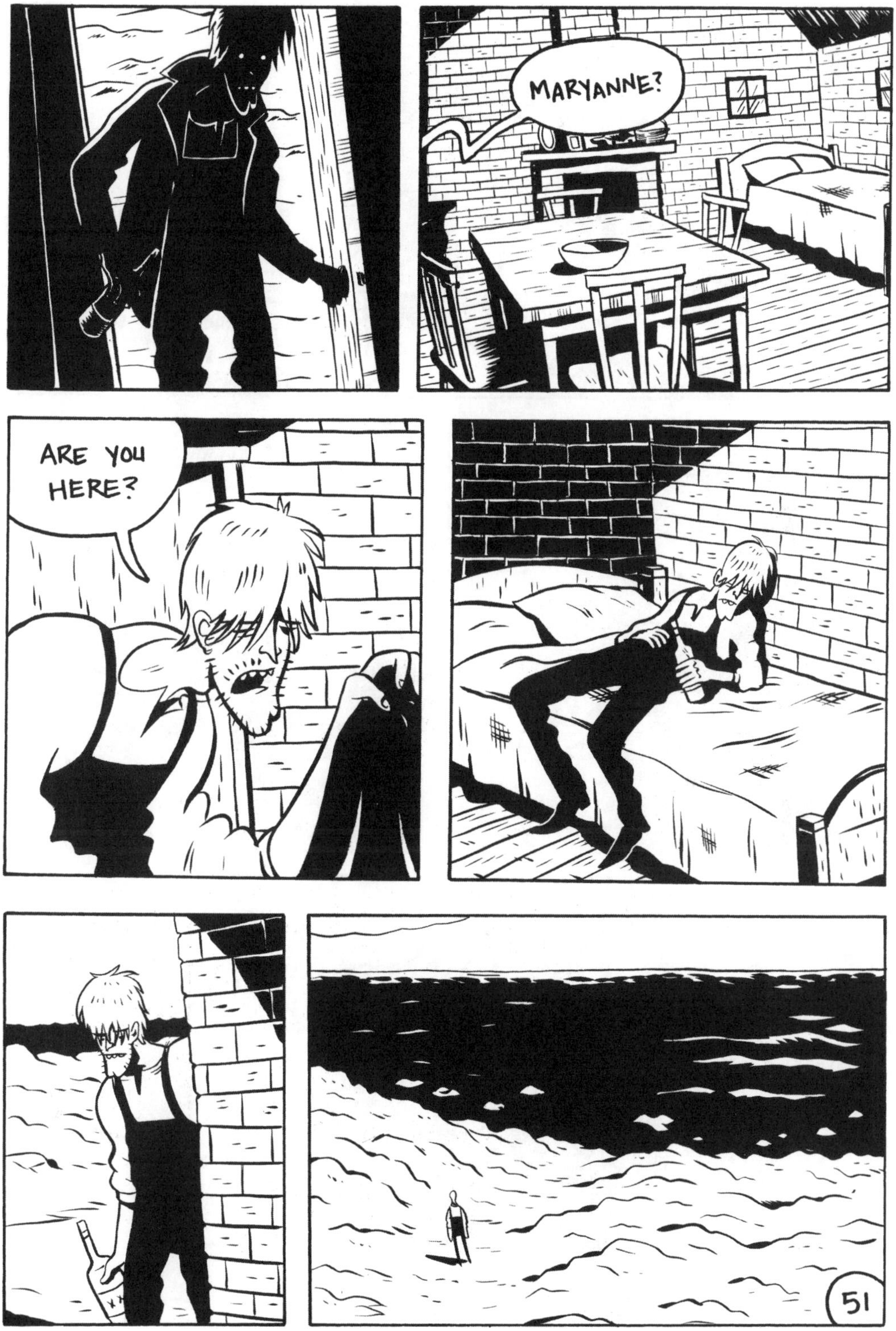
MARYANNE?
ARE YOU HERE?

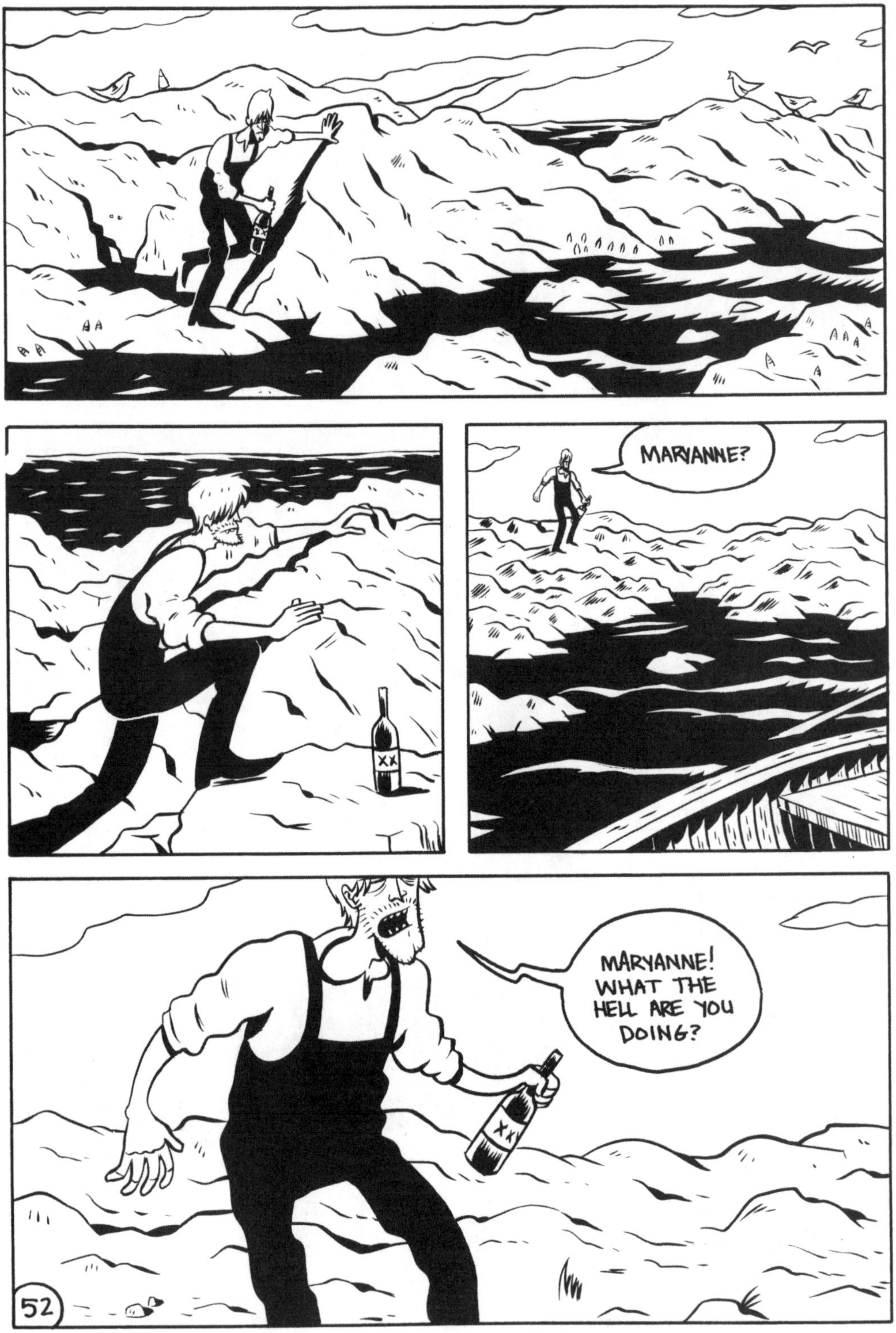
MARYANNE?
MARYANNE! WHAT THE HELL ARE YOU DOING?
52

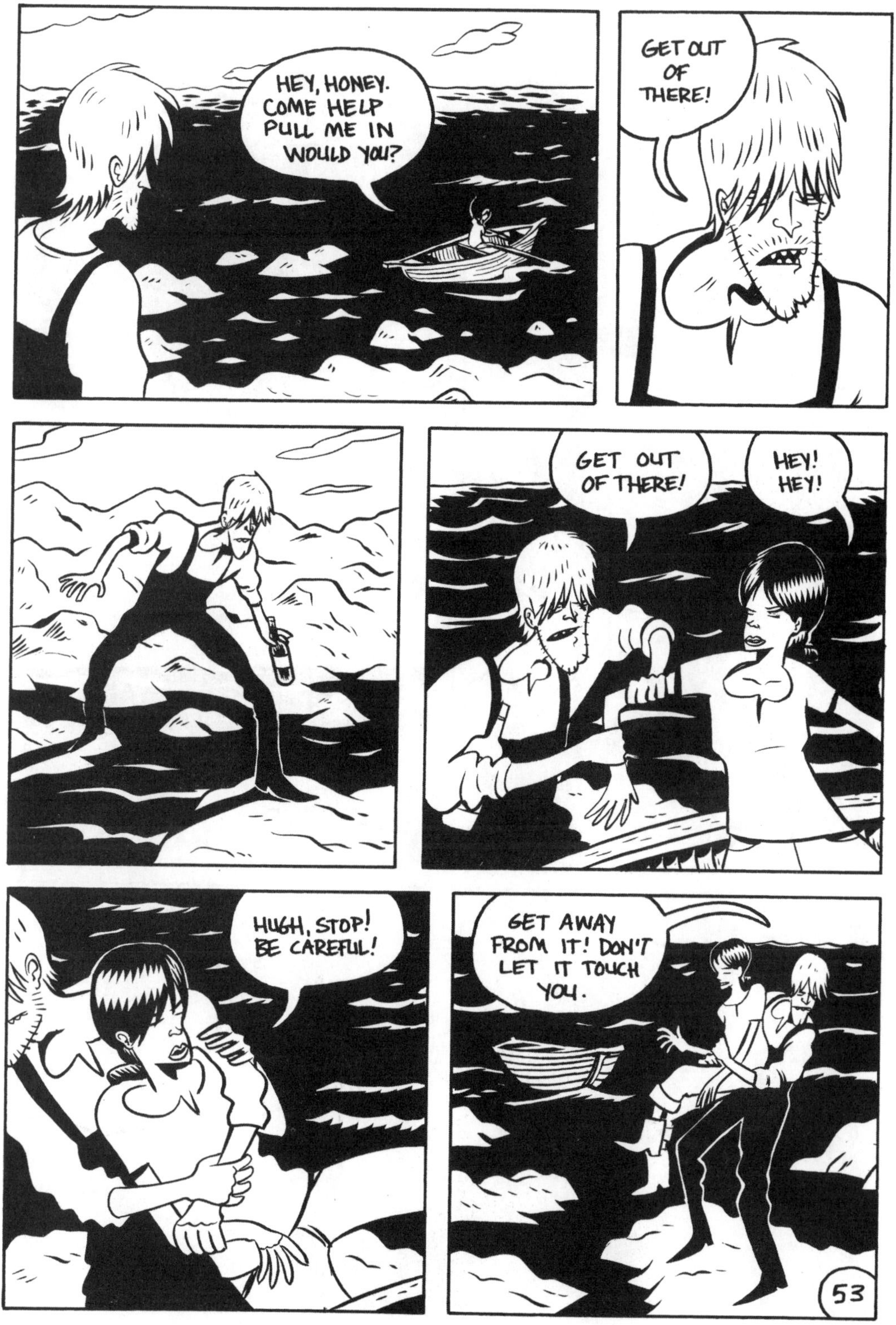
HEY, HONEY. COME HELP PULL ME IN WOULD YOU?
GET OUT OF THERE!
GET OUT OF THERE!
HEY! HEY!
HUGH, STOP! BE CAREFUL!
GET AWAY FROM IT! DON'T LET IT TOUCH YOU.

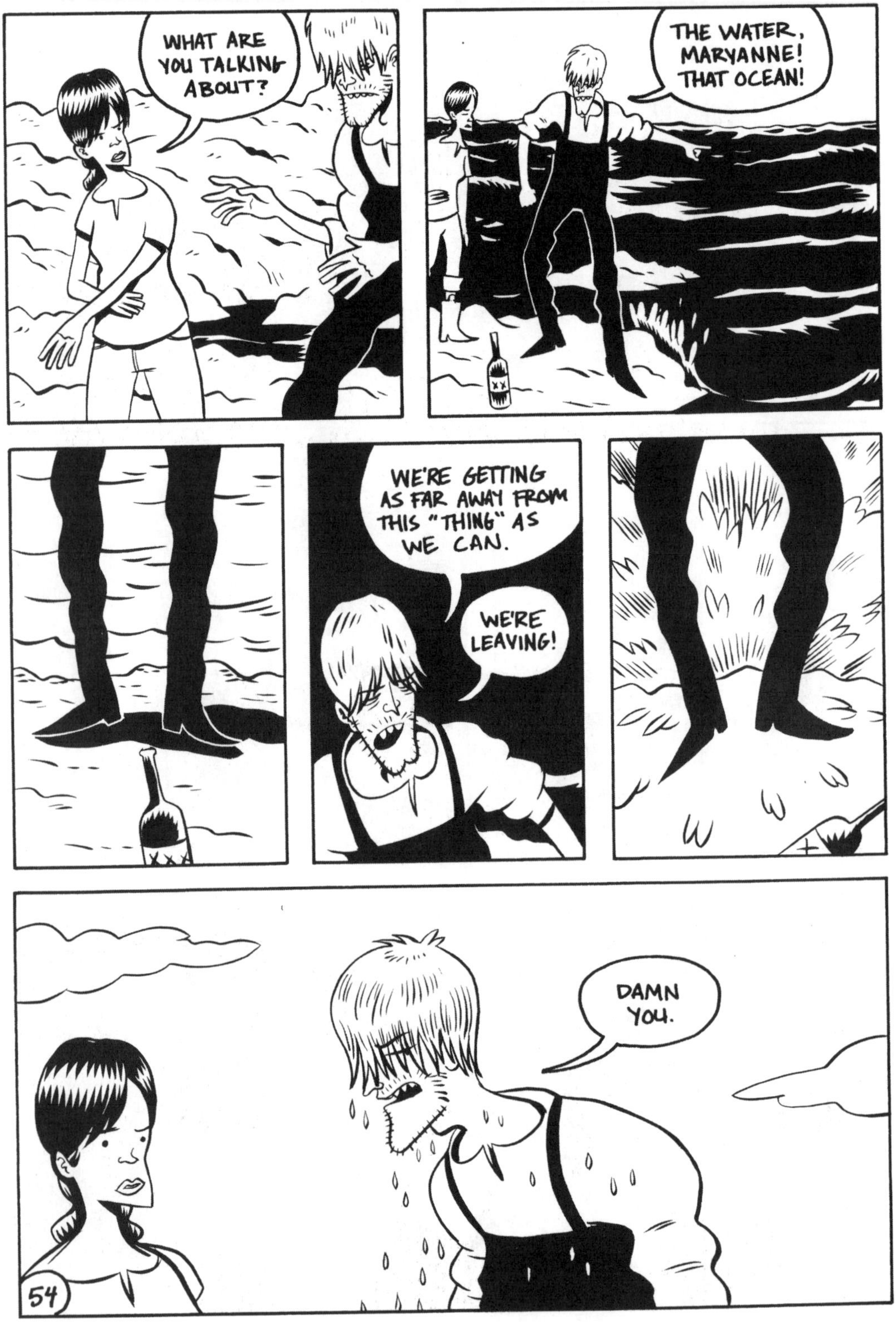
WHAT ARE YOU TALKING ABOUT?
THE WATER, MARYANNE! THAT OCEAN!
WE'RE GETTING AS FAR AWAY FROM THIS "THING" AS WE CAN.
WE'RE LEAVING!
DAMN YOU.

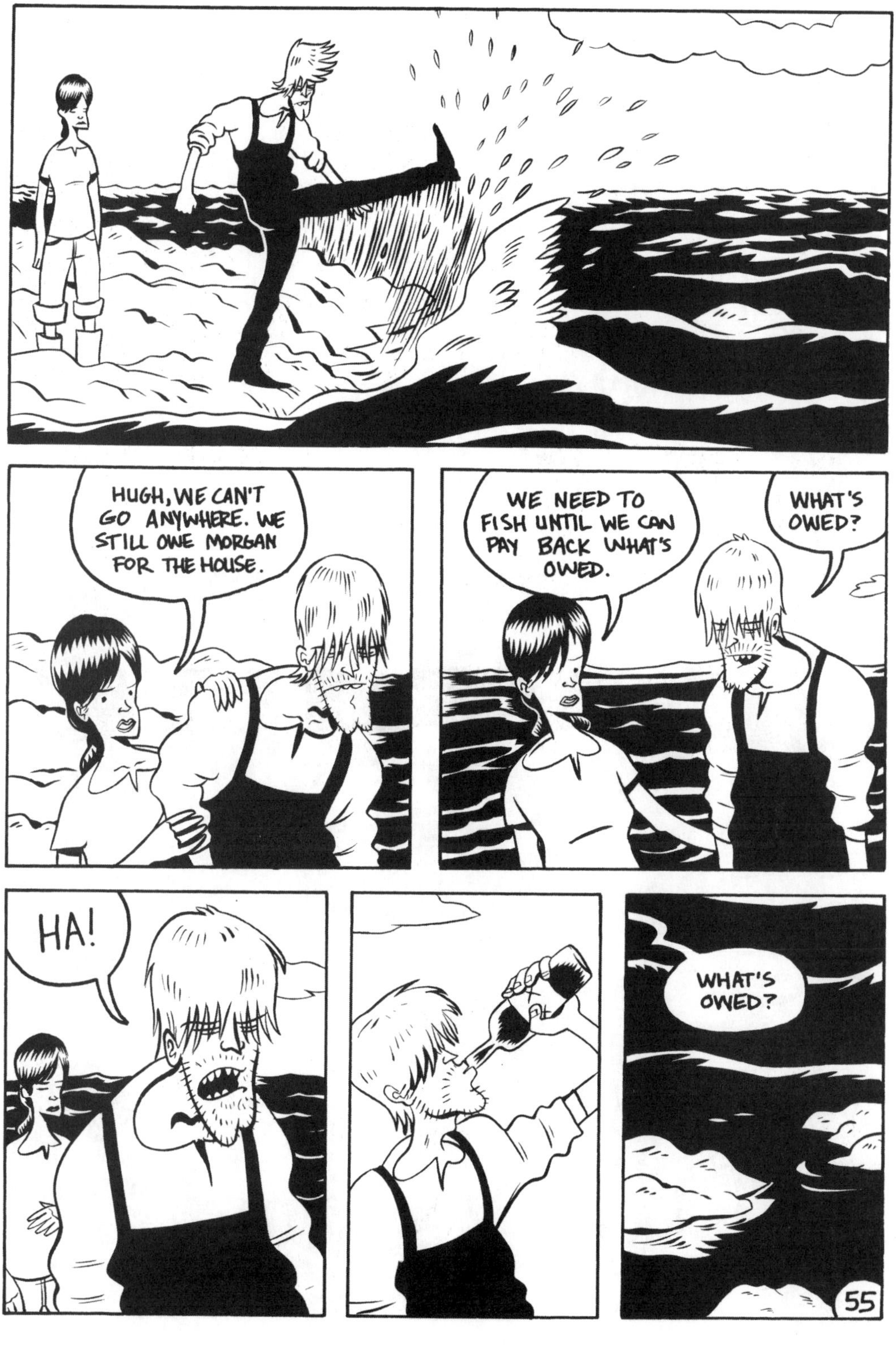
HUGH, WE CAN'T GO ANYWHERE. WE STILL OWE MORGAN FOR THE HOUSE.
WE NEED TO FISH UNTIL WE CAN PAY BACK WHAT'S OWED.
WHAT'S OWED?
HA!
WHAT'S OWED?

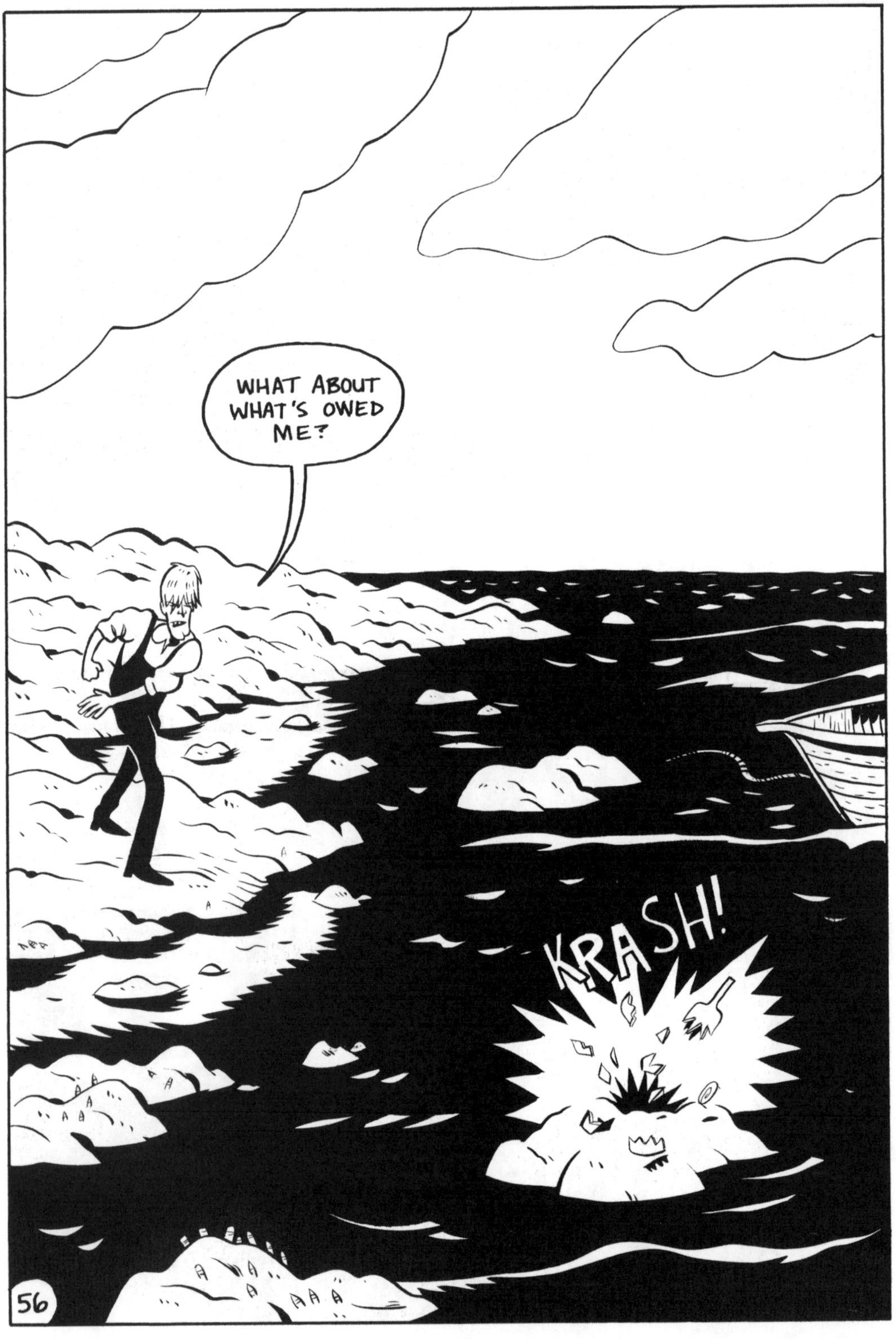
WHAT ABOUT WHAT'S OWED ME?
KRASH!

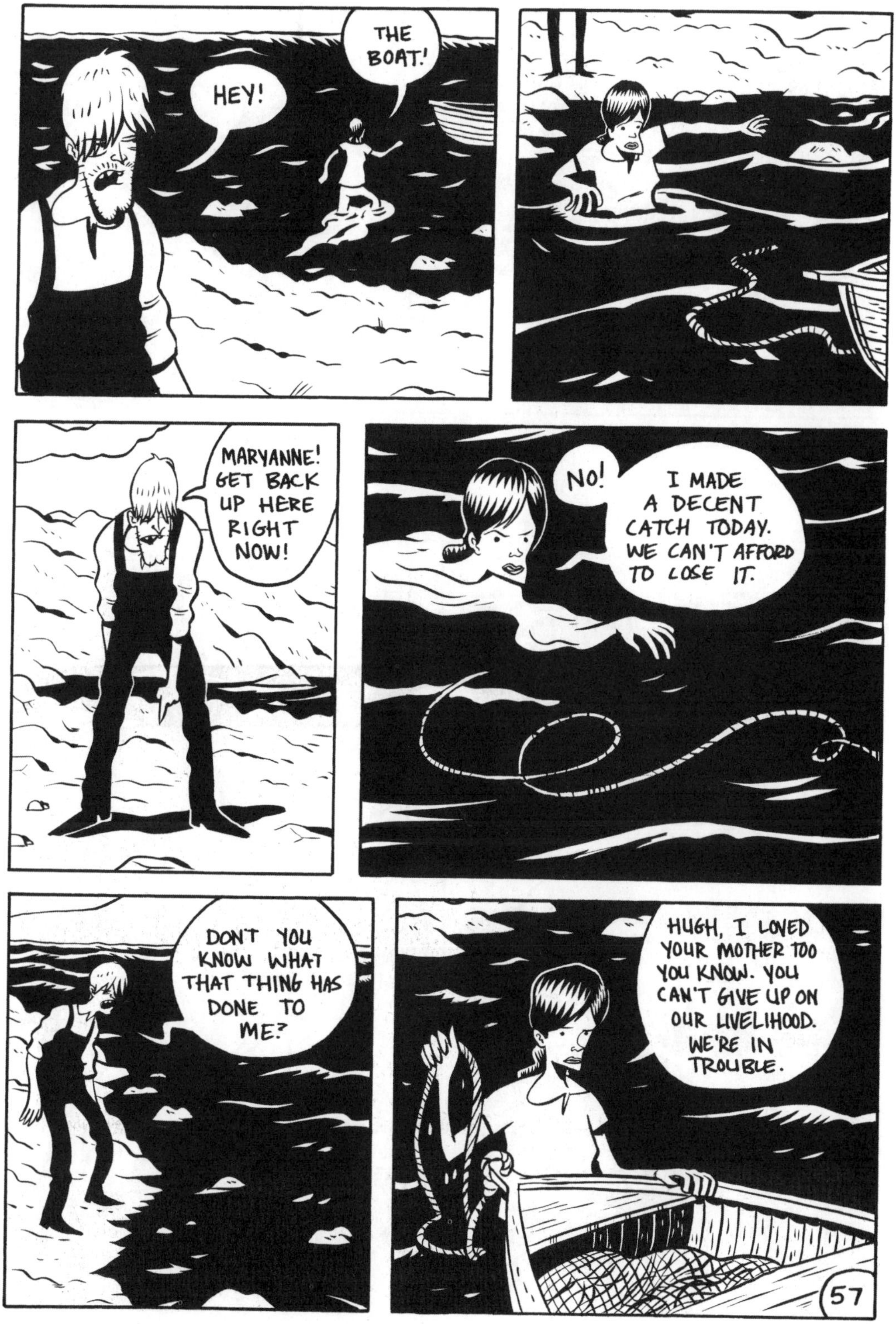
HEY!
THE BOAT!
MARYANNE! GET BACK UP HERE RIGHT NOW!
NO!
I MADE A DECENT CATCH TODAY. WE CAN'T AFFORD TO LOSE IT.
DON'T YOU KNOW WHAT THAT THING HAS DONE TO ME?
HUGH, I LOVED YOUR MOTHER TOO YOU KNOW. YOU CAN'T GIVE UP ON OUR LIVELIHOOD. WE'RE IN TROUBLE.

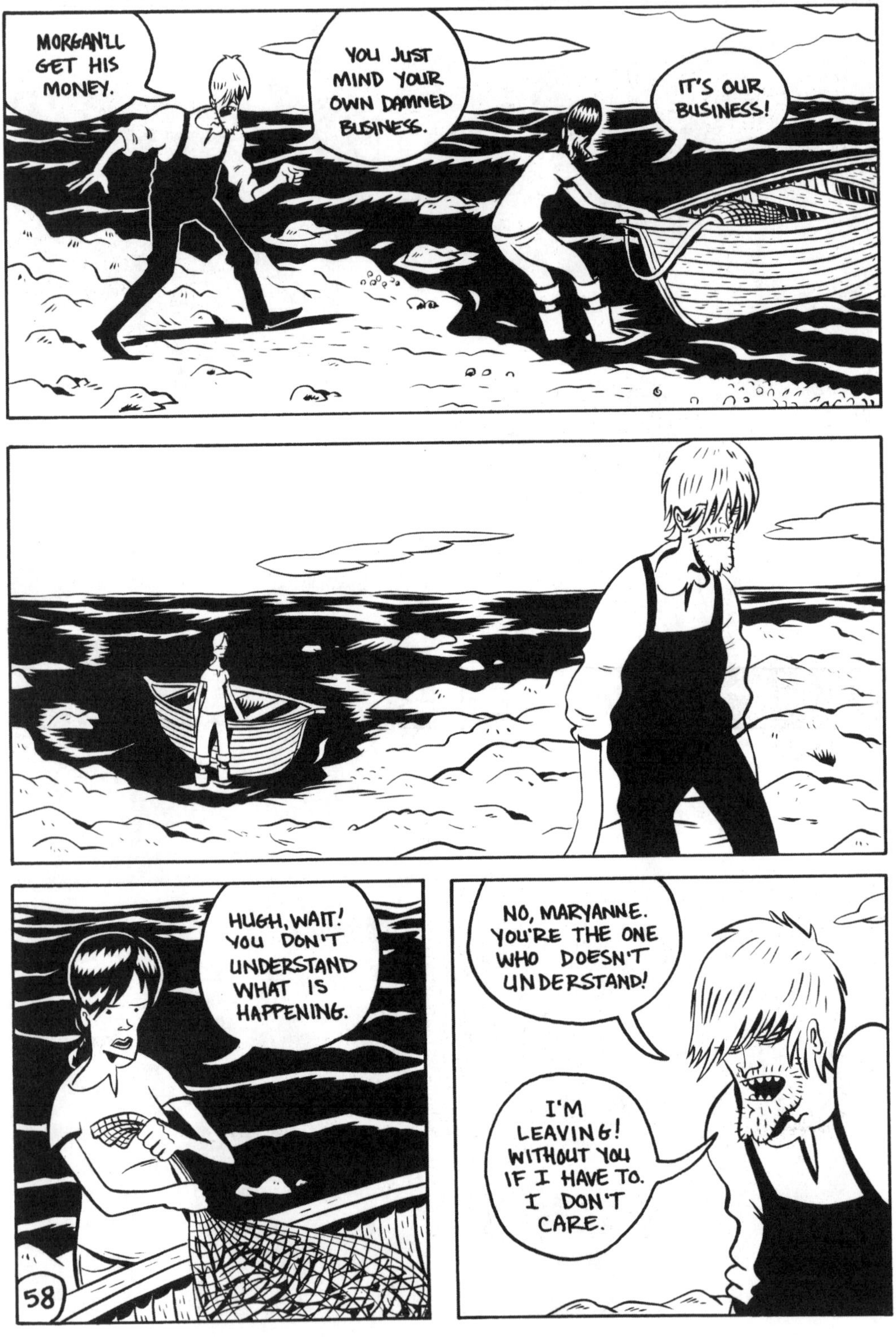
MORGAN'LL GET HIS MONEY.
YOU JUST MIND YOUR OWN DAMNED BUSINESS.
IT'S OUR BUSINESS!
HUGH, WAIT! YOU DON'T UNDERSTAND WHAT IS HAPPENING.
NO, MARYANNE. YOU'RE THE ONE WHO DOESN'T UNDERSTAND!
I'M LEAVING! WITHOUT YOU IF I HAVE TO. I DON'T CARE.

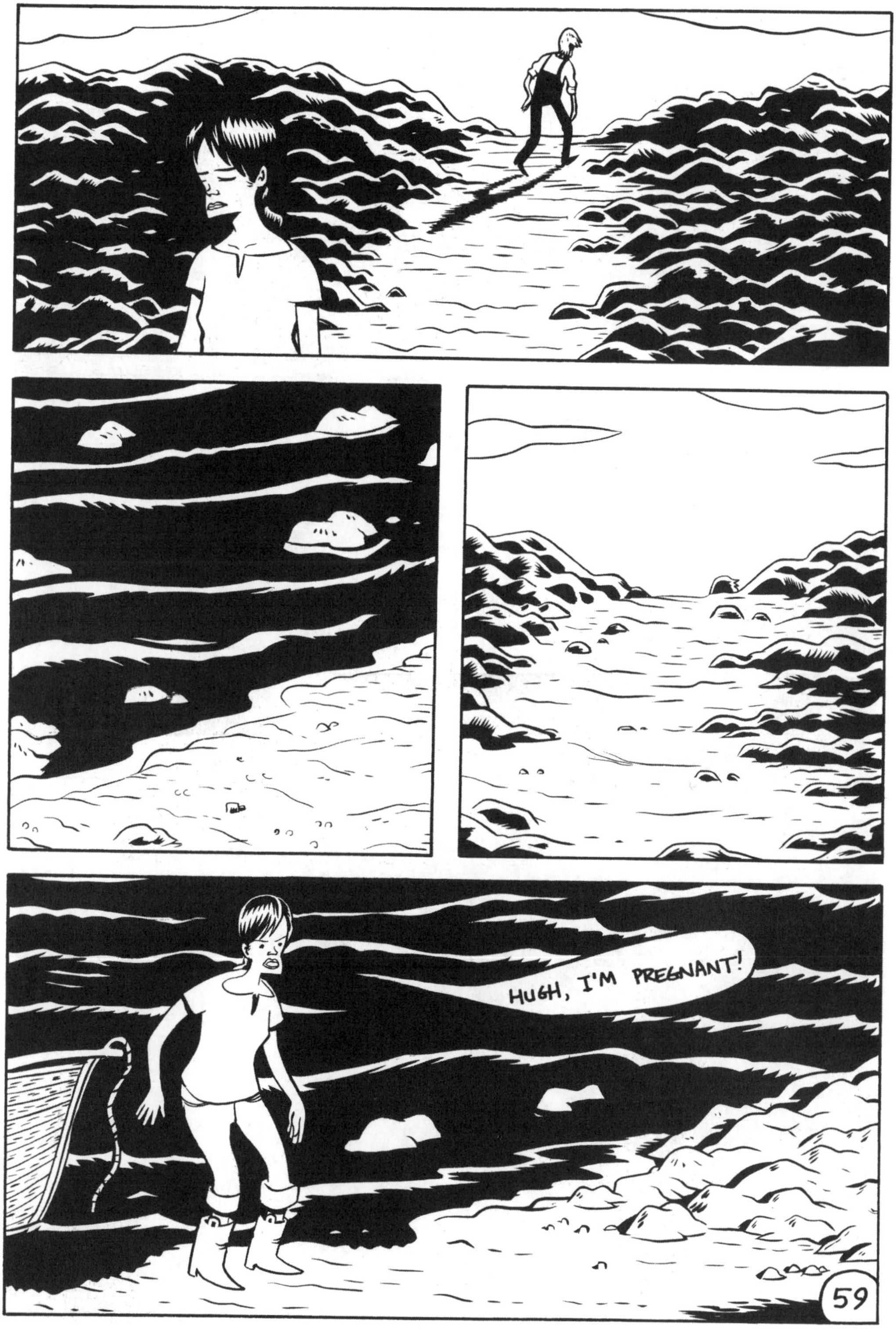
HUGH, I'M PREGNANT!

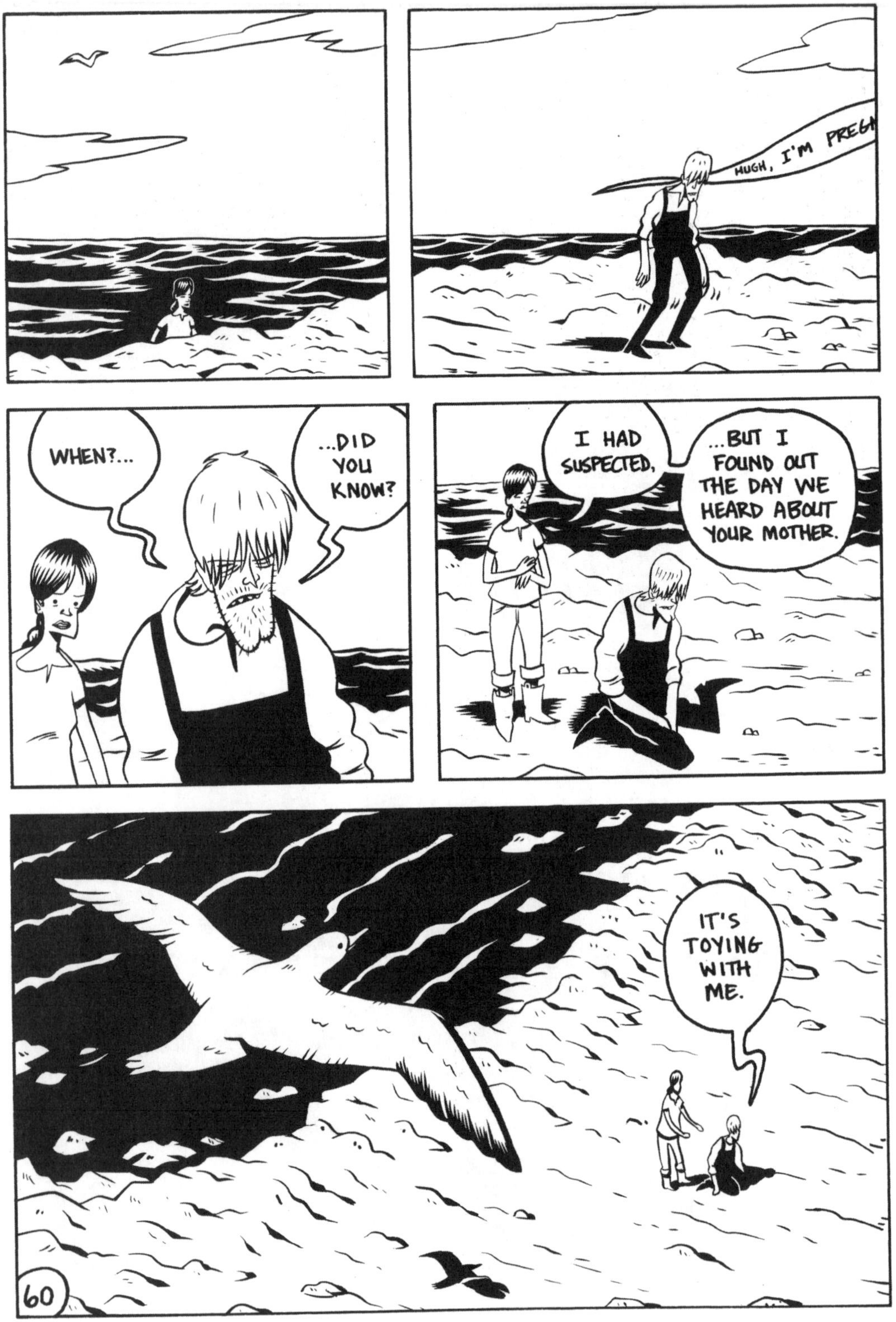
HUGH, I'M PREGN
WHEN?...
...DID YOU KNOW?
I HAD SUSPECTED,
...BUT I FOUND OUT THE DAY WE HEARD ABOUT YOUR MOTHER.
IT'S TOYING WITH ME.

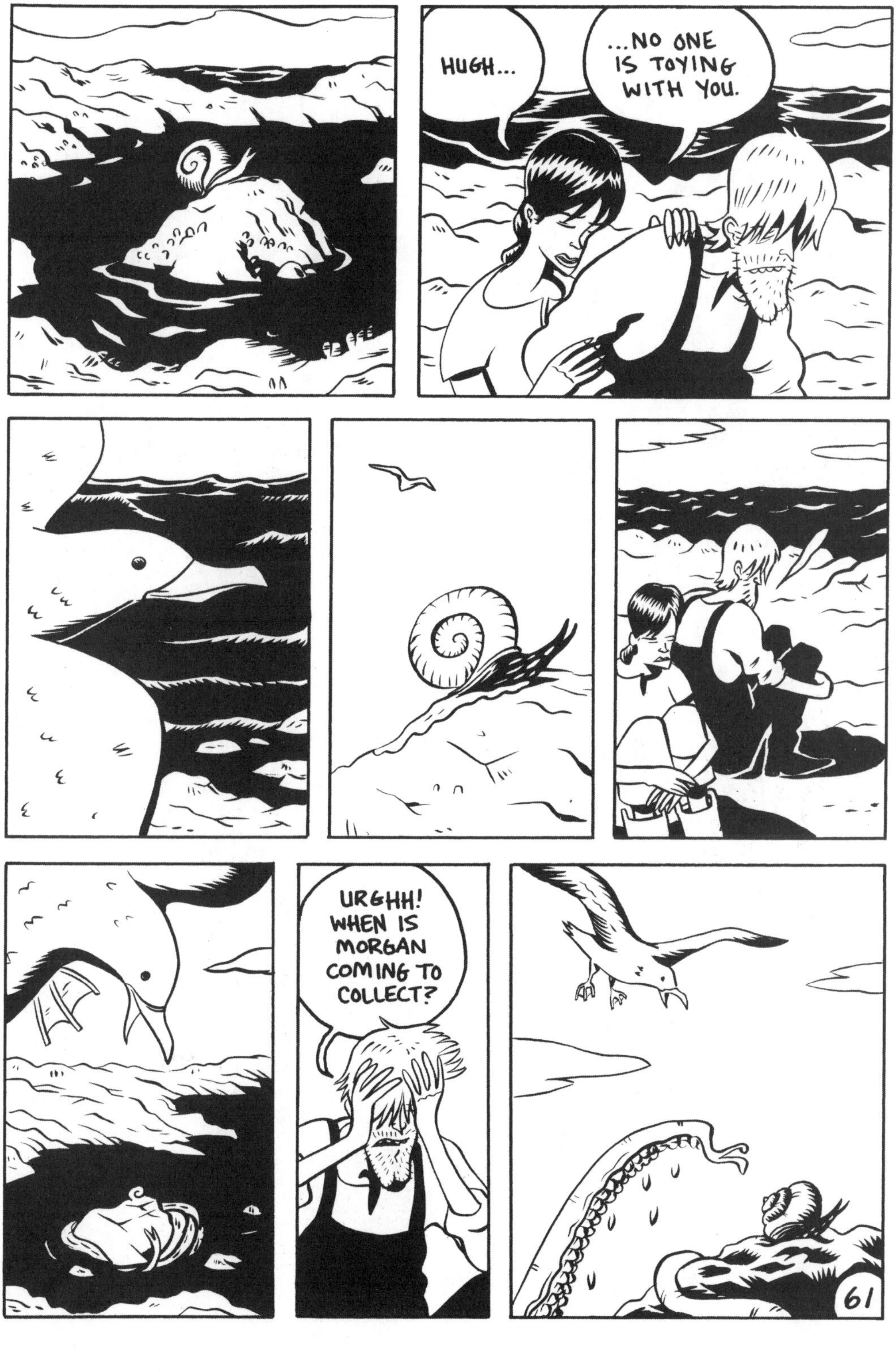
HUGH...
...NO ONE IS TOYING WITH YOU.
URGHH! WHEN IS MORGAN COMING TO COLLECT?

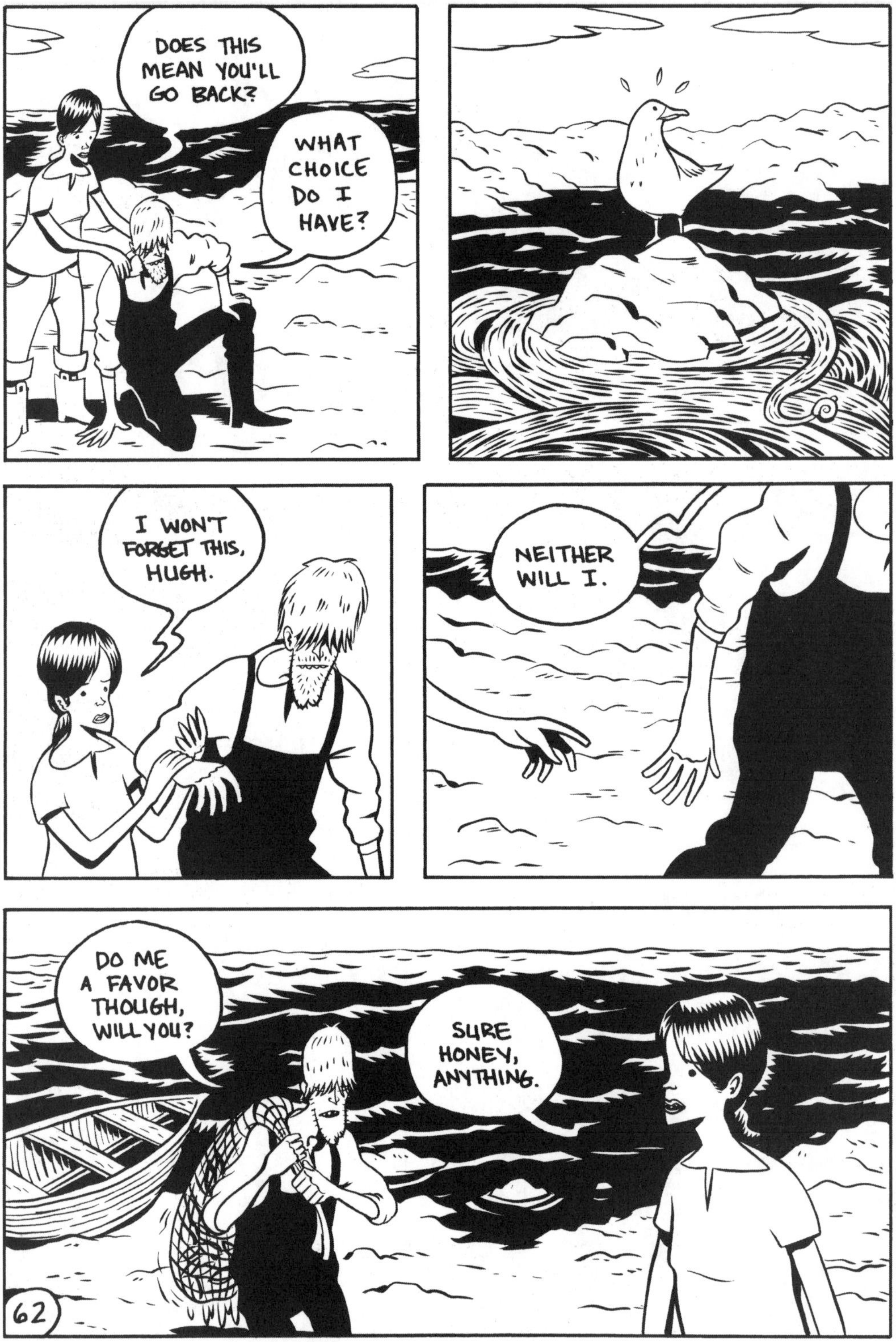
DOES THIS MEAN YOU'LL GO BACK?
WHAT CHOICE DO I HAVE?
I WON'T FORGET THIS, HUGH.
NEITHER WILL I.
DO ME A FAVOR THOUGH, WILL YOU?
SURE HONEY, ANYTHING.

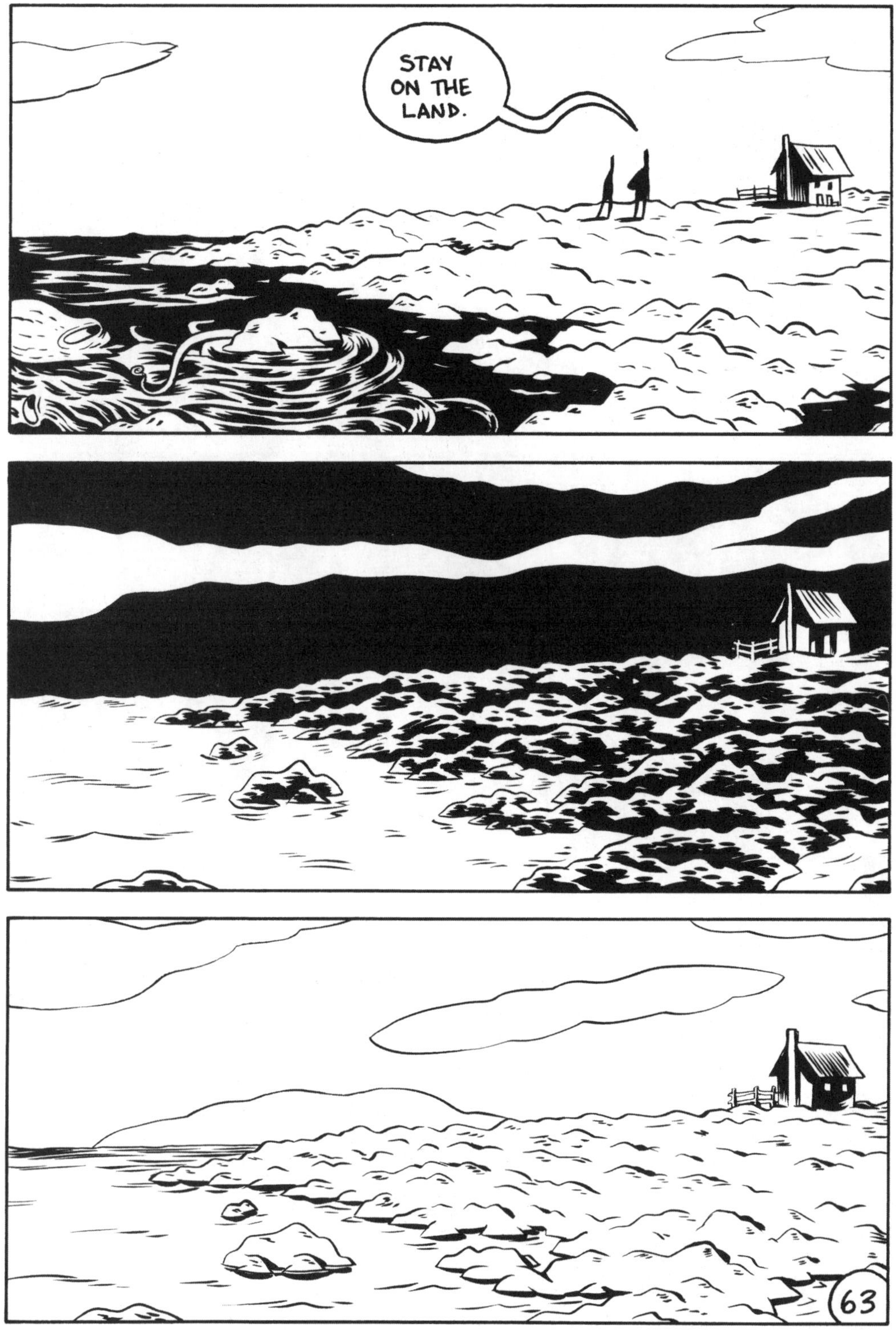
STAY ON THE LAND.

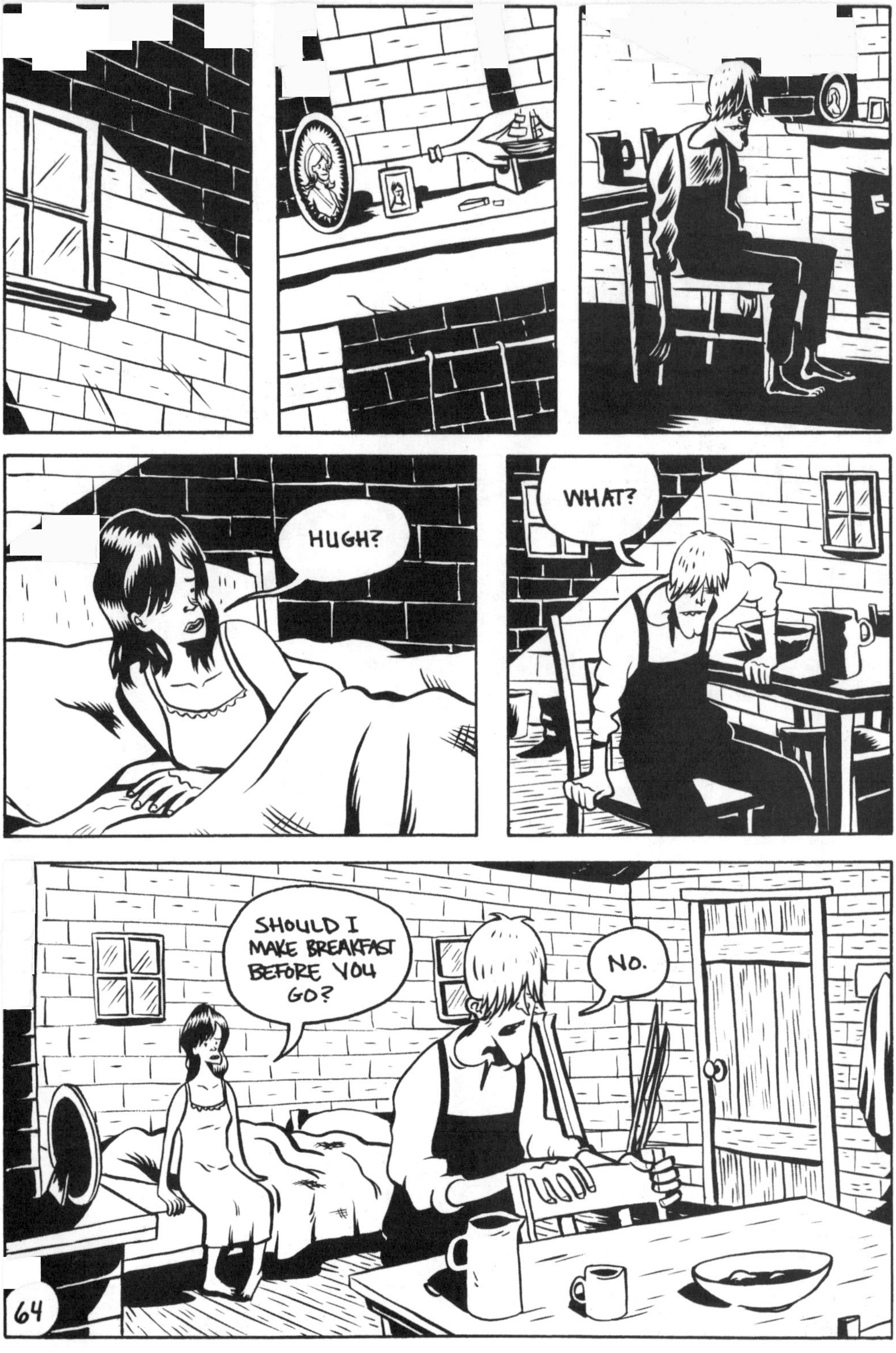
HUGH?
WHAT?
SHOULD I MAKE BREAKFAST BEFORE YOU GO?
NO.

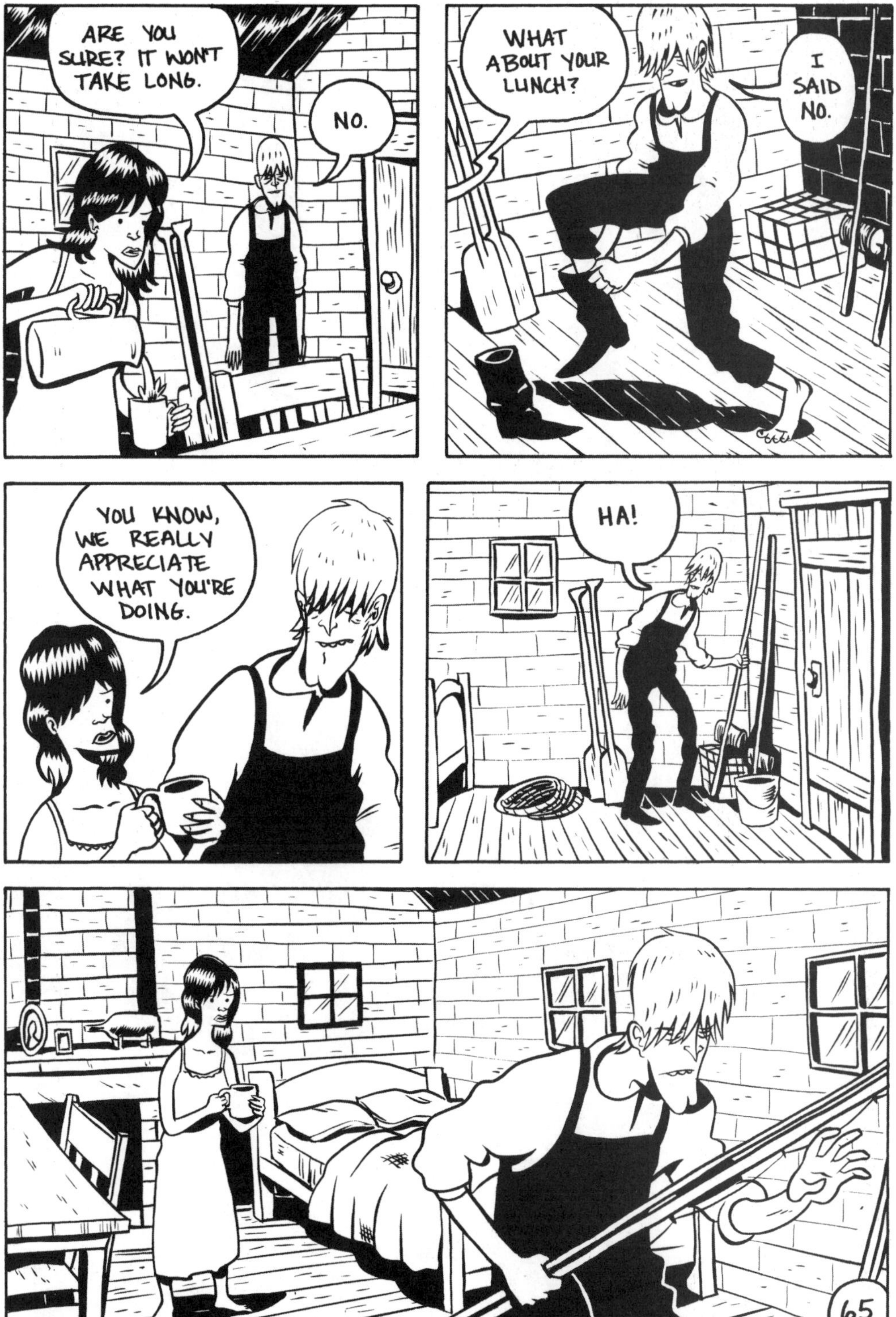
ARE YOU SURE? IT WON'T TAKE LONG.
NO.
WHAT ABOUT YOUR LUNCH?
I SAID NO.
YOU KNOW, WE REALLY APPRECIATE WHAT YOU'RE DOING.
HA!

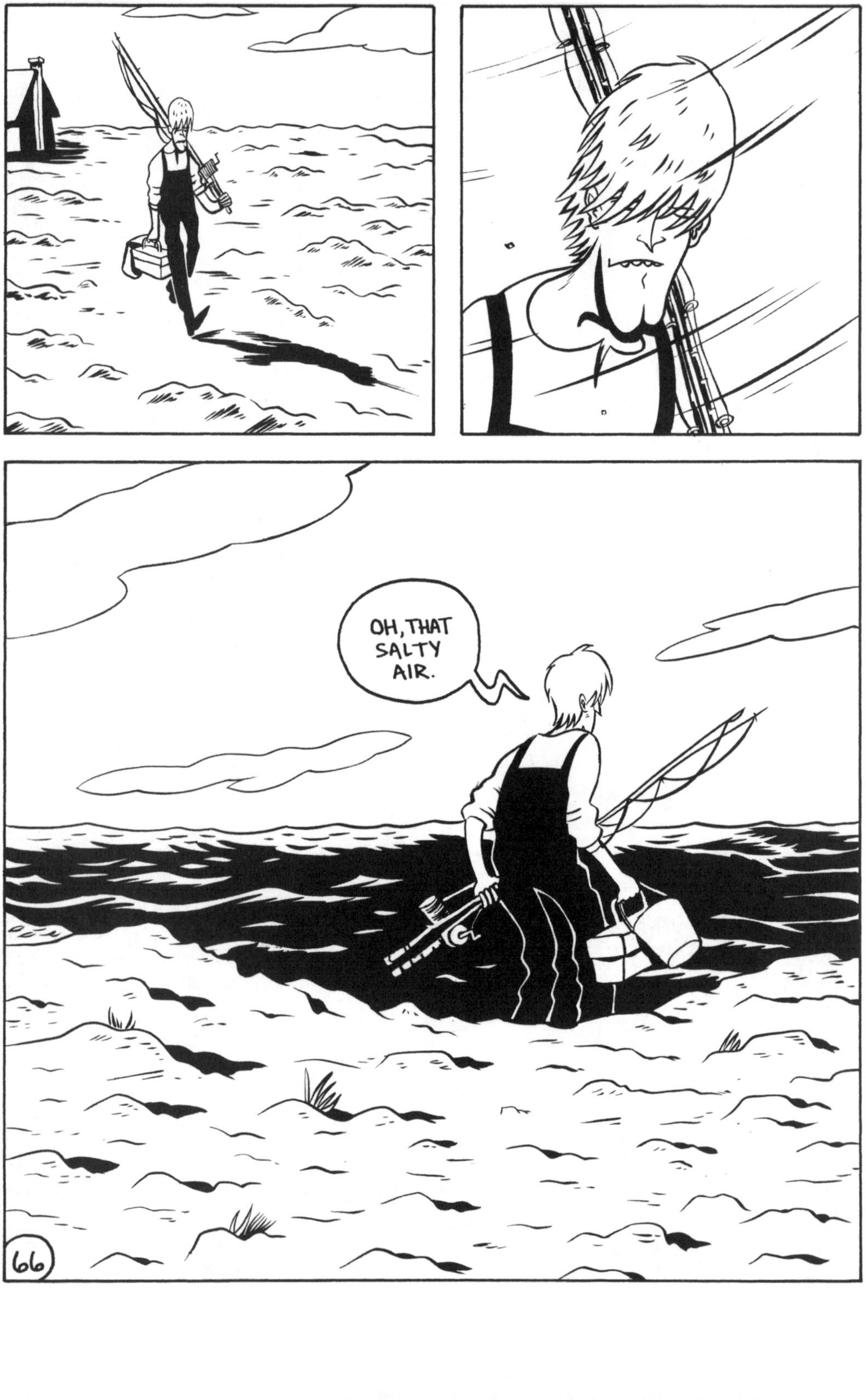
OH, THAT SALTY AIR.

JUST A FEW FISH...

...THAT'S ALL.

67

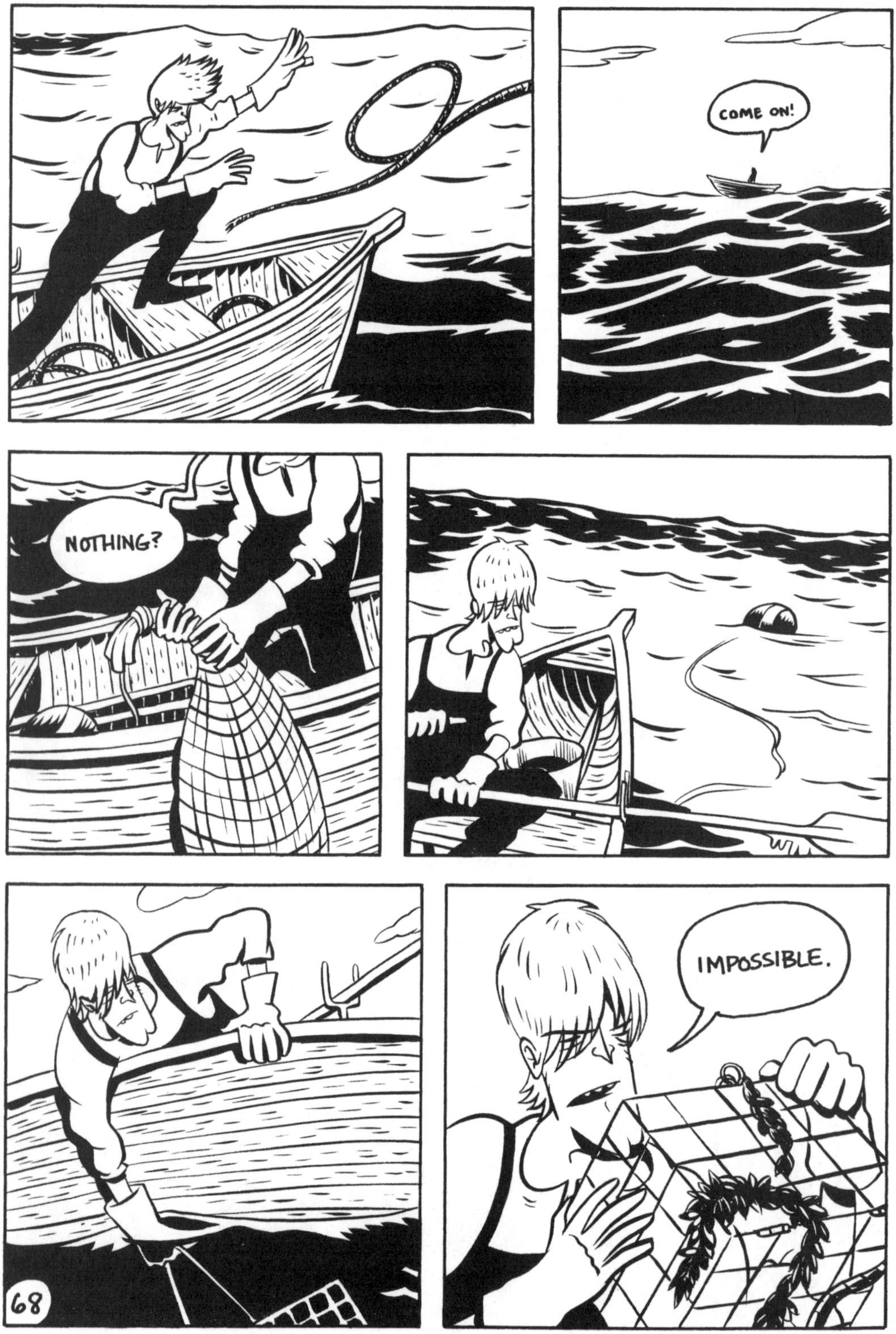
COME ON!
NOTHING?
IMPOSSIBLE.

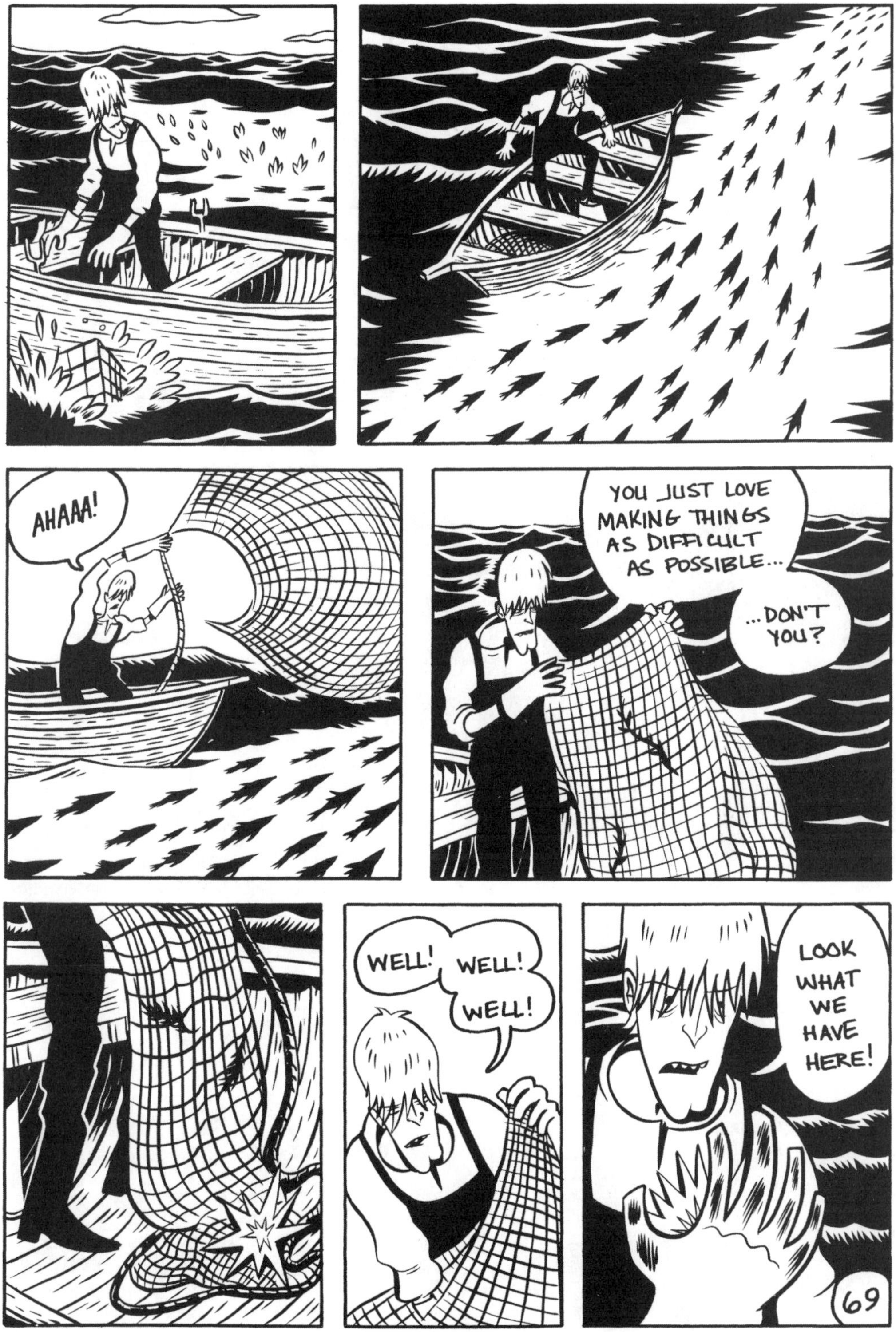
AHAAA!
YOU JUST LOVE MAKING THINGS AS DIFFICULT AS POSSIBLE...
...DON'T YOU?
WELL! WELL! WELL!
LOOK WHAT WE HAVE HERE!

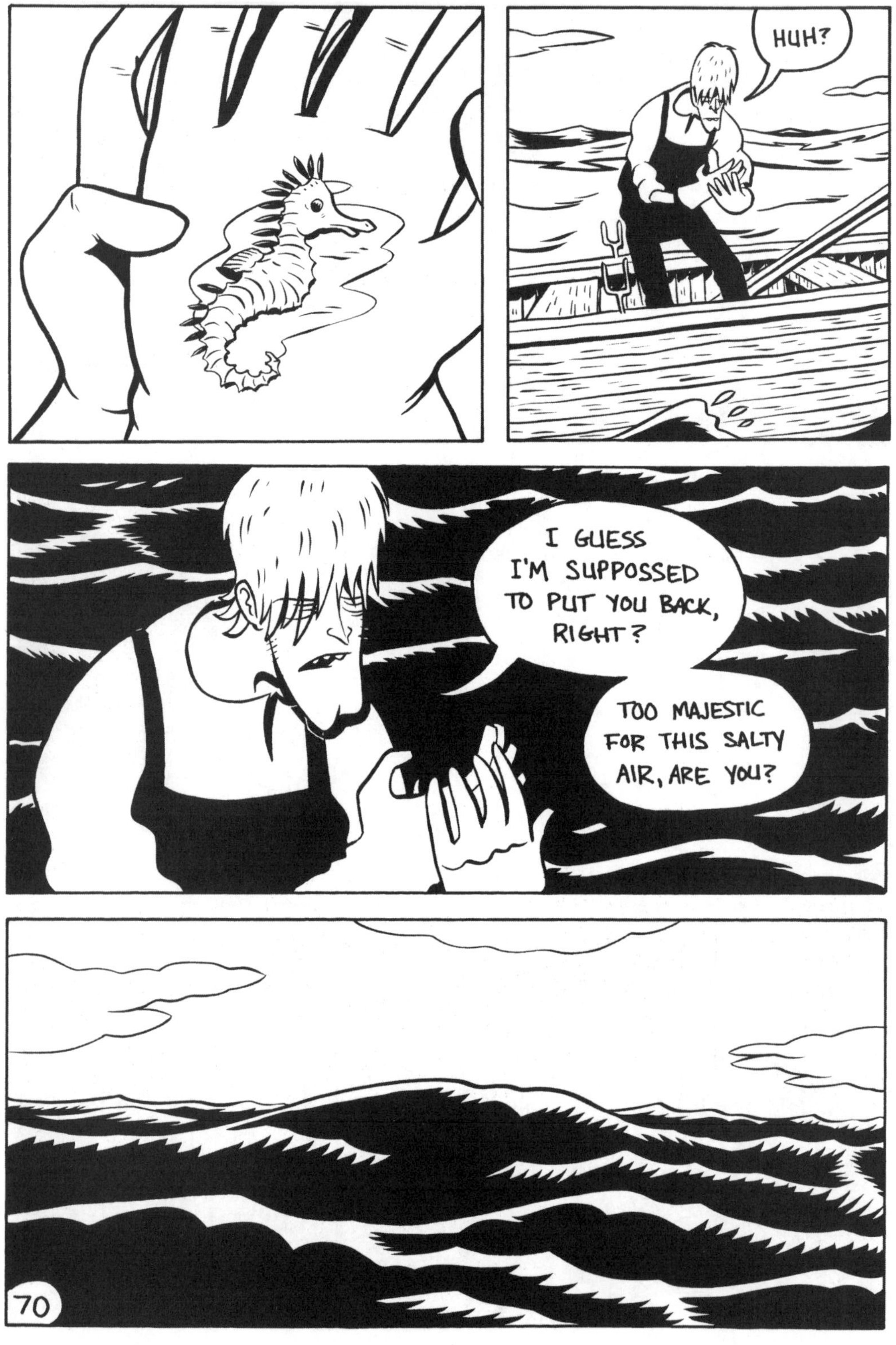
HUH?
I GUESS I'M SUPPOSSED TO PUT YOU BACK, RIGHT?
TOO MAJESTIC FOR THIS SALTY AIR, ARE YOU?

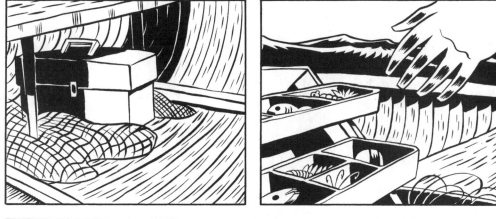

WELL, SO WAS SHE.

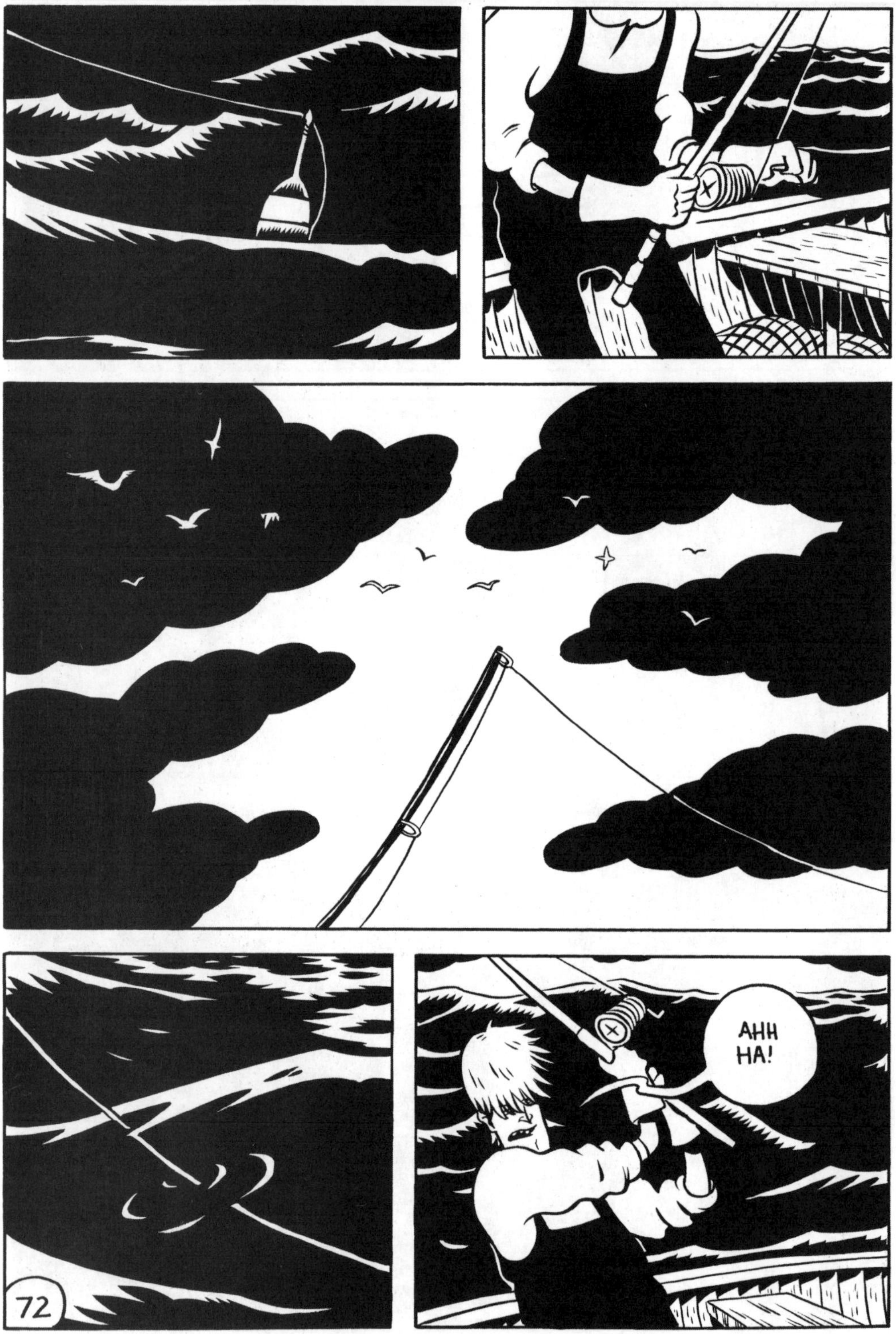
AHH
HA!

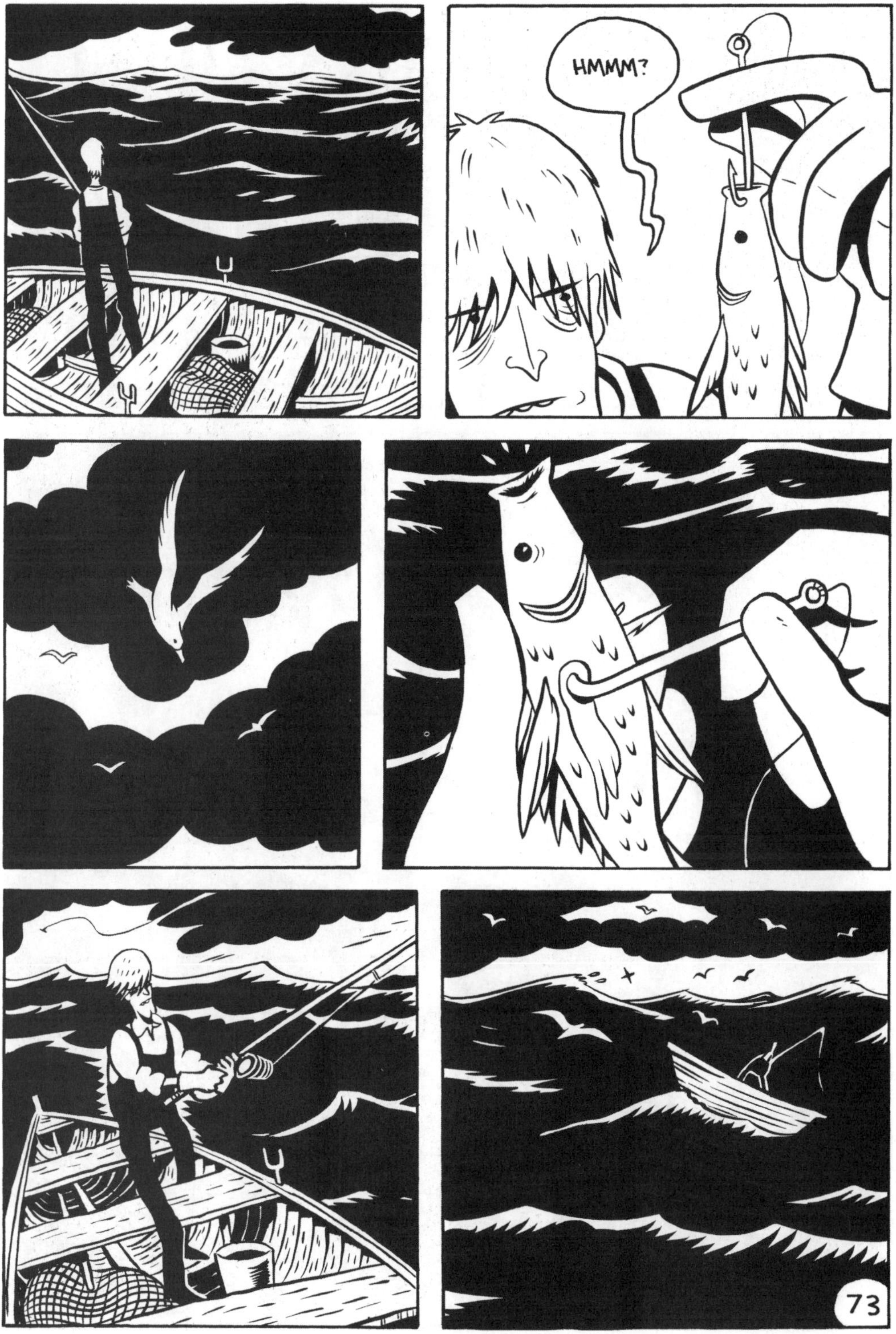
HMMM?

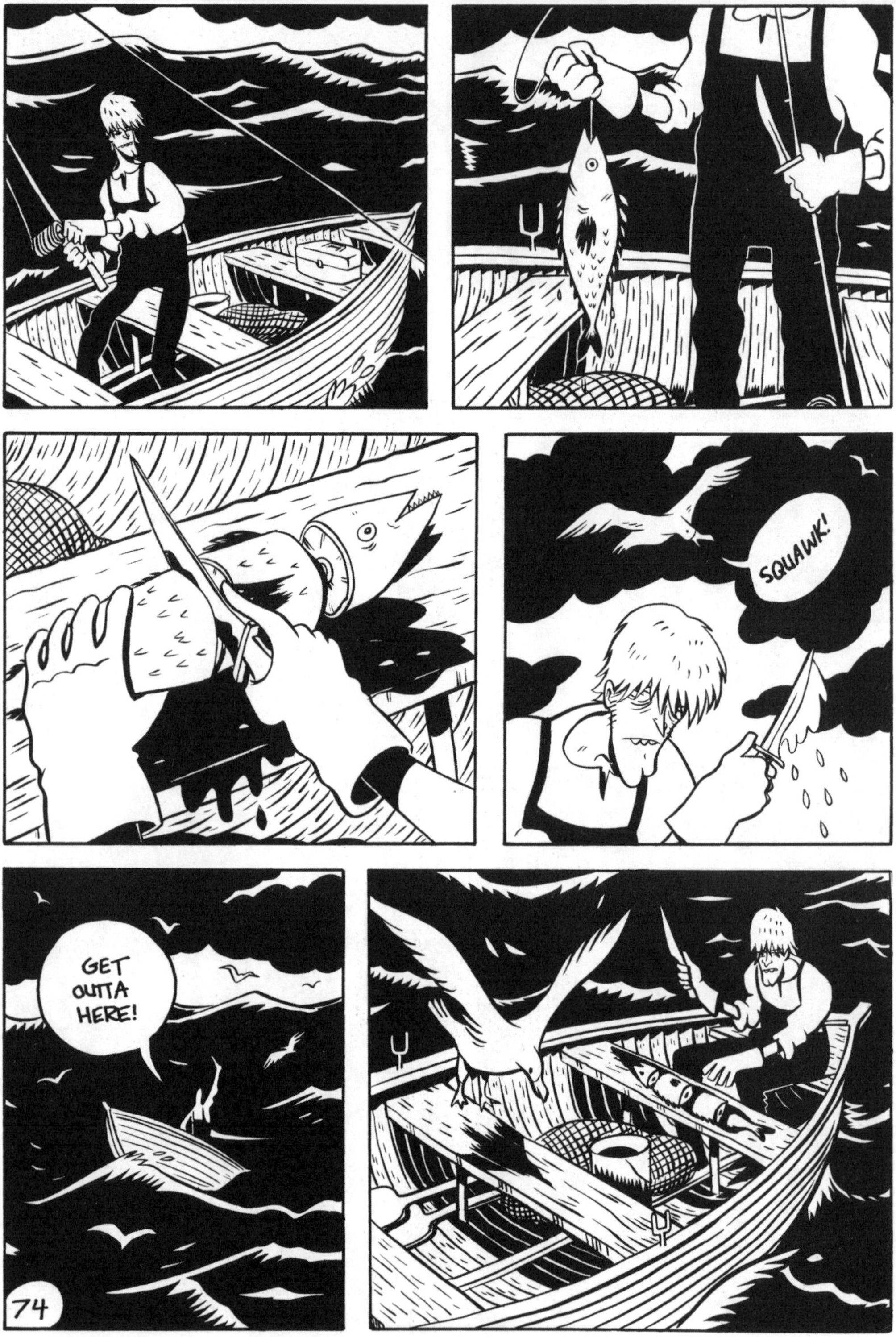
SQUAWK!
GET OUTTA HERE!

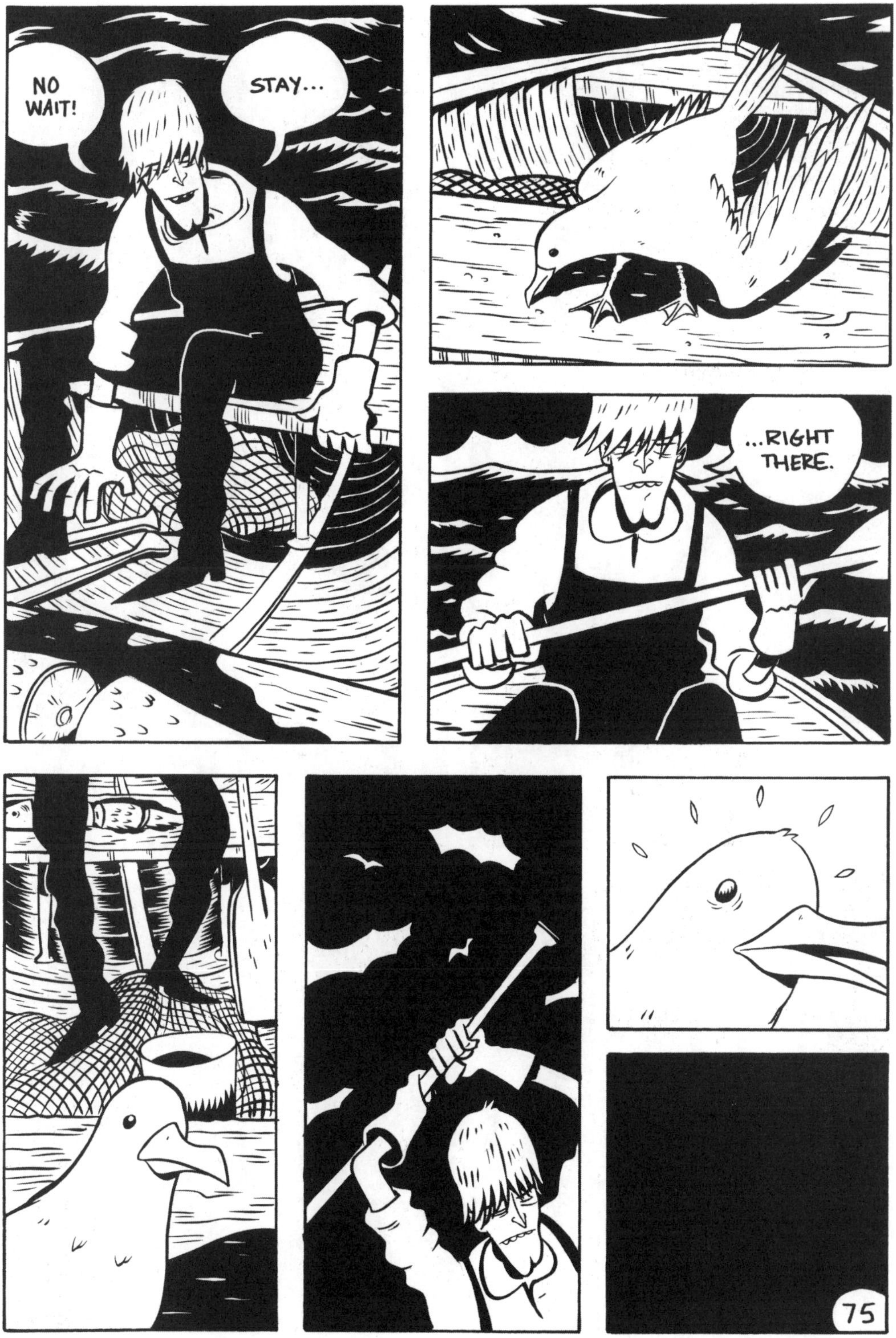
NO WAIT!
STAY...
...RIGHT THERE.

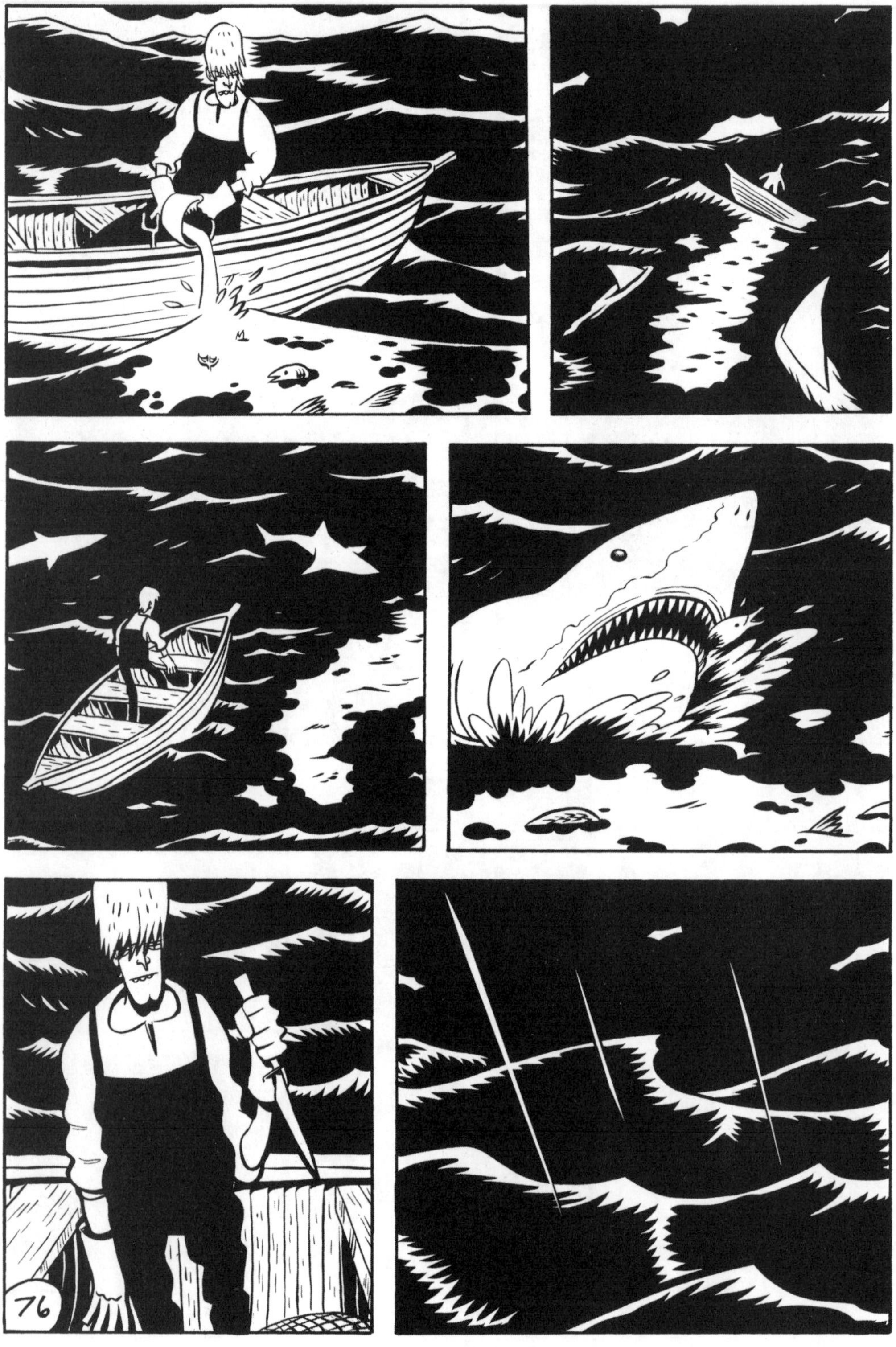

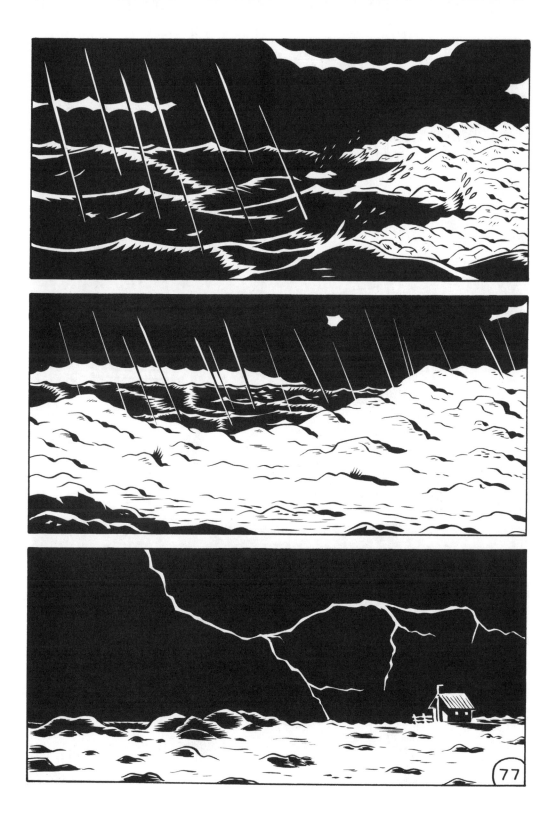

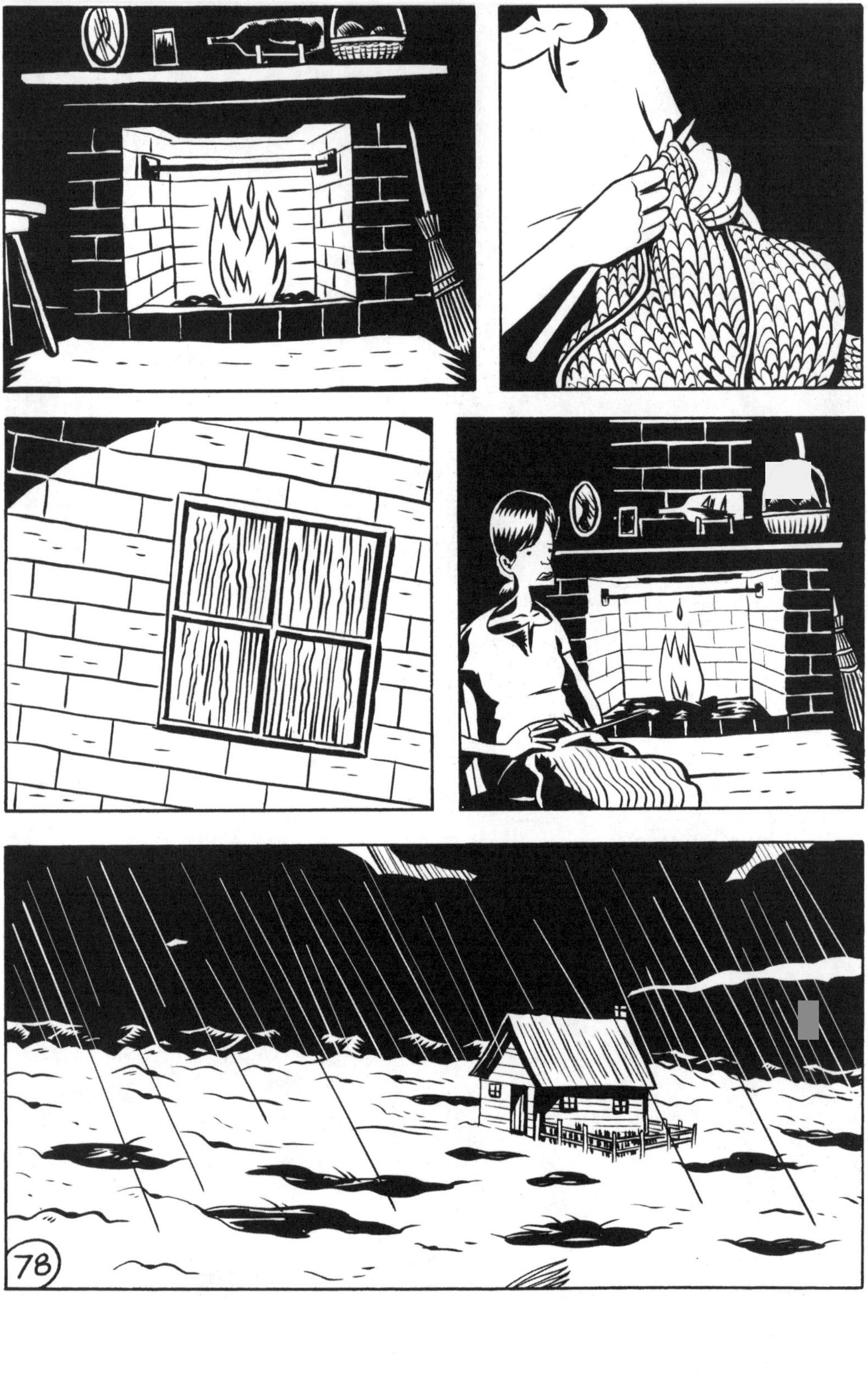

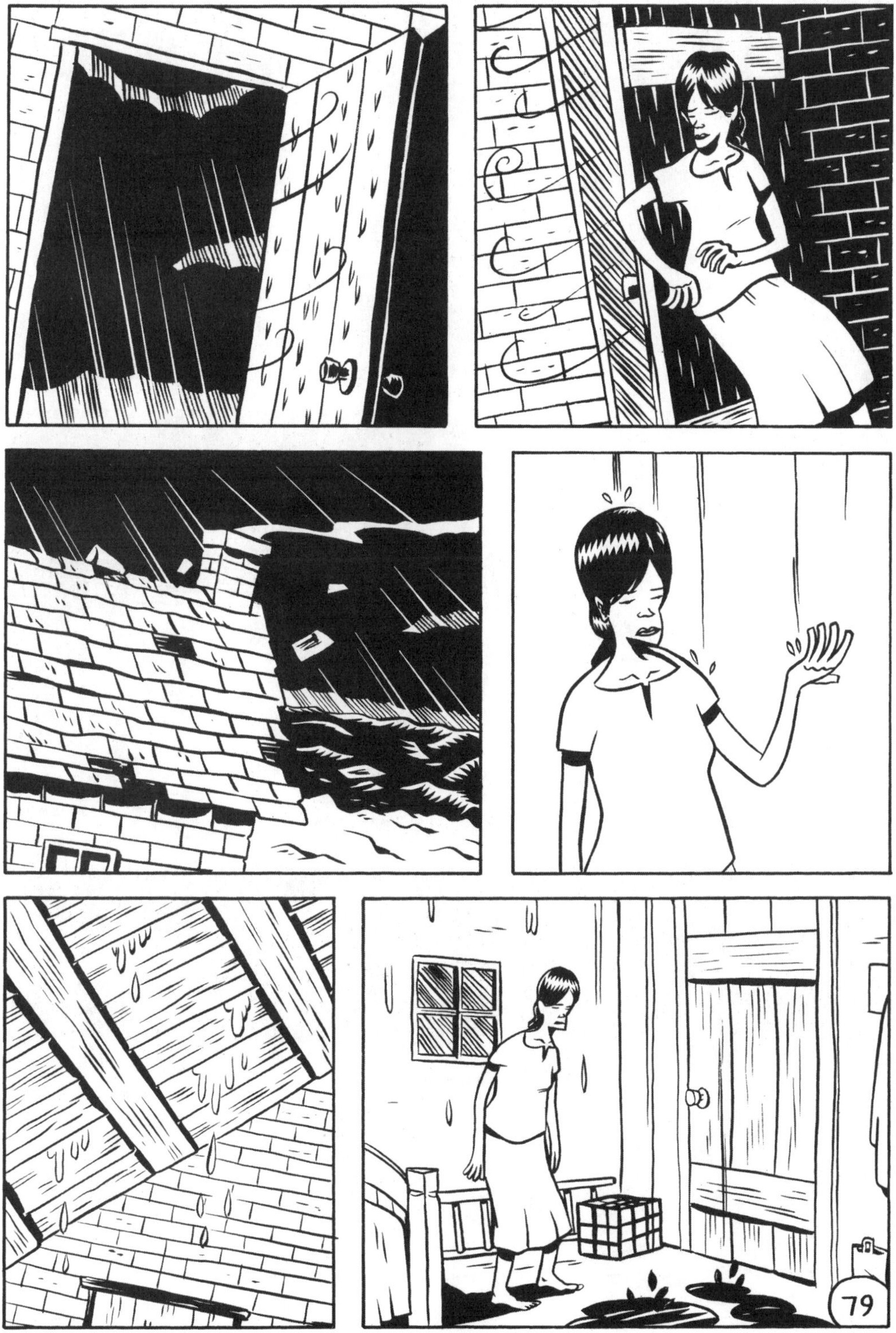
79

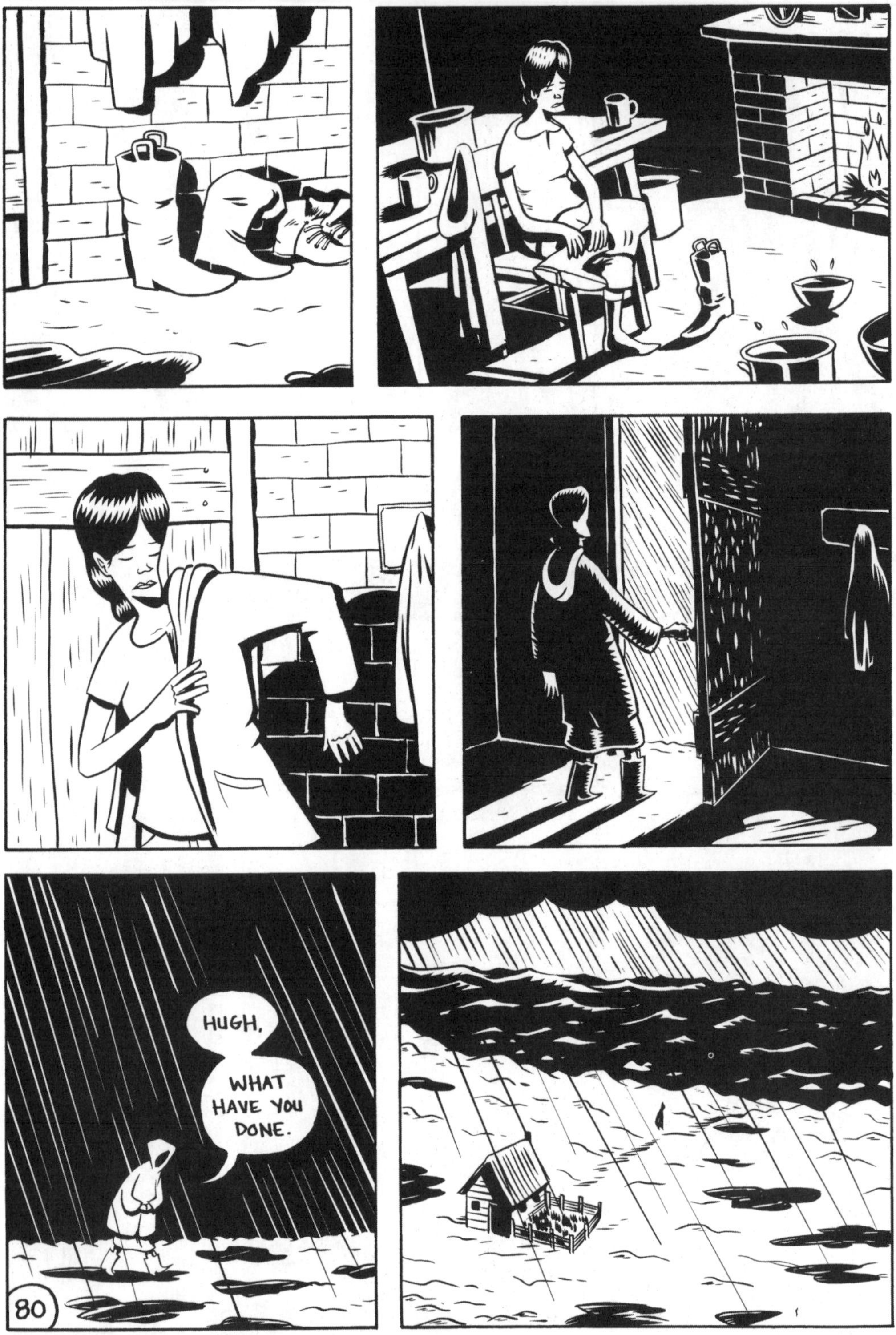
HUGH.
WHAT HAVE YOU DONE.

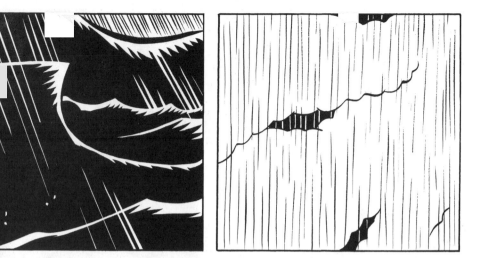

81

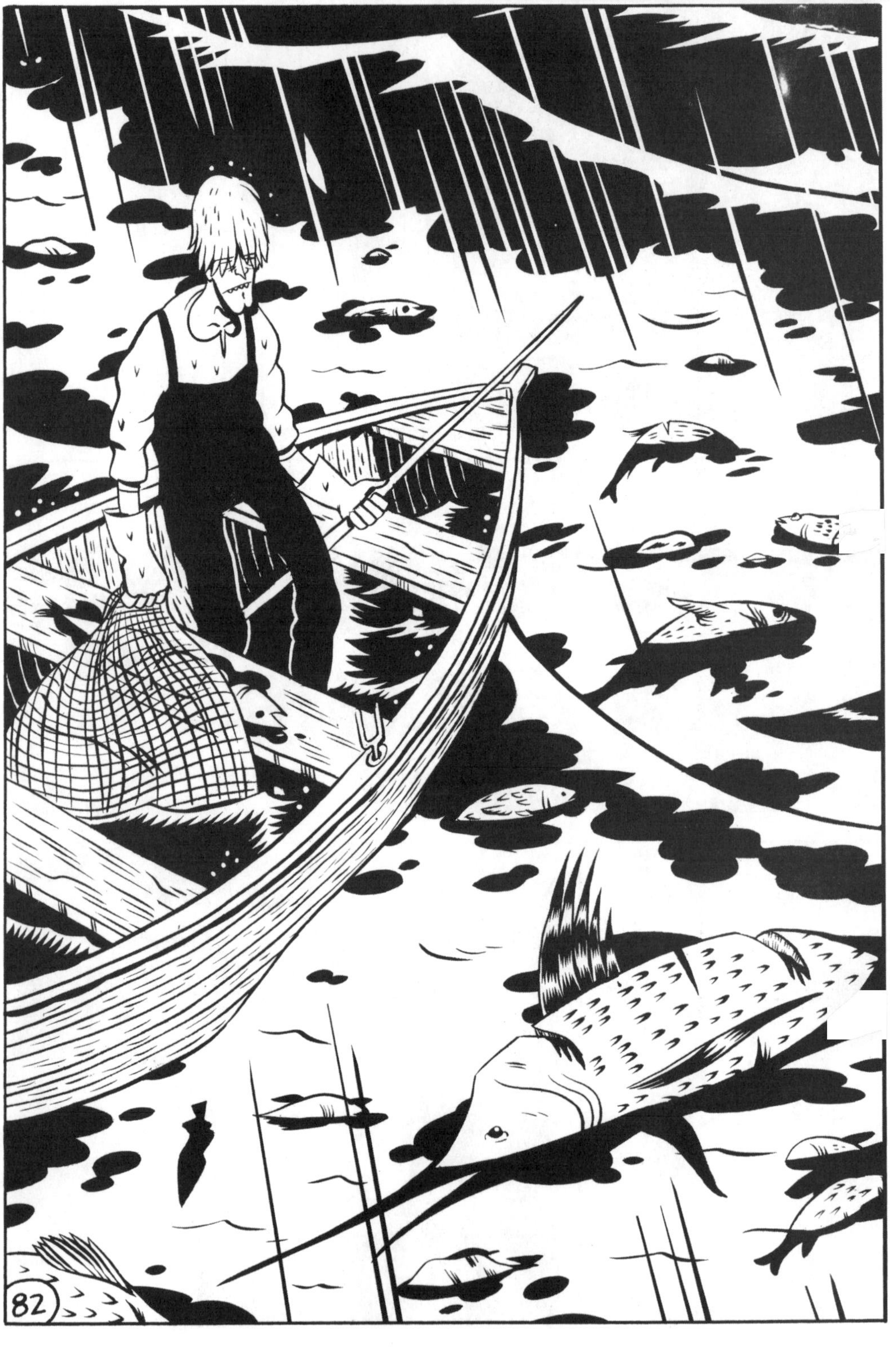

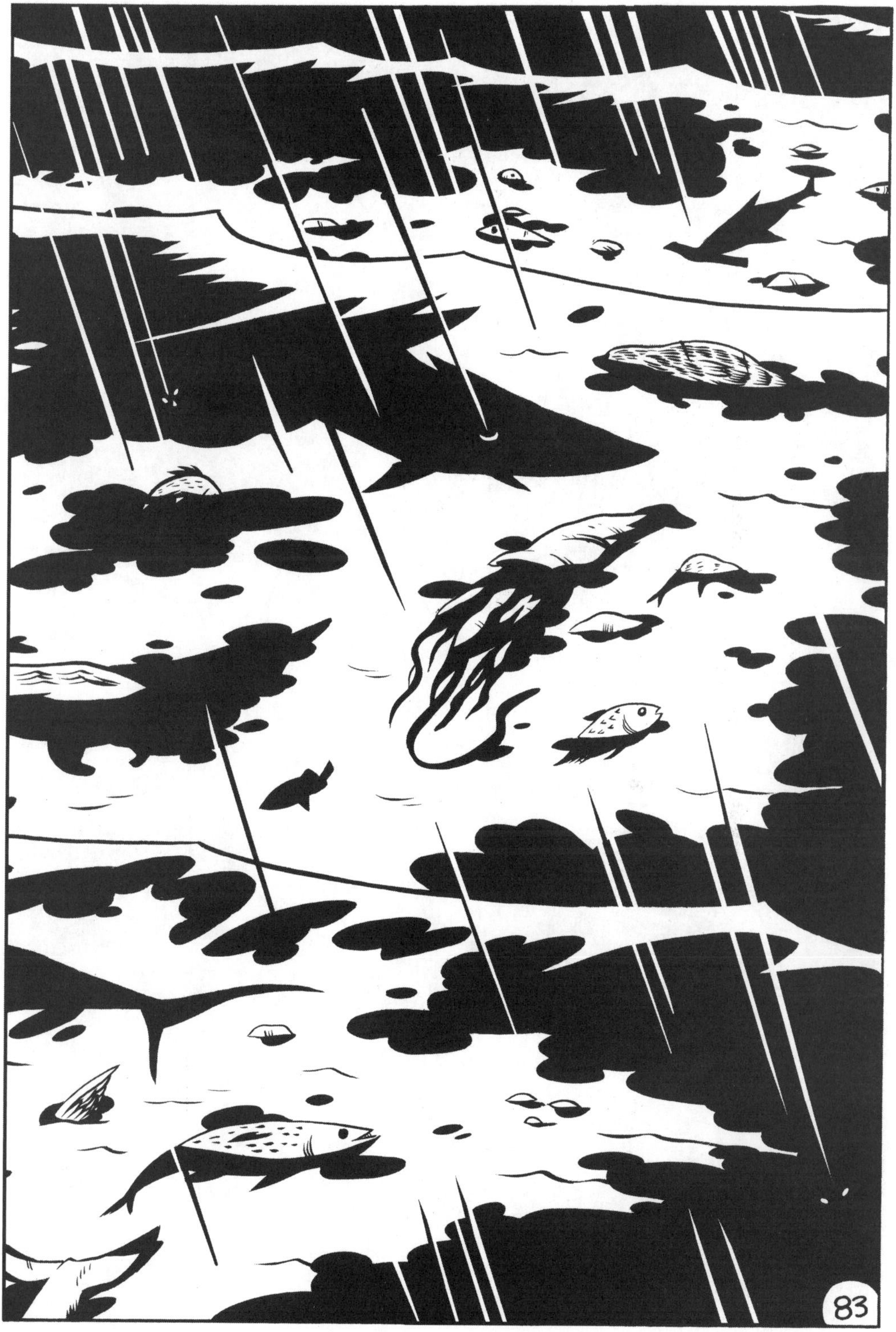

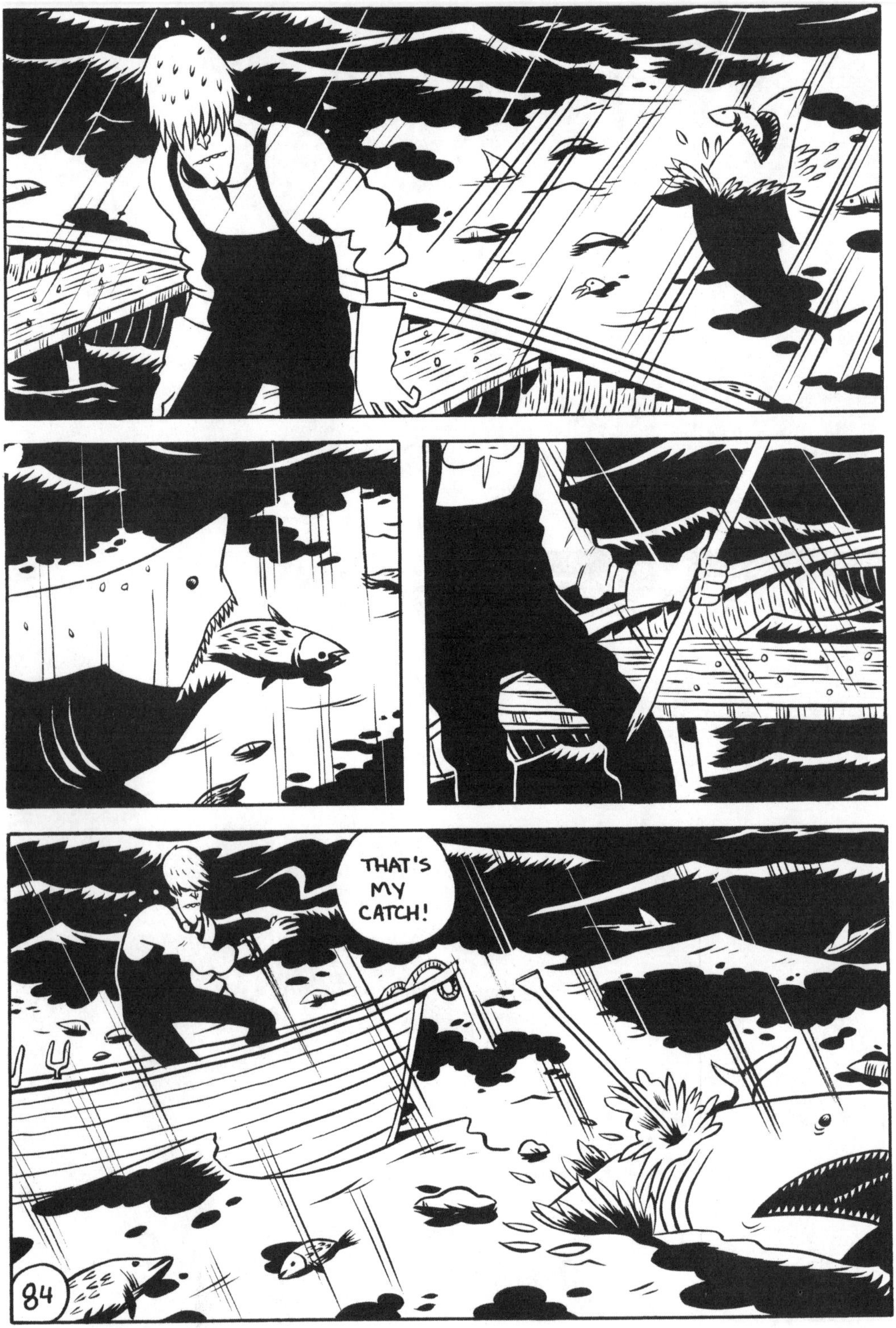
THAT'S MY CATCH!

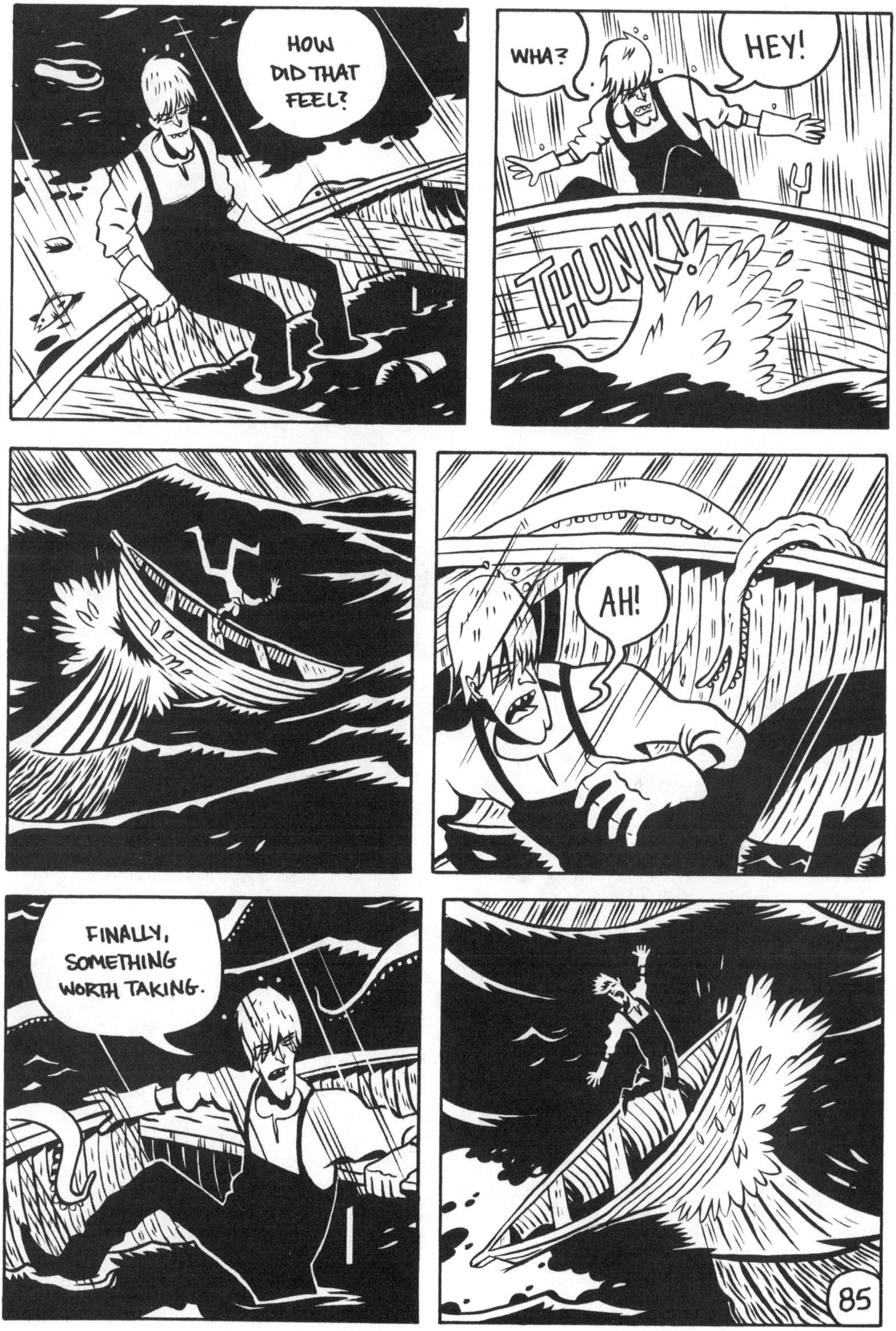
HOW DID THAT FEEL?
WHA?
HEY!
THUNK!
AH!
FINALLY, SOMETHING WORTH TAKING.

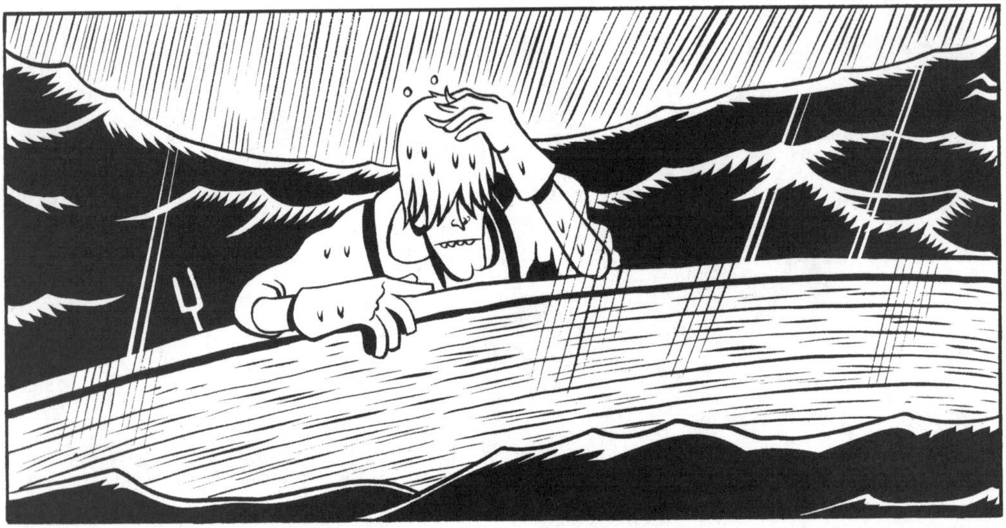

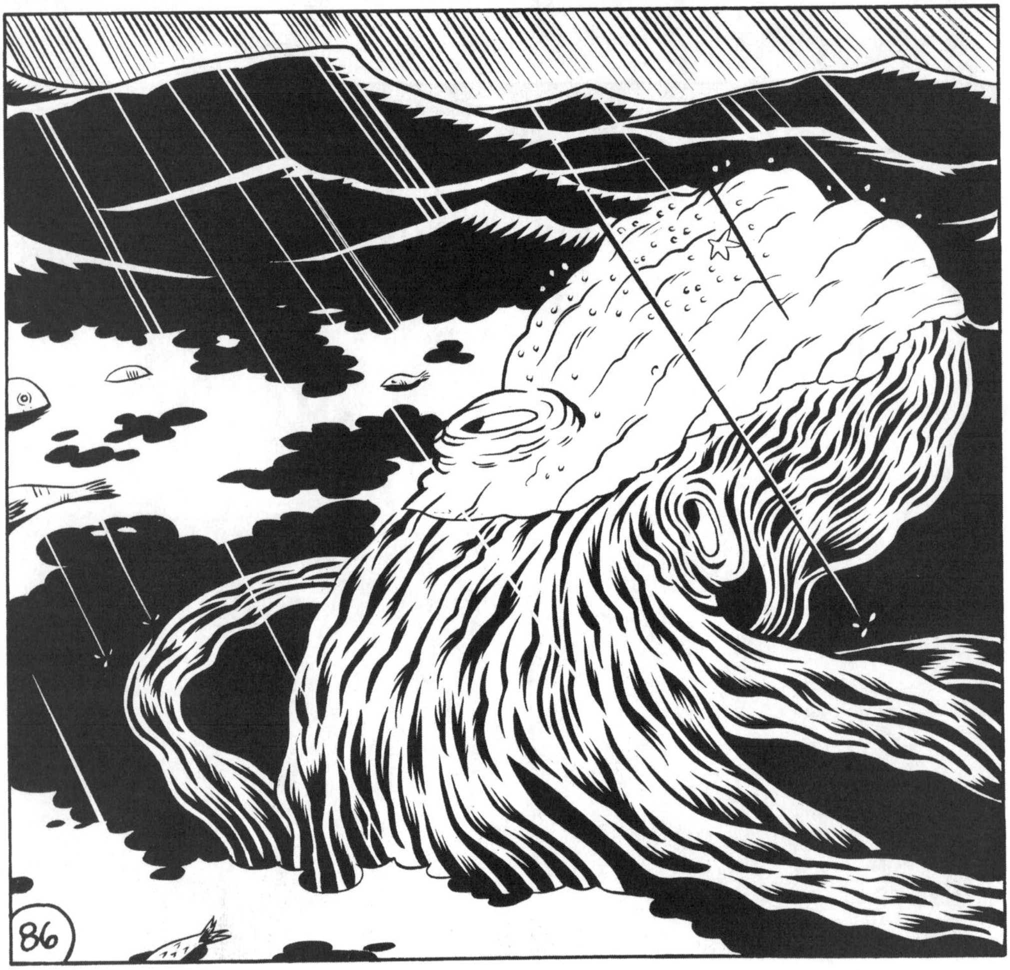

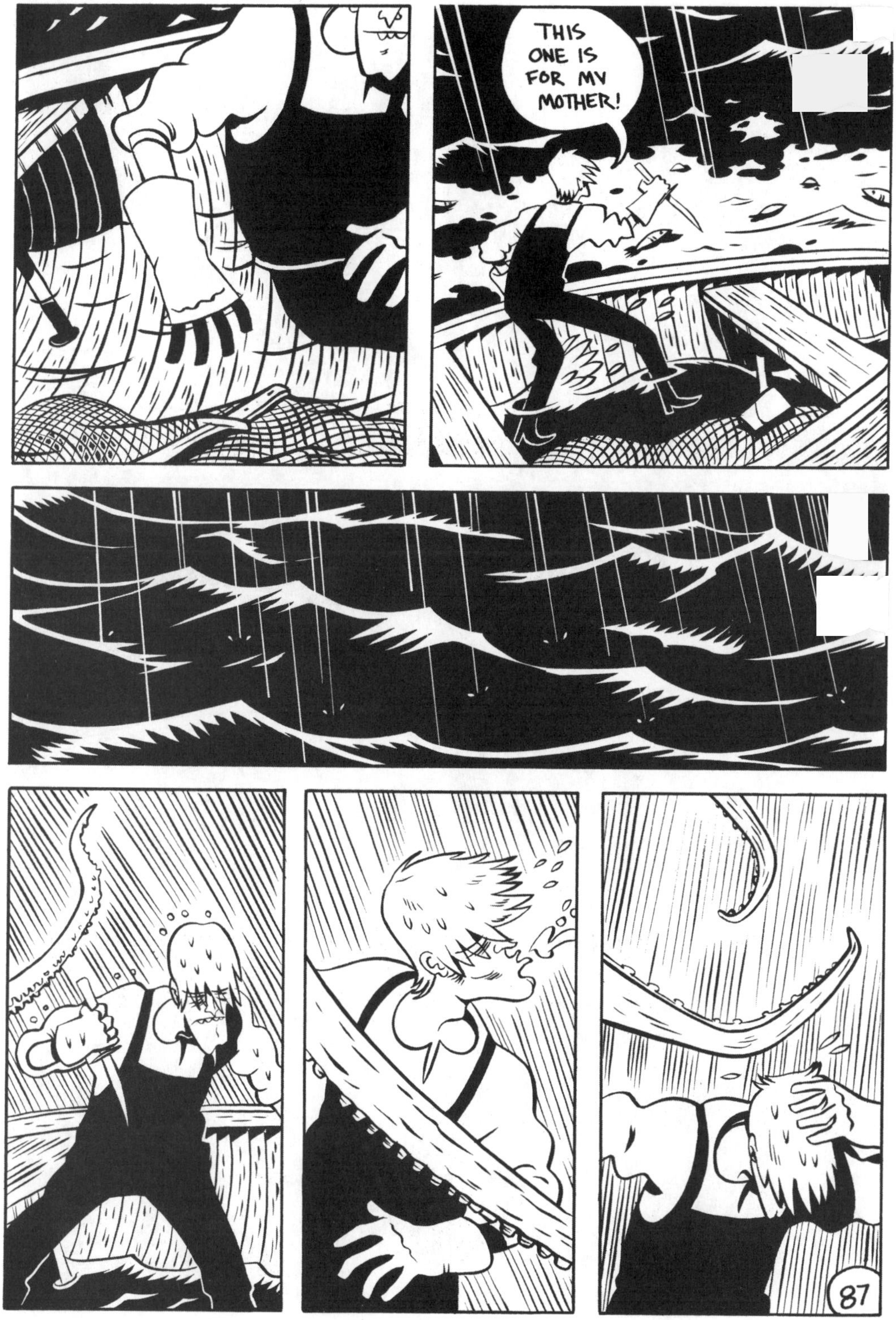
THIS ONE IS FOR MY MOTHER!

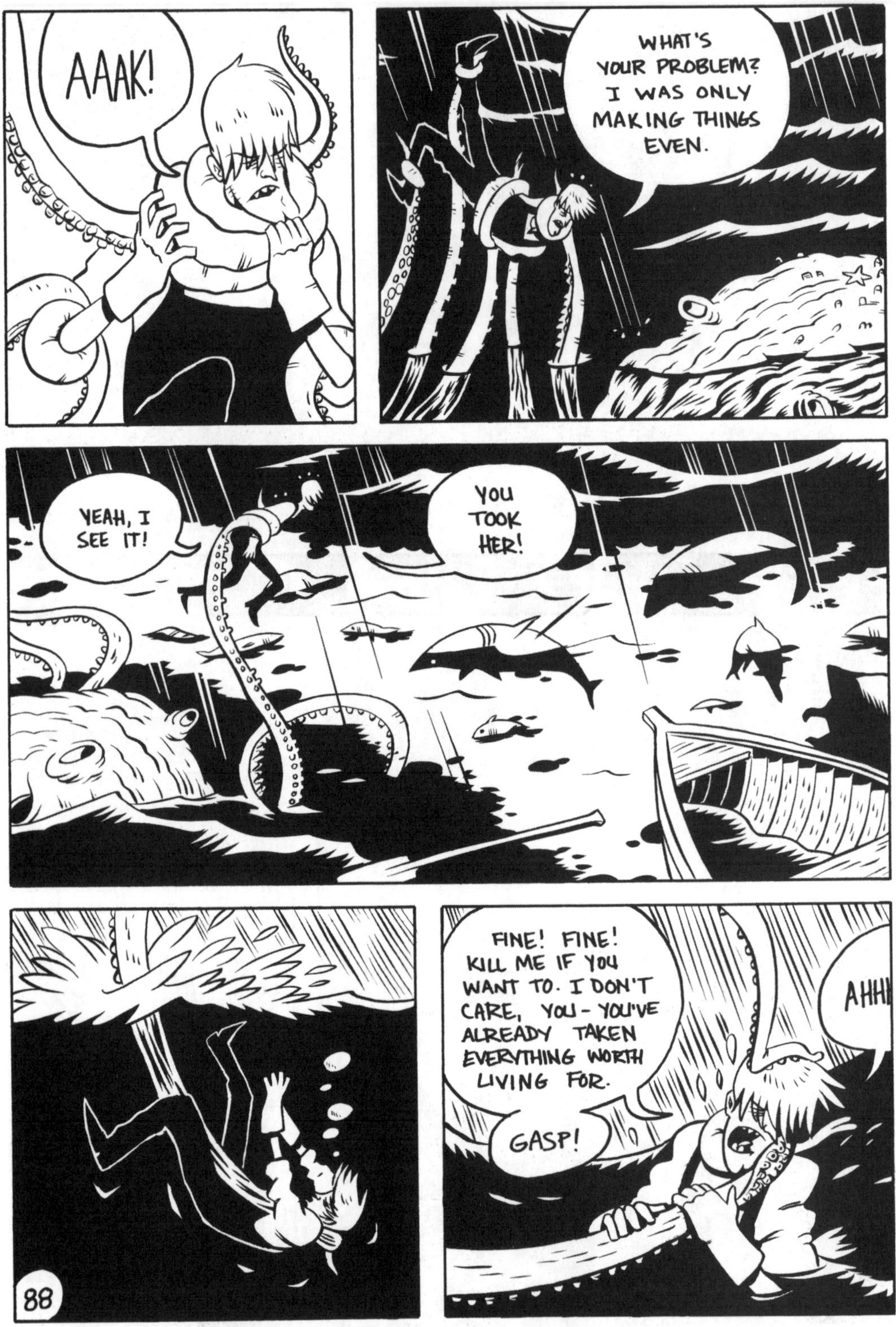
AAAK!
WHAT'S YOUR PROBLEM? I WAS ONLY MAKING THINGS EVEN.
YEAH, I SEE IT!
YOU TOOK HER!
FINE! FINE! KILL ME IF YOU WANT TO. I DON'T CARE, YOU- YOU'VE ALREADY TAKEN EVERYTHING WORTH LIVING FOR.
AHH
GASP!

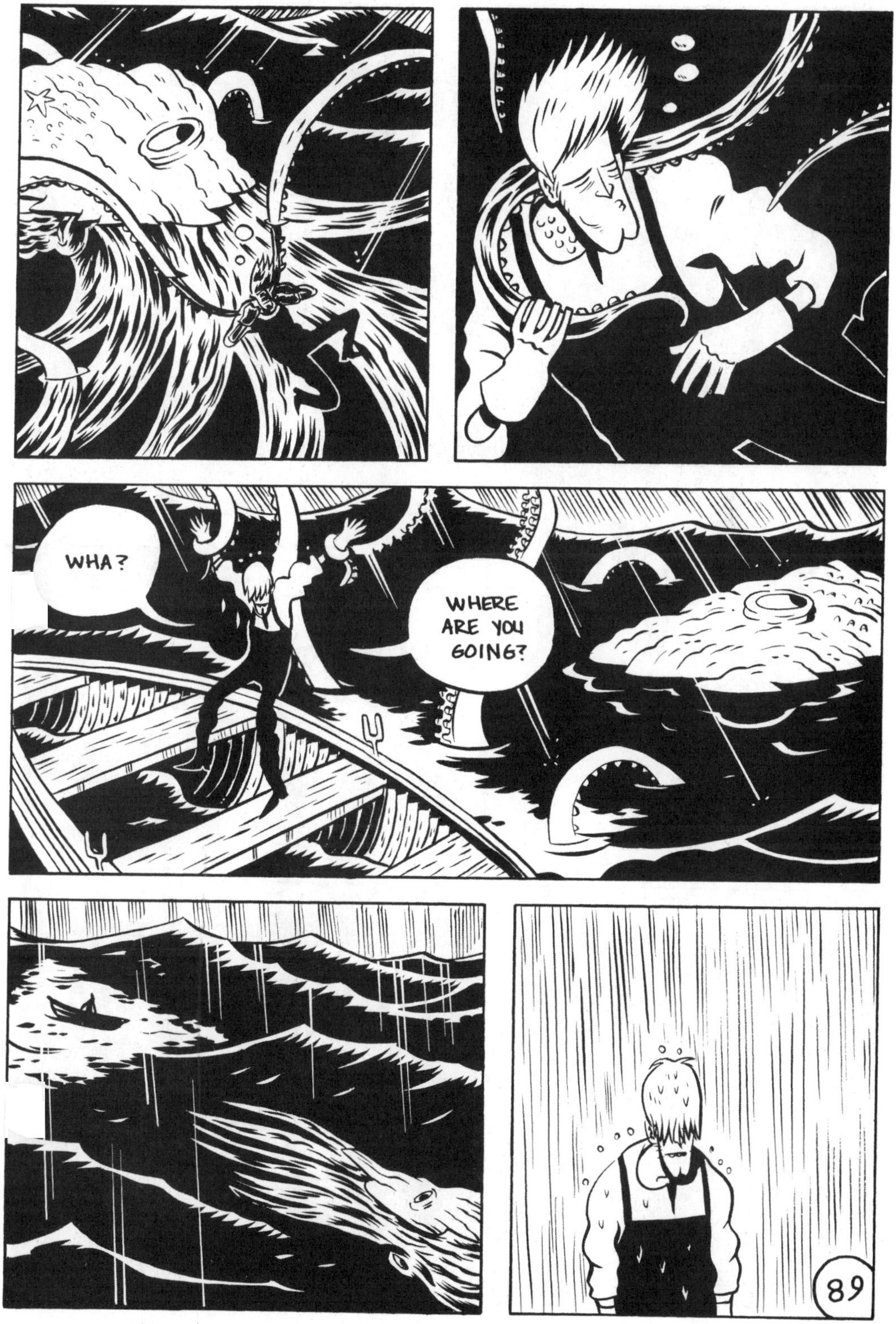
WHA?
WHERE ARE YOU GOING?

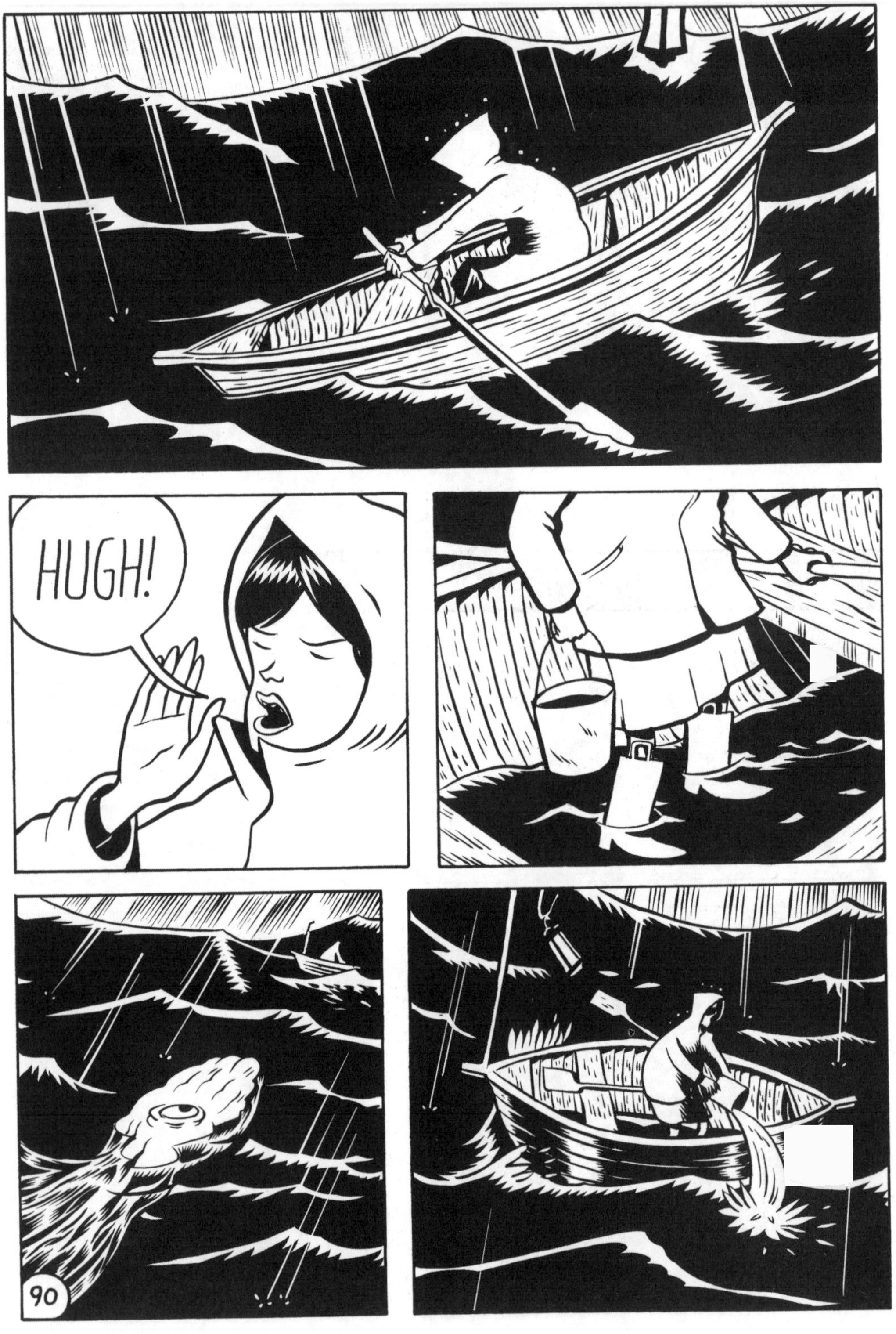
HUGH!

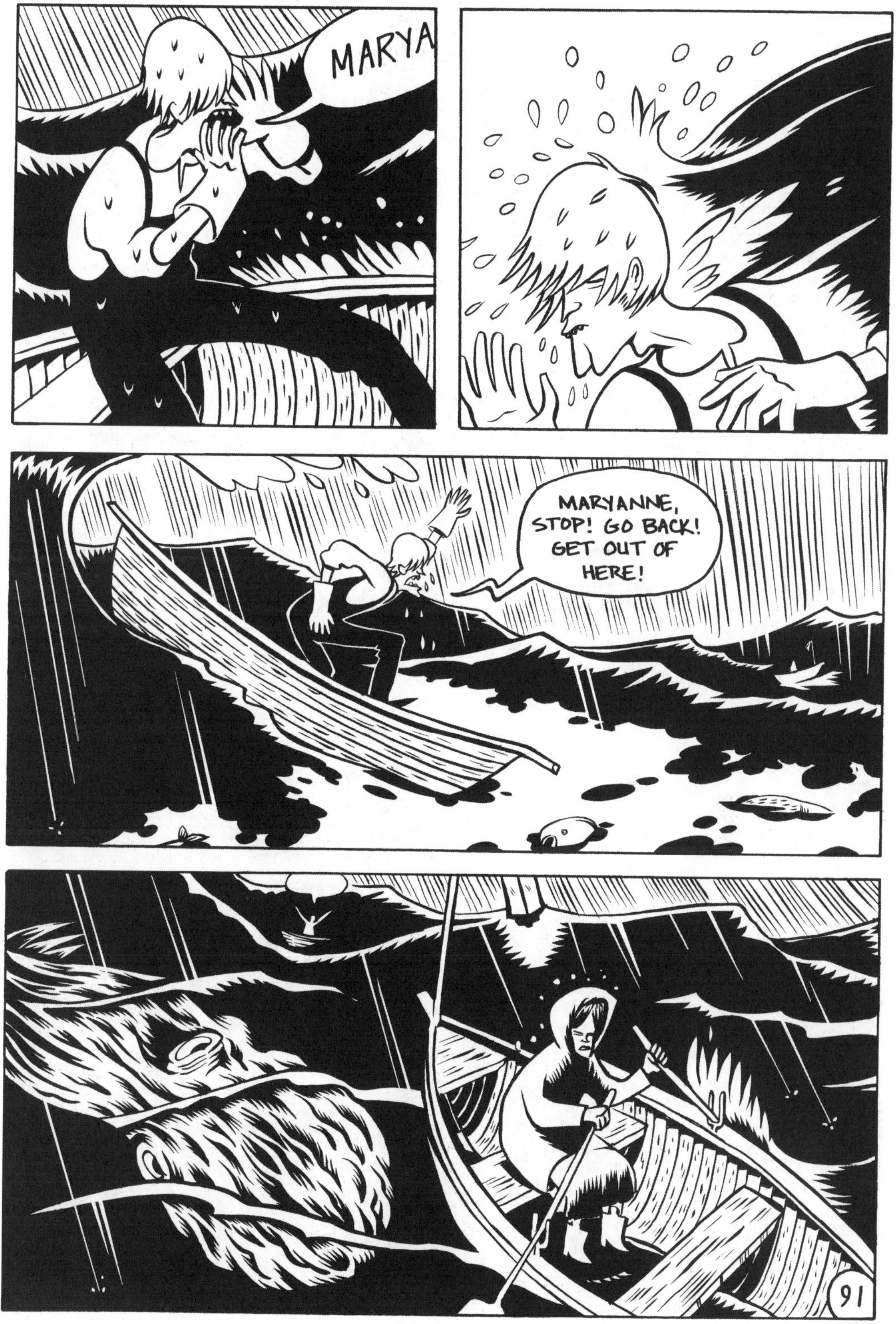
MARYA
MARYANNE, STOP! GO BACK! GET OUT OF HERE!

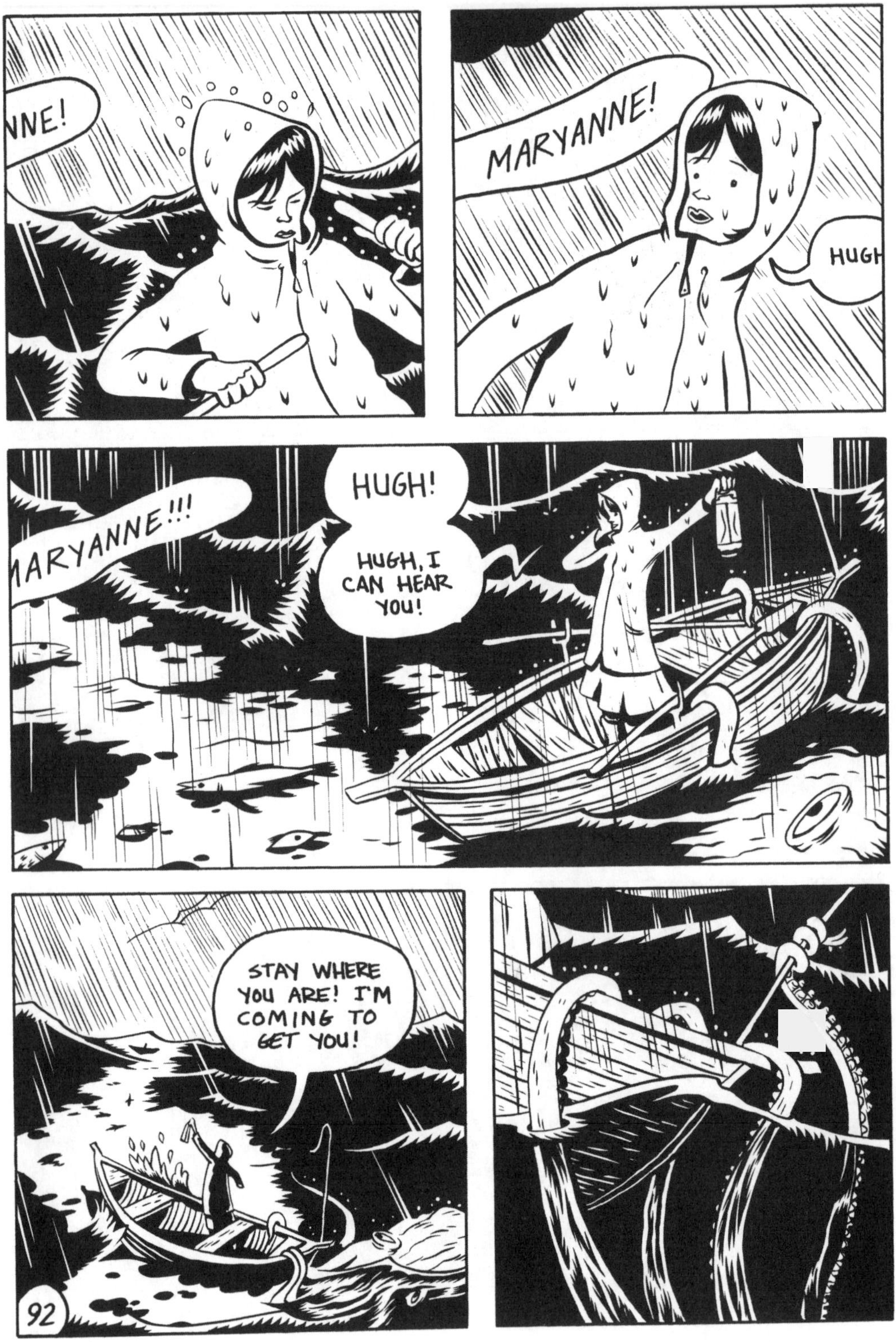
NNE!
MARYANNE!
HUGH
MARYANNE!!!
HUGH!
HUGH, I CAN HEAR YOU!
STAY WHERE YOU ARE! I'M COMING TO GET YOU!

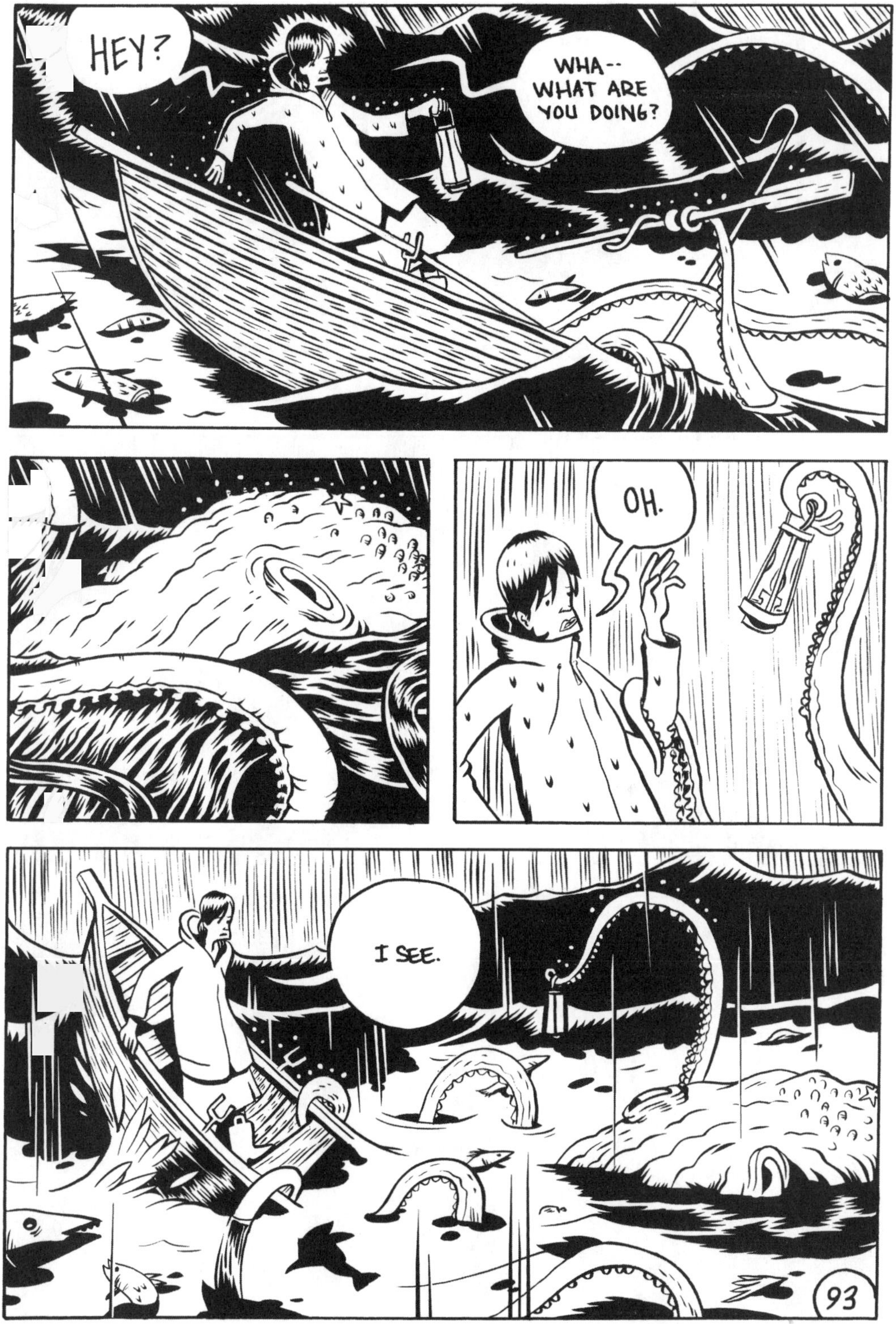
HEY?
WHA-- WHAT ARE YOU DOING?
OH.
I SEE.
93

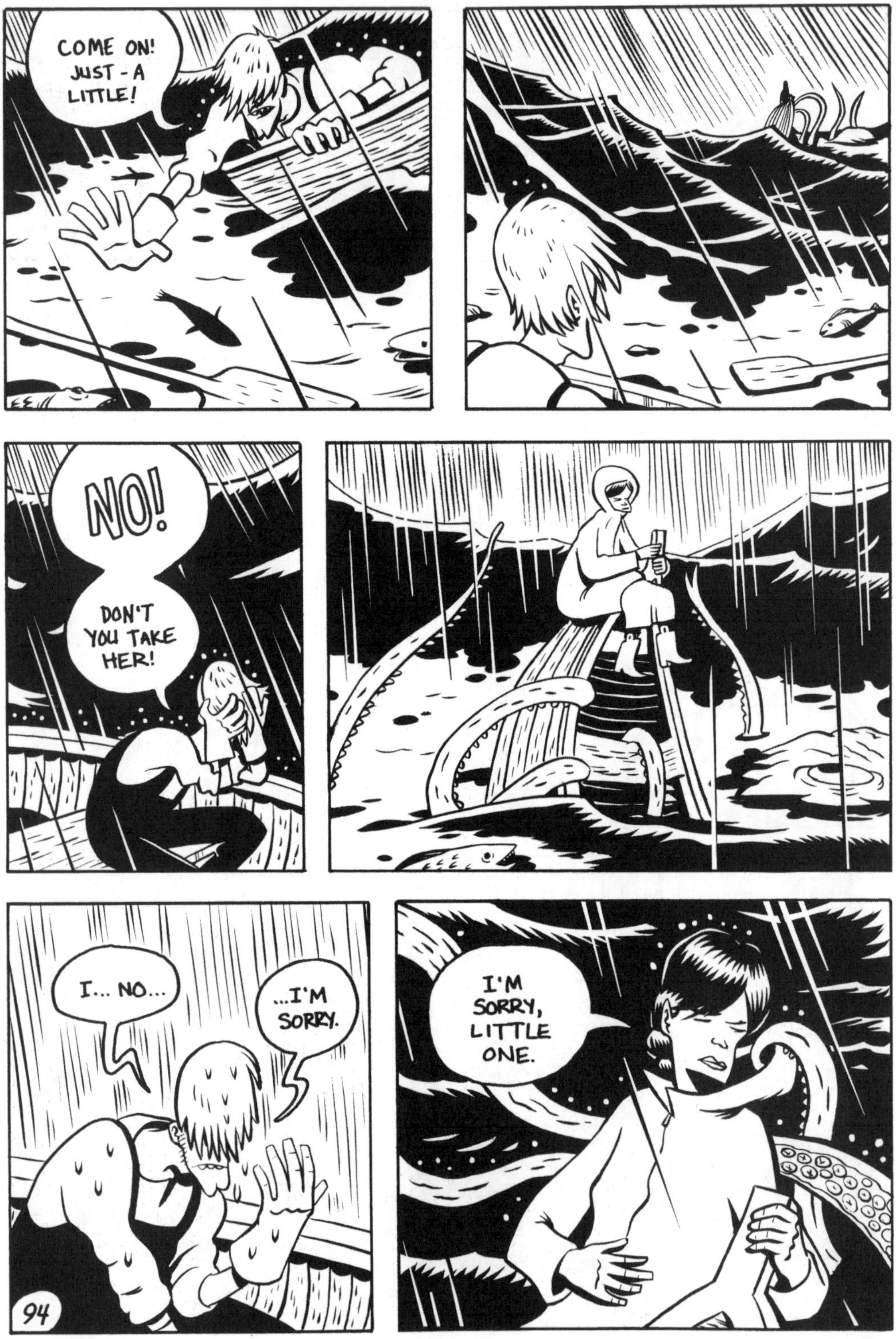
COME ON! JUST - A LITTLE!
NO!
DON'T YOU TAKE HER!
I... NO...
...I'M SORRY.
I'M SORRY, LITTLE ONE.

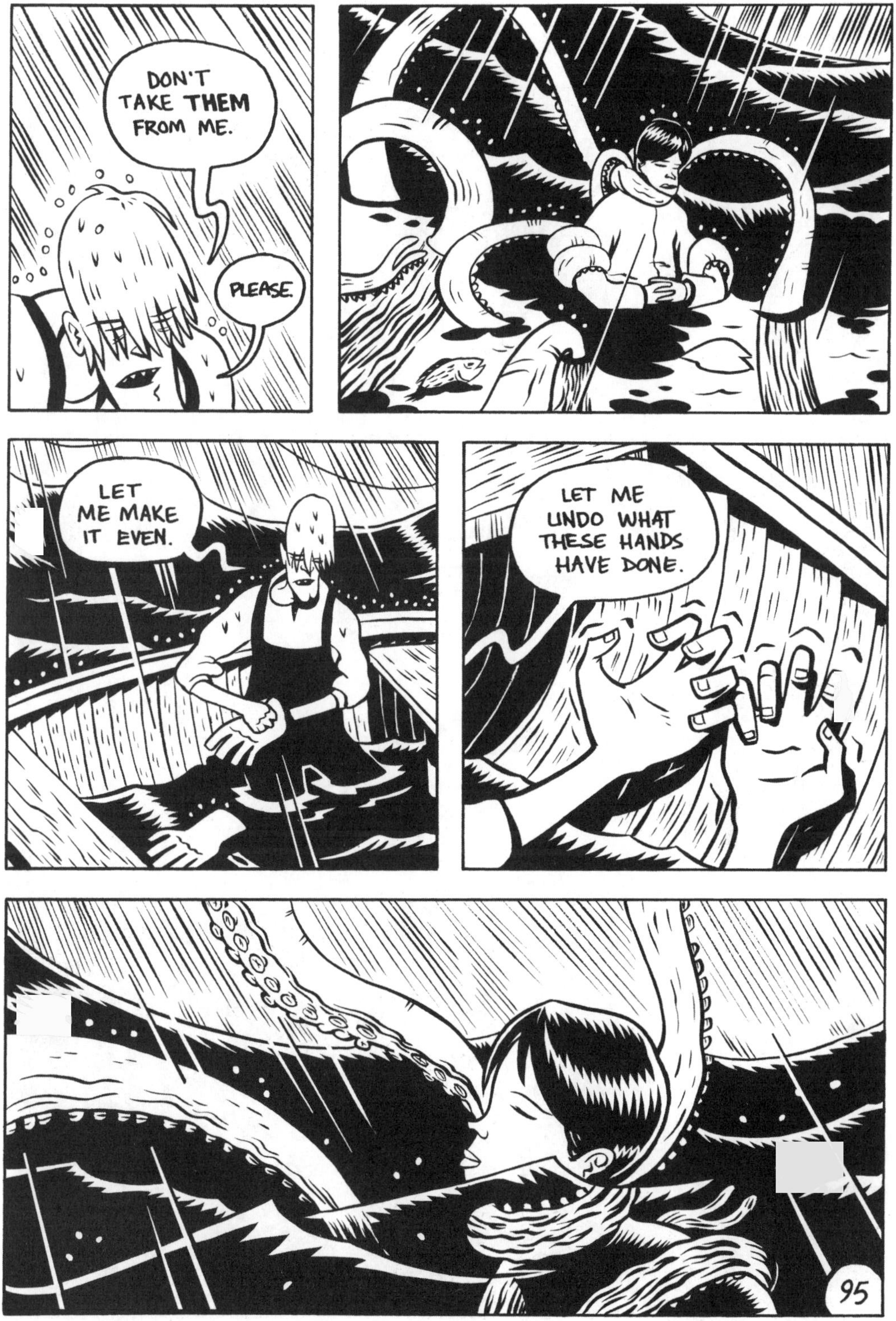
DON'T TAKE THEM FROM ME.
PLEASE.
LET ME MAKE IT EVEN.
LET ME UNDO WHAT THESE HANDS HAVE DONE.

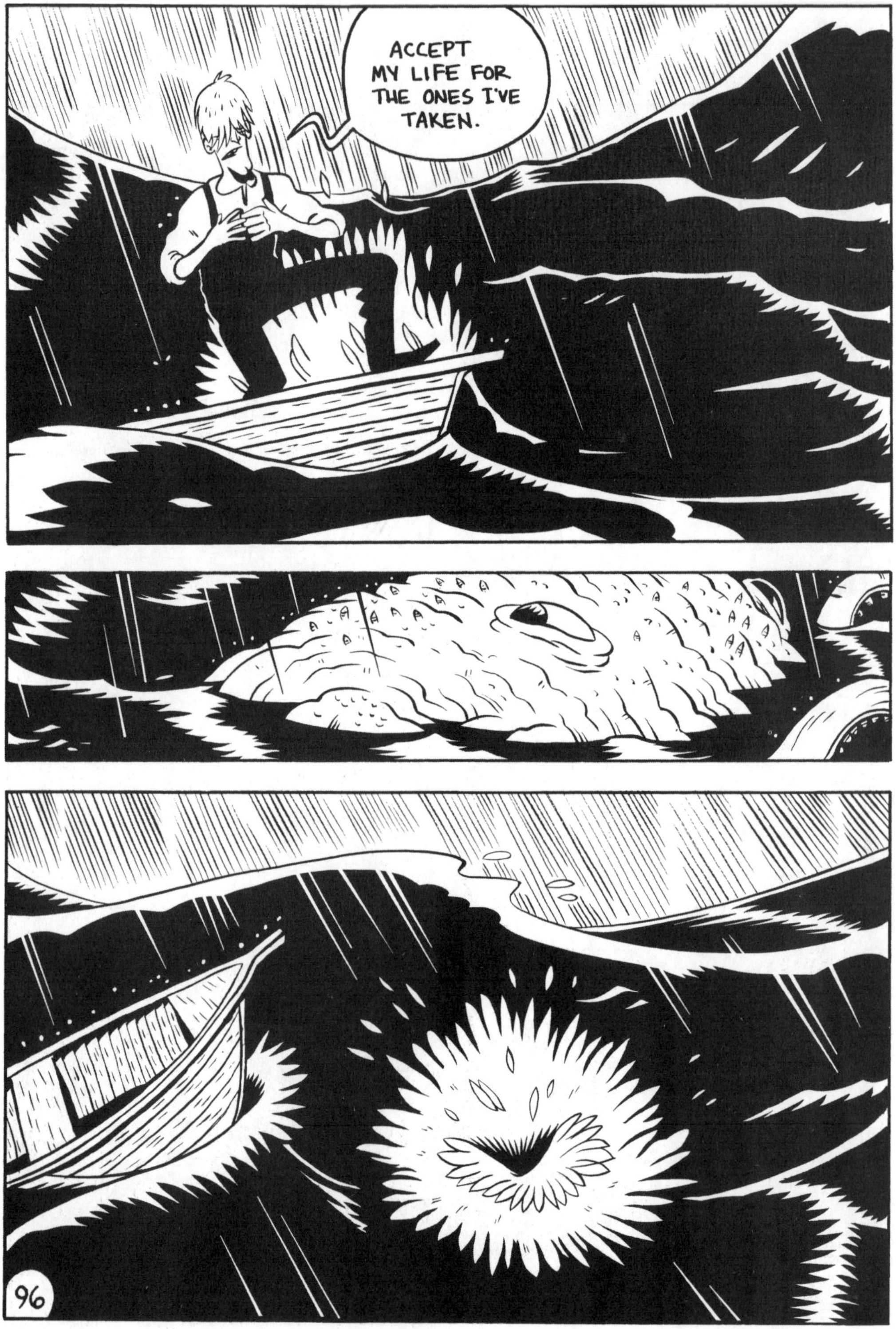
ACCEPT MY LIFE FOR THE ONES I'VE TAKEN.

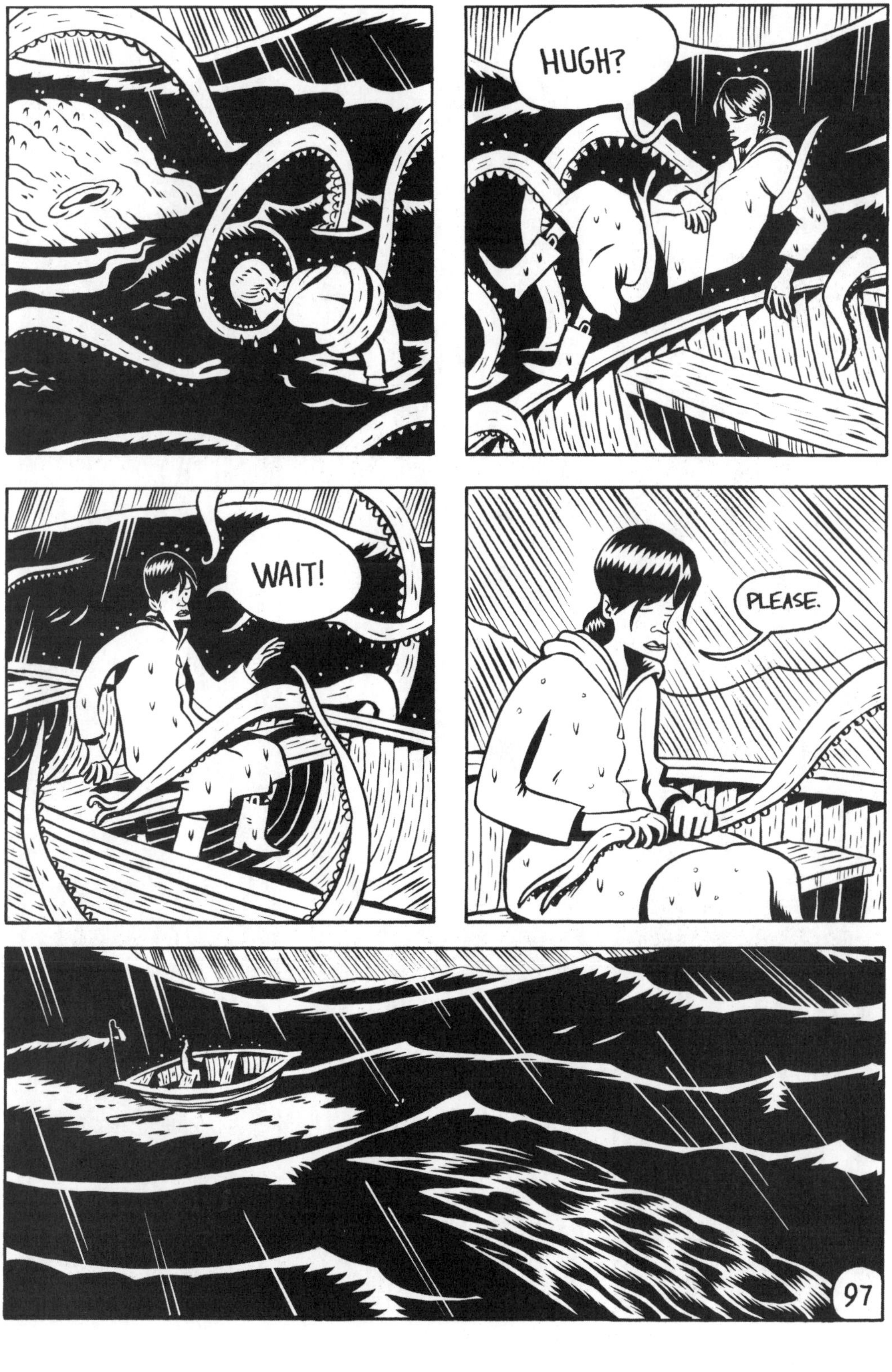
HUGH?
WAIT!
PLEASE.

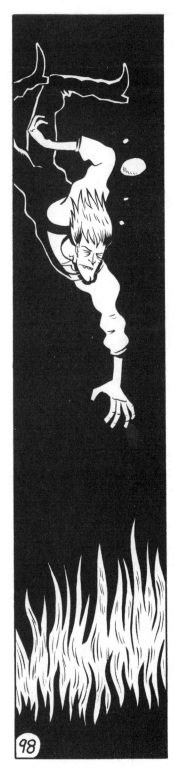

98

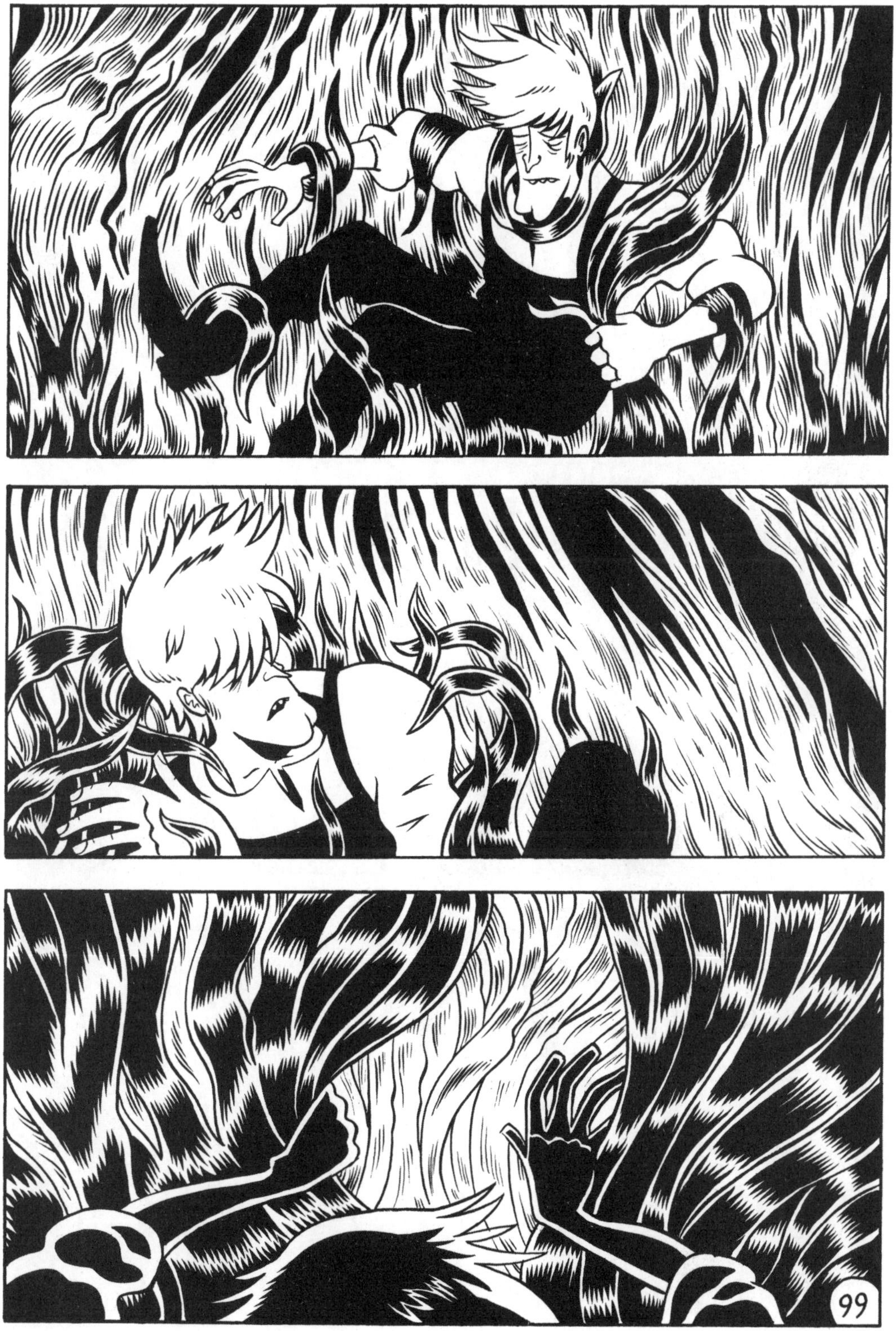

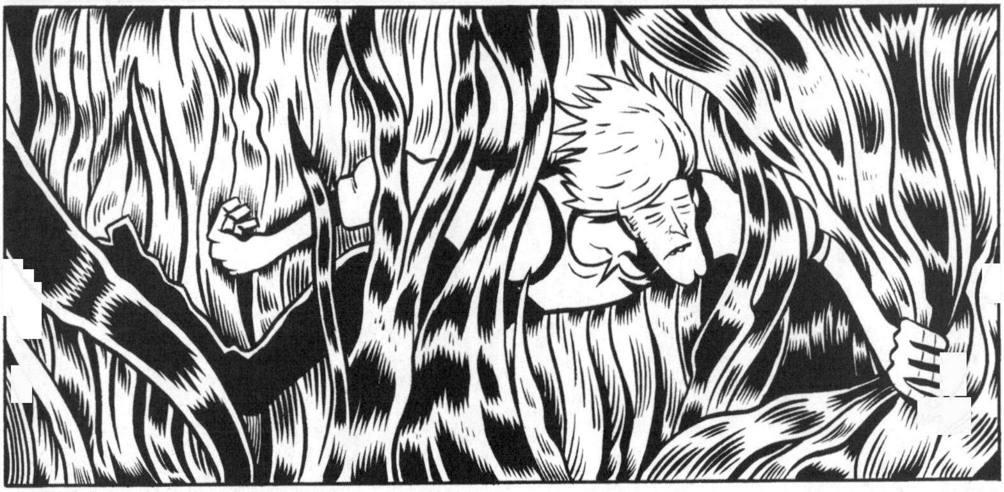

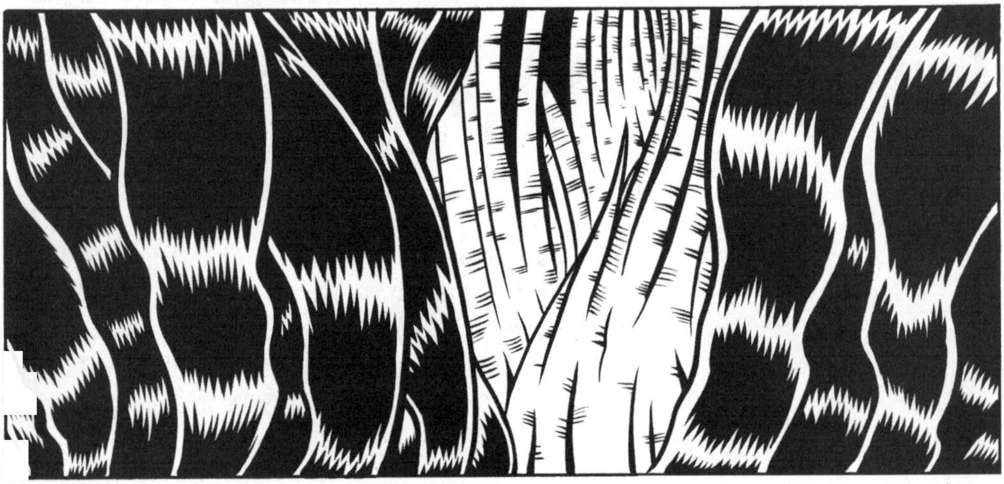

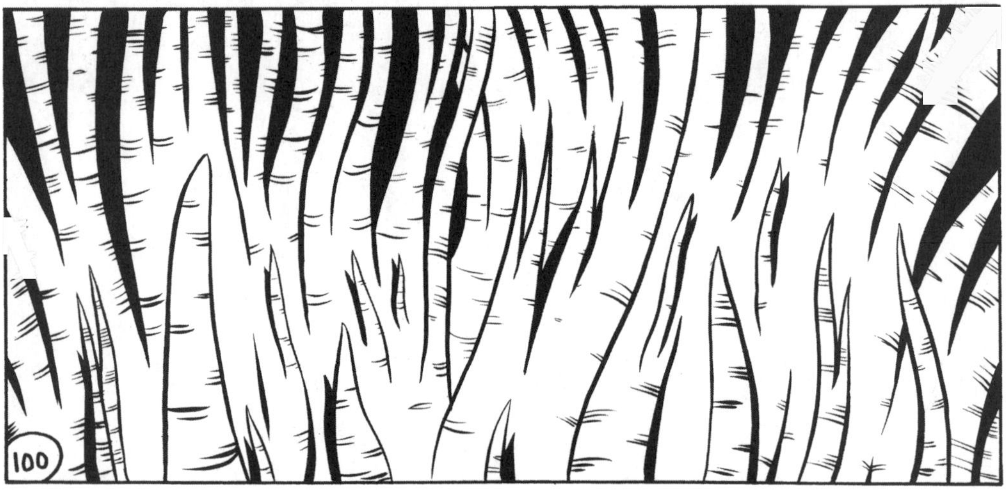

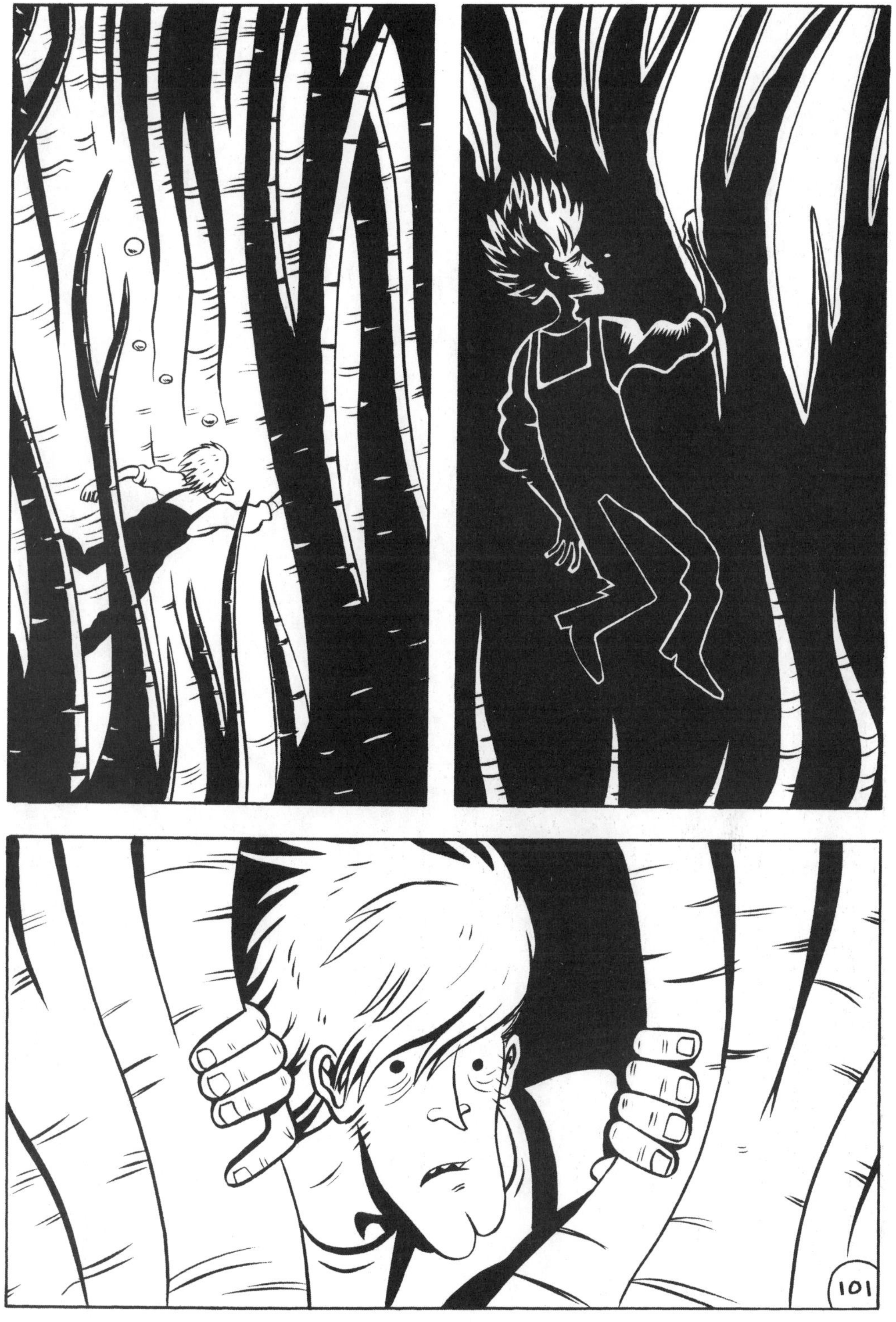

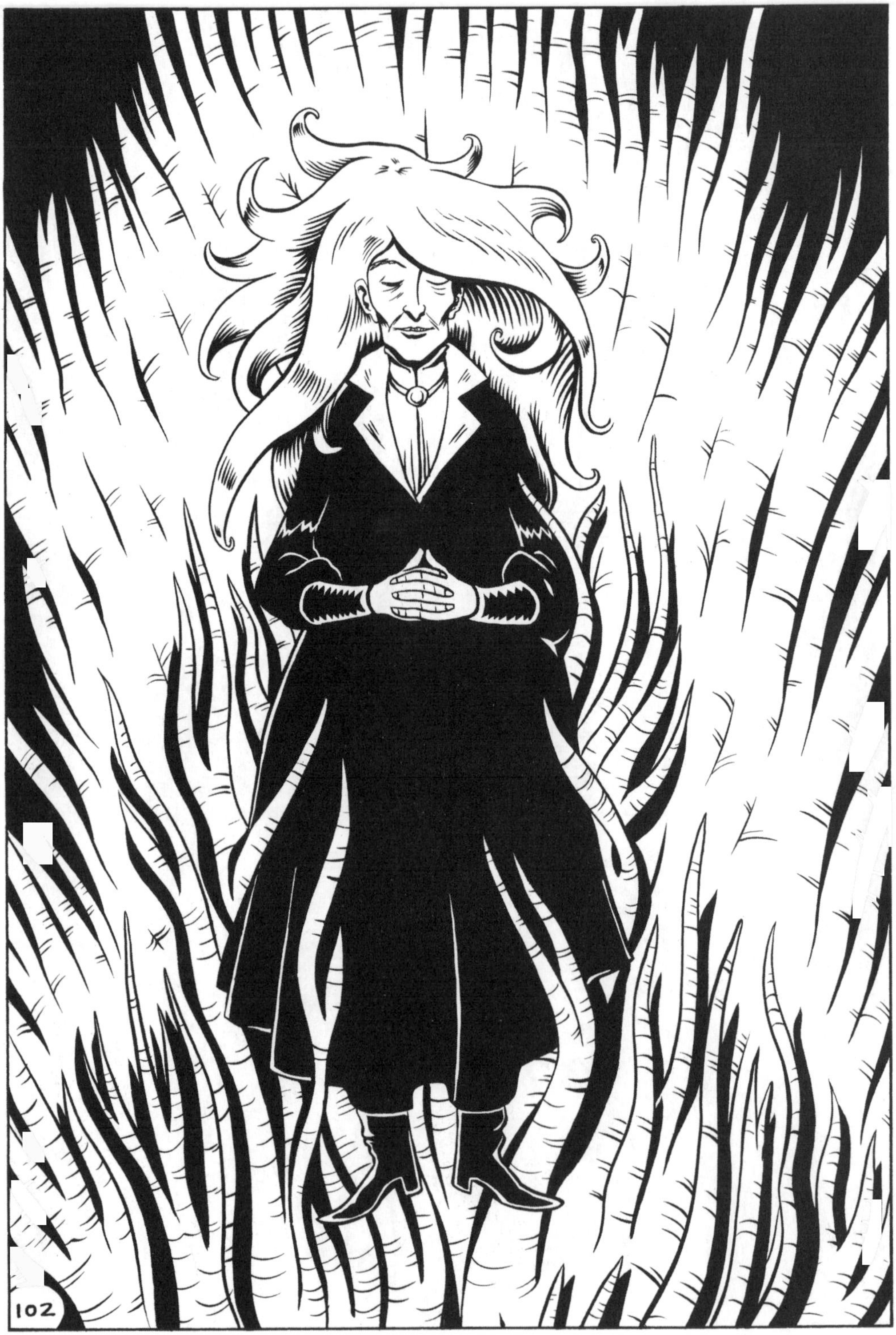
102

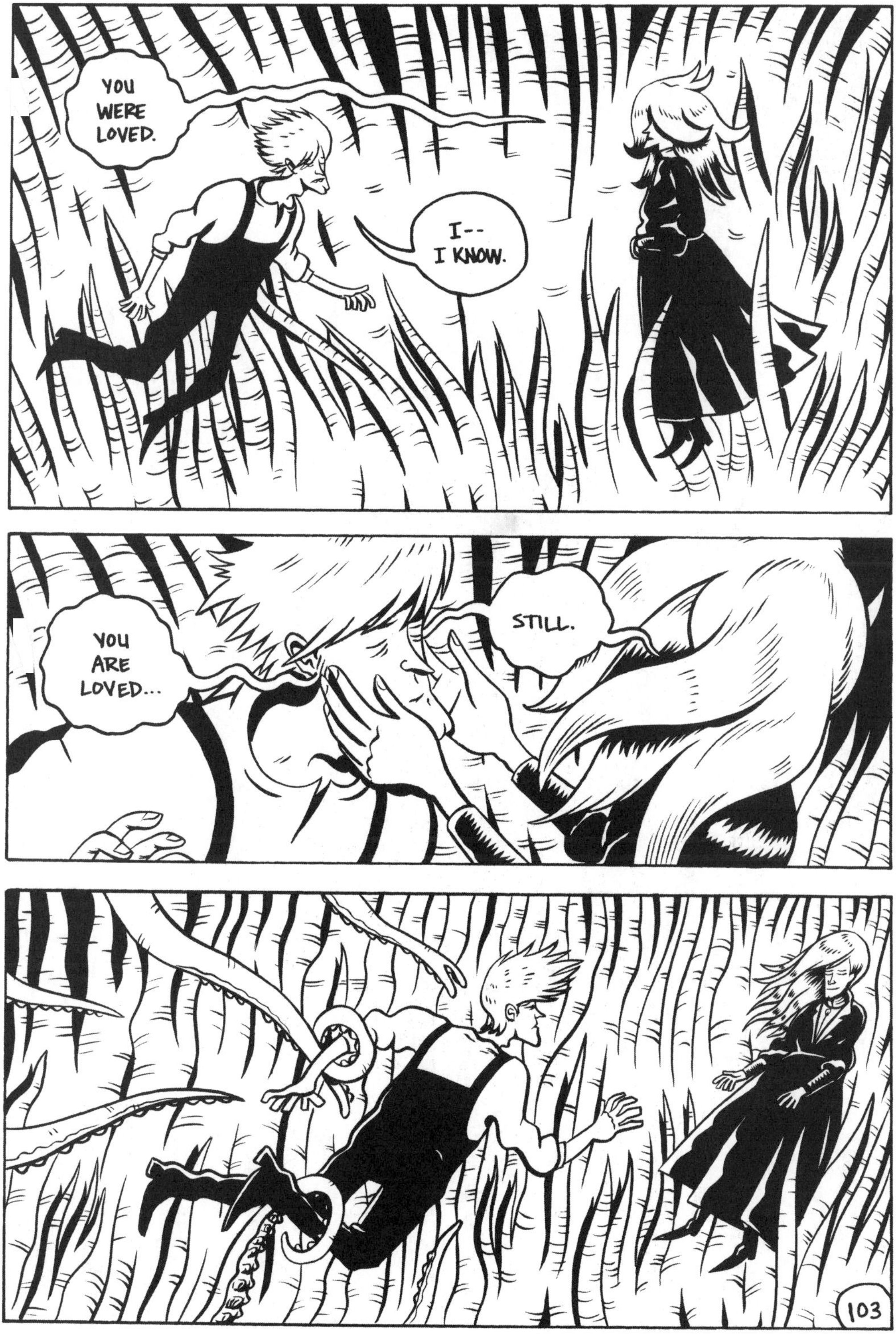
YOU WERE LOVED.
I-- I KNOW.
YOU ARE LOVED...
STILL.
103

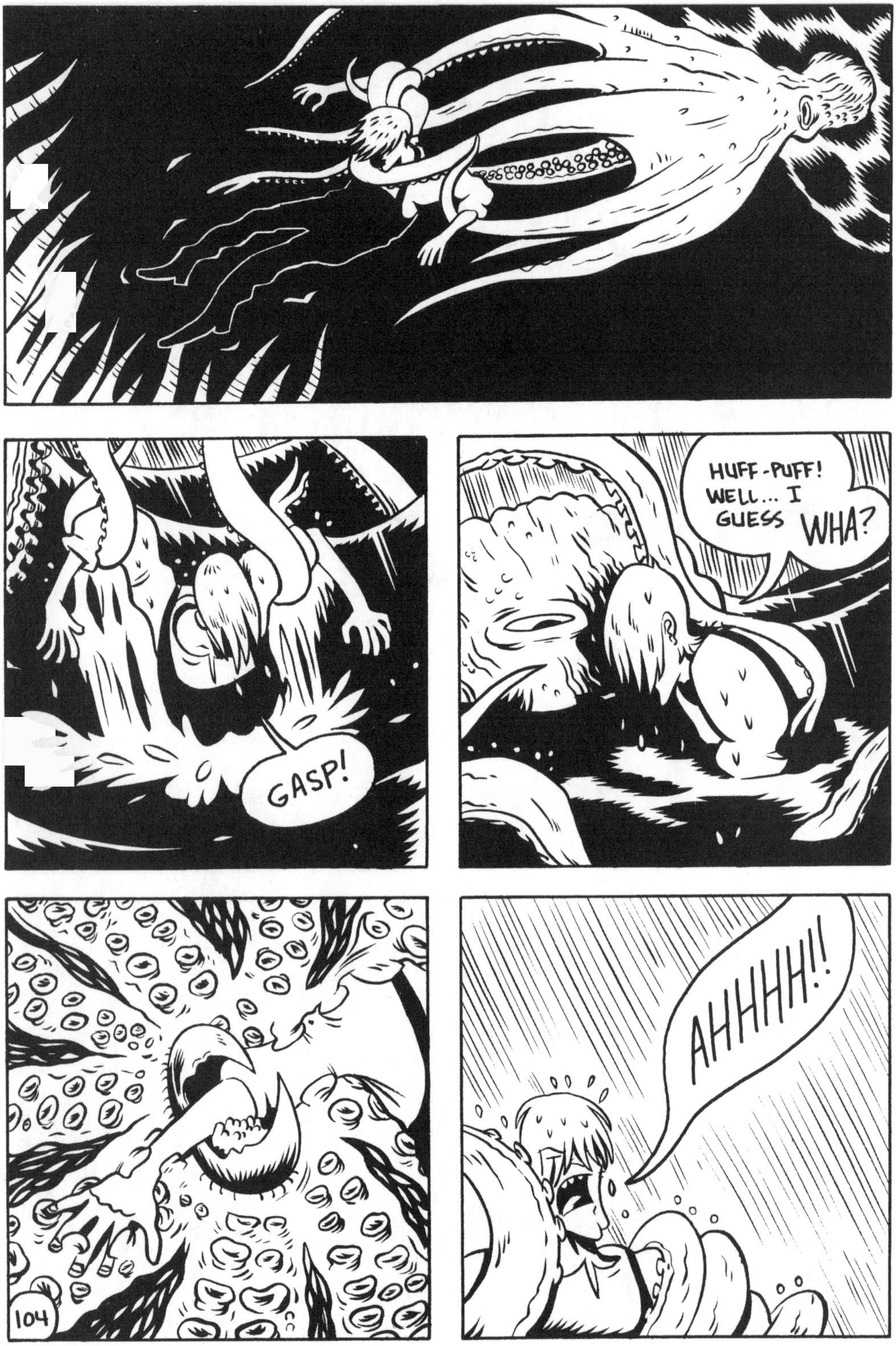
GASP!
HUFF-PUFF! WELL... I GUESS
WHA?
AHHHH!!

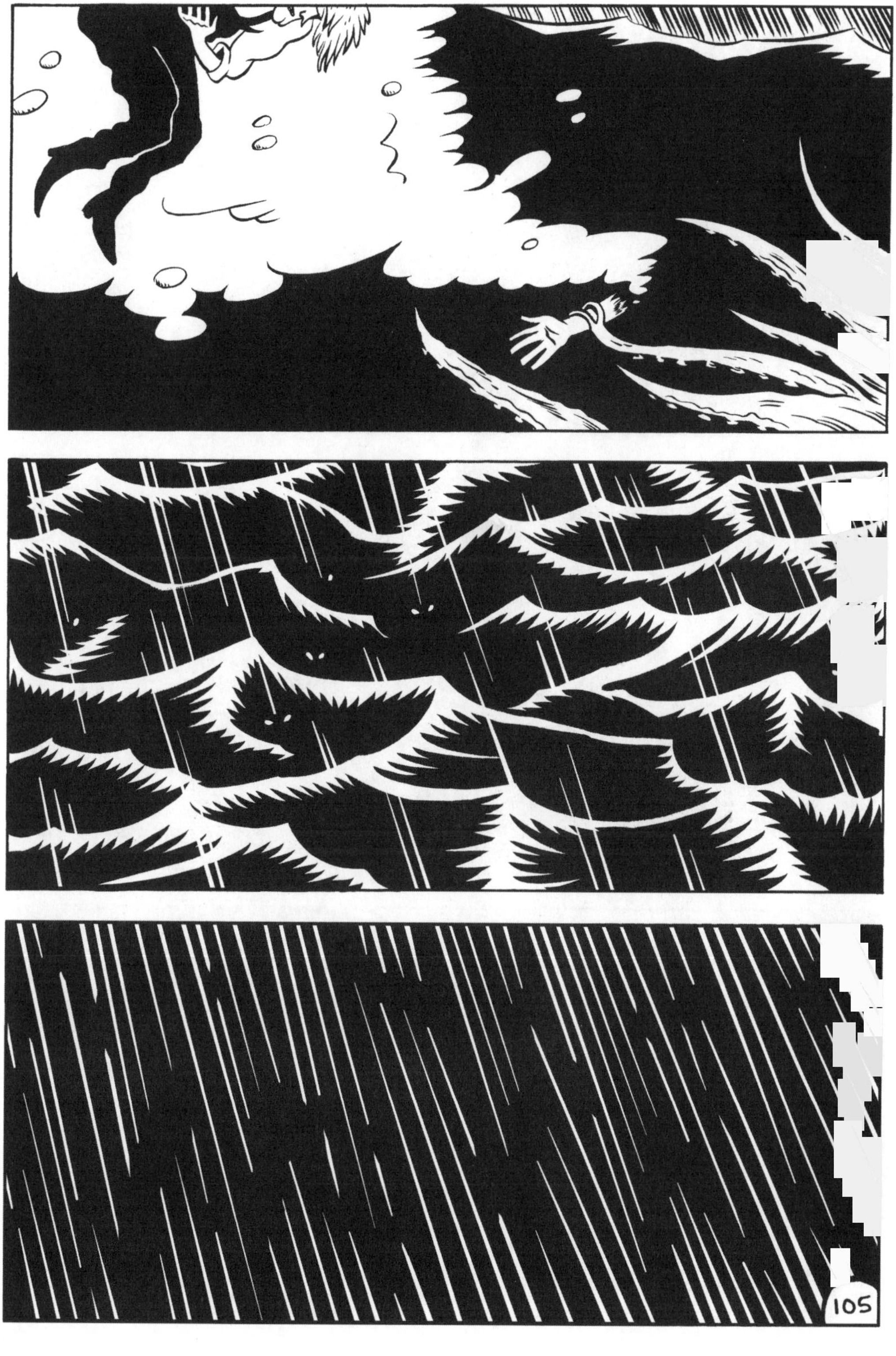

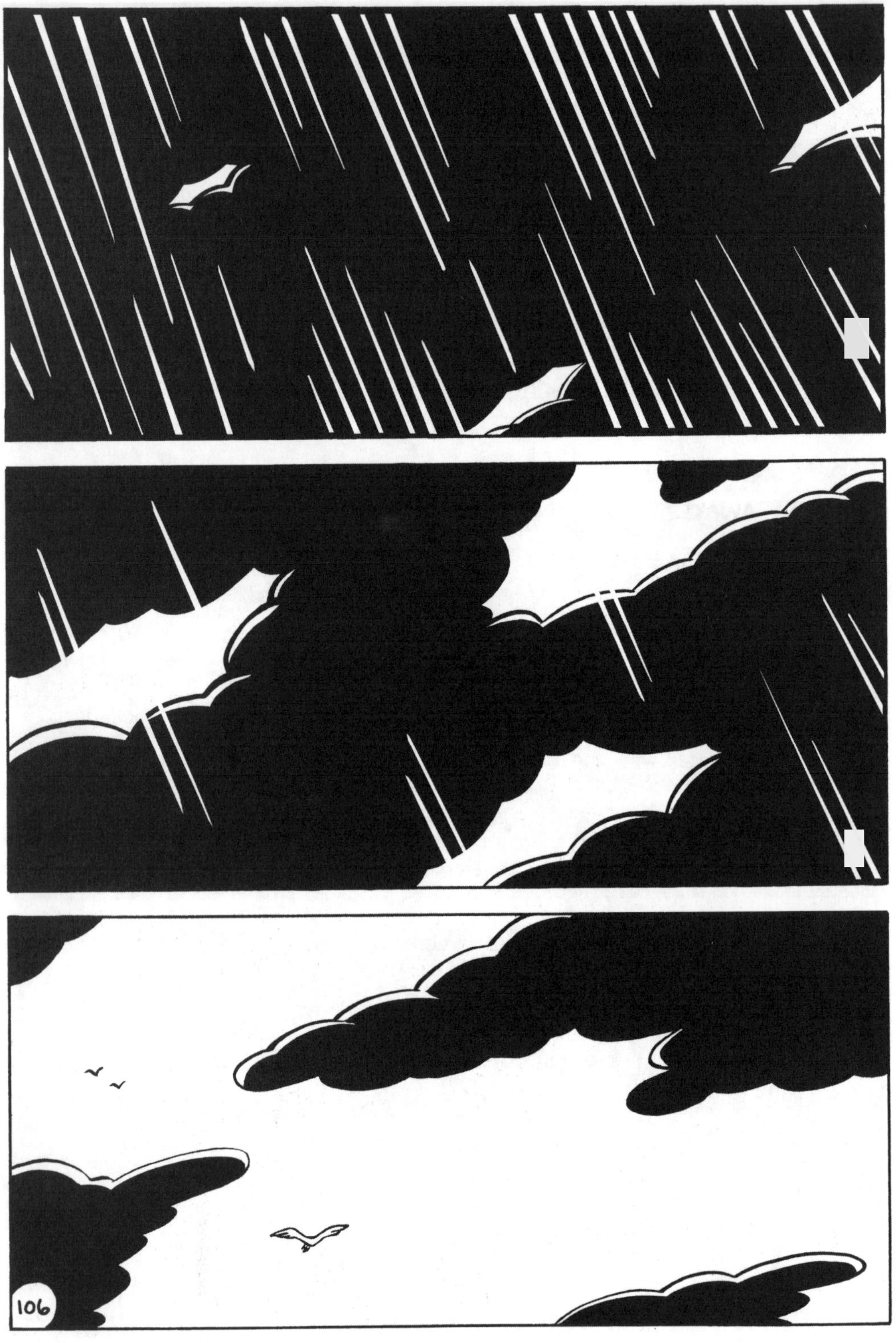

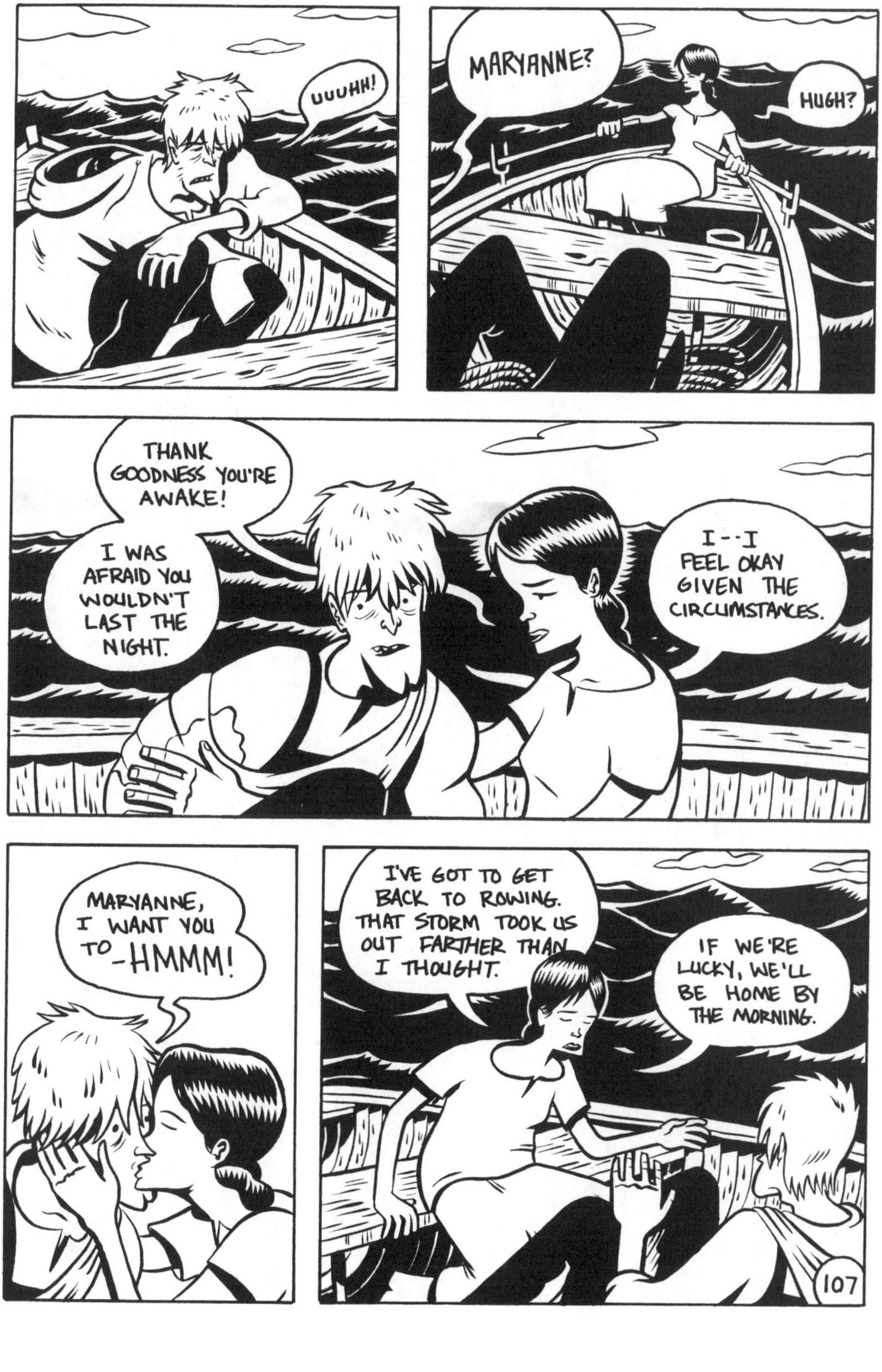
UUUHH!
MARYANNE?
HUGH?
THANK GOODNESS YOU'RE AWAKE!
I WAS AFRAID YOU WOULDN'T LAST THE NIGHT.
I--I FEEL OKAY GIVEN THE CIRCUMSTANCES.
MARYANNE, I WANT YOU TO-HMMM!
I'VE GOT TO GET BACK TO ROWING. THAT STORM TOOK US OUT FARTHER THAN I THOUGHT.
IF WE'RE LUCKY, WE'LL BE HOME BY THE MORNING.
107

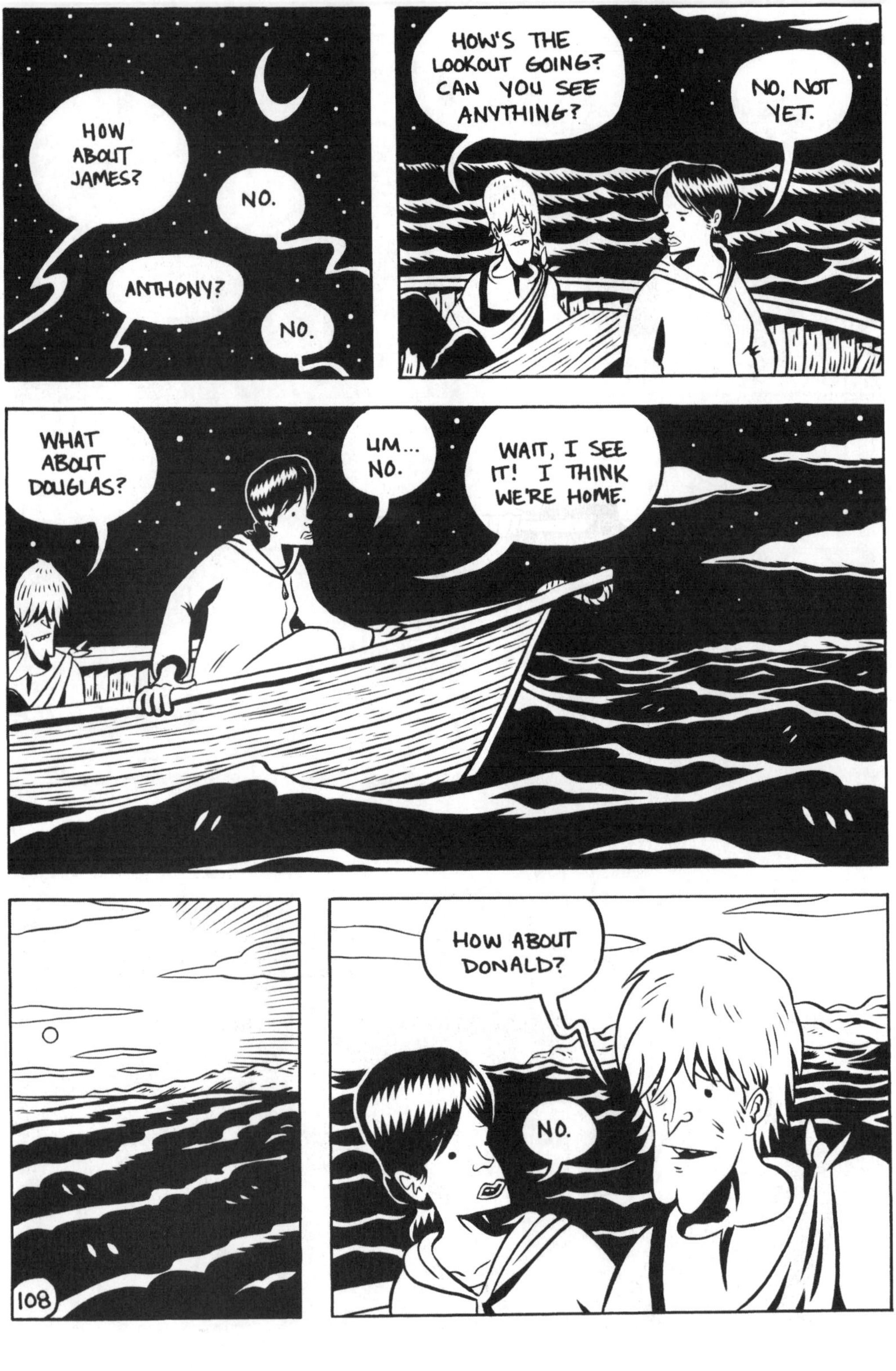
HOW ABOUT JAMES?
NO.
ANTHONY?
NO.
HOW'S THE LOOKOUT GOING? CAN YOU SEE ANYTHING?
NO, NOT YET.
WHAT ABOUT DOUGLAS?
UM... NO.
WAIT, I SEE IT! I THINK WE'RE HOME.
HOW ABOUT DONALD?
NO.

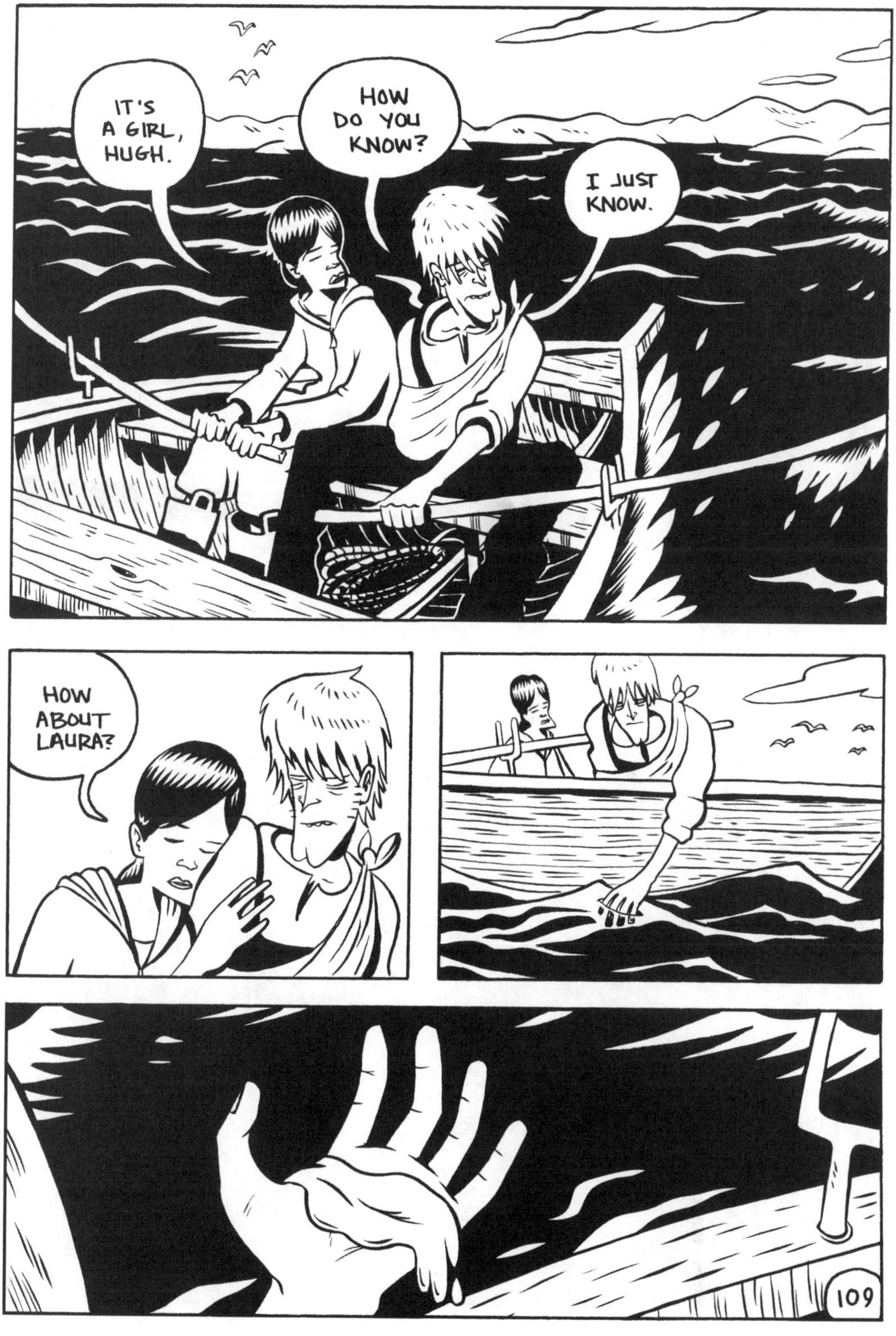
IT'S A GIRL, HUGH.
HOW DO YOU KNOW?
I JUST KNOW.
HOW ABOUT LAURA?

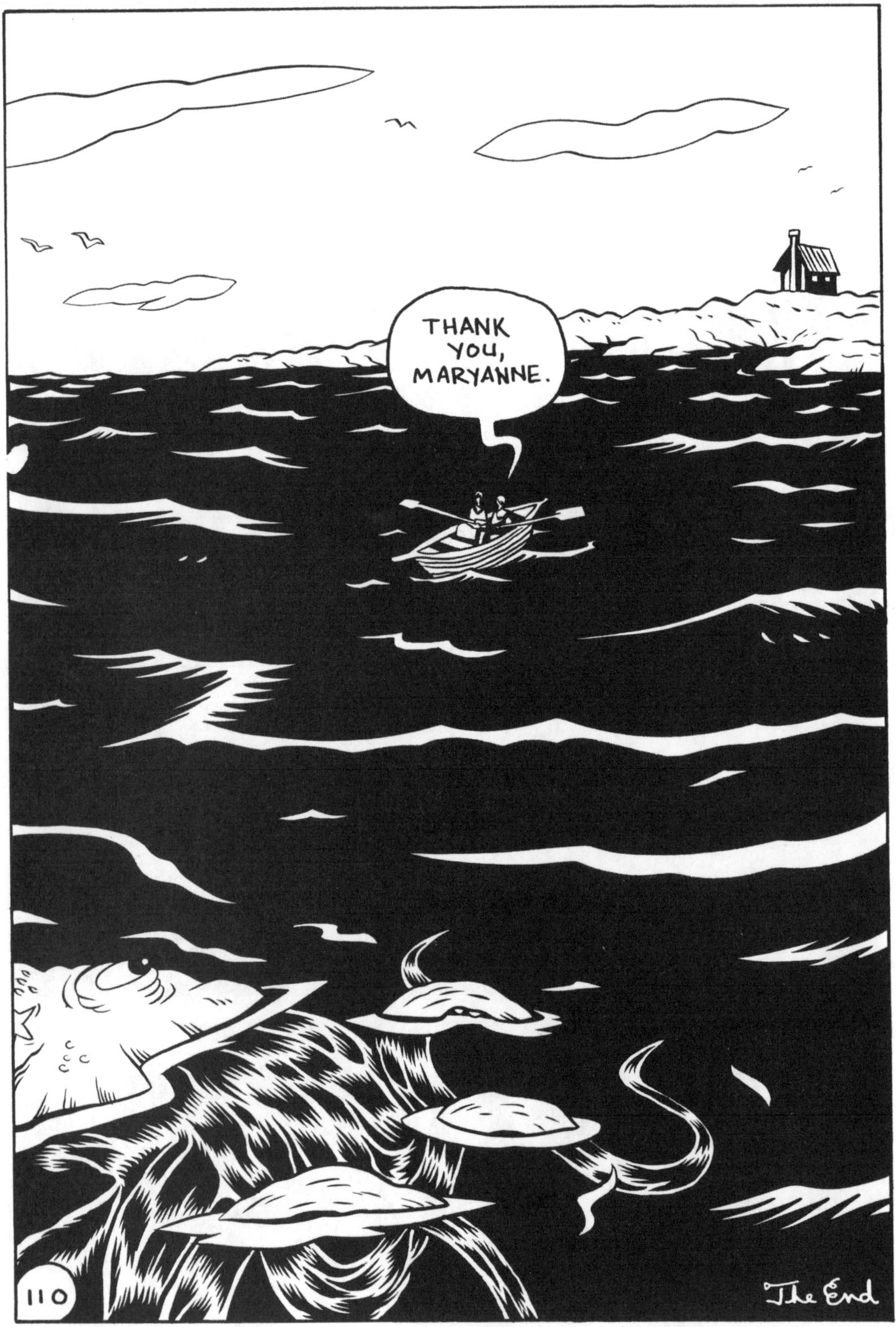
THANK YOU, MARYANNE.
The End

for
Laura
Sievert

I'd like to thank the following people for their love and support during the most difficult three years of my life. Without your help this book would not have been possible.

Vincent Stall
Brett Vonschlosser
Maxeem Konrardy
Ke Jiang
Stad Petosky
Scott Bibus
Abbey Aichinger
John Peacock
Chris Staros
Brett Warnock
Julia Vickerman
Zander Cannon
Kevin Cannon
the Sieverts
the Dillons

Thank You.

Tim Sievert was born
in Davenport, Iowa in
1983. In 2001 he moved
to Minneapolis, Minnesota
to study cartooning.

That Salty Air is his
very first graphic novel,
and he hopes that you
enjoyed reading it
as much as he
enjoyed making it.